# Lecture Notes in Computer Science     10303

Commenced Publication in 1973
Founding and Former Series Editors:
Gerhard Goos, Juris Hartmanis, and Jan van Leeuwen

More information about this series at http://www.springer.com/series/7408

Simone Barbosa · Panos Markopoulos
Fabio Paternò · Simone Stumpf
Stefano Valtolina (Eds.)

# End-User Development

6th International Symposium, IS-EUD 2017
Eindhoven, The Netherlands, June 13–15, 2017
Proceedings

Springer

*Editors*
Simone Barbosa
Pontifical Catholic University of
  Rio de Janeiro
Rio de Janeiro
Brazil

Panos Markopoulos
Eindhoven University of Technology
Eindhoven
The Netherlands

Fabio Paternò
C.N.R. - ISTI
Pisa
Italy

Simone Stumpf
City University of London
London
UK

Stefano Valtolina
Università degli Studi di Milano
Milan
Italy

ISSN 0302-9743                ISSN 1611-3349   (electronic)
Lecture Notes in Computer Science
ISBN 978-3-319-58734-9        ISBN 978-3-319-58735-6   (eBook)
DOI 10.1007/978-3-319-58735-6

Library of Congress Control Number: 2017940385

LNCS Sublibrary: SL2 – Programming and Software Engineering

Printed on acid-free paper

This Springer imprint is published by Springer Nature
The registered company is Springer International Publishing AG
The registered company address is: Gewerbestrasse 11, 6330 Cham, Switzerland

# Preface

This volume is the proceedings of IS-EUD 2017, the 6th International Symposium on End-User Development, which was held in Eindhoven, The Netherlands during June 13–15, 2017.

End-user development is a field that aims to empower end users who are not necessarily experts in software development, to create or modify their software to address their own specific needs. It is an interdisciplinary field that traditionally relates to areas such as psychology of programming, empirical studies in software engineering, and human–computer interaction. Recent technological trends like ubiquitous computing, tangible and embodied interaction, the Internet of Things, on-line communities, and crowd sourcing have renewed interest in end-user development, which emerges as an approach to empower end users to control and changes their role from a passive audience to active creators of their technological habitat.

IS-EUD is a bi-annual event that gathers researchers interested in extending our knowledge about how to design end-user development technologies and to provide scientific accounts of phenomena surrounding end-user development practices. IS-EUD cuts across application areas such as ubiquitous and wearable computing, online communities, domotics, ambient and assisted living robotics, games, etc.

IS-EUD 2017 in Eindhoven invited contributions on the topics of empowerment and materiality, on how EUD technologies can empower end users to magnify their reach and control over the physical world, to allow them to engage actively in societal trends and transformations. The theme of the conference was "that was business, this is personal," aiming to emphasize the personal involvement and engagement of end users, the application of end-user programming beyond the professional environment looking also at discretionary use of technologies. Papers and submissions in all categories addressed this specific theme together with topics that have been traditionally covered by the broader area of end-user development such as domain-specific tools, spreadsheets, and end-user aspects.

IS-EUD 2017 collected research contributions as papers, short papers, work-in-progress, demonstrations and doctoral consortium papers that described:

- New, simple, and efficient environments for end-user development
- New processes and methods for designing open-ended solutions and empowering users to cover the last mile of software development
- Case studies and design implications on challenges and practices of end-user development and user creativity
- Theoretical concepts and foundations for the field of end-user development

The paper track received 26 submissions of full and short papers, of which we accepted ten full papers and three short papers after a rigorous double-blind review process.

The program was opened and closed by two invited keynote talks, in areas where end-user development is becoming increasingly interesting: games for civic involvement and crowd sourcing.

Ben Schouten (Eindhoven University of Technology) gave a lecture on "Play and Civic Interaction Design" addressing a changing perspective on design, one in which users are defined as social and economical actors who co-create products and services. Steven Dow (Department of Cognitive Science at UC San Diego) discussed the need to advance fundamental knowledge and technologies for "collective innovation," where groups collectively explore and refine solutions for big problem spaces.

We are happy to sustain the tradition of high-quality papers reporting on advances in this specialized field of human–computer interaction. This preface was written in anticipation of an energizing and inspiring event, with a rich program that aspired to fuel further research in end-user development for the symposium attendants as well as the broader readership of this volume.

April 2017

Simone Barbosa
Panos Markopoulos
Fabio Paternò
Simone Stumpf
Stefano Valtolina

# Organization

## Steering Committee

| | |
|---|---|
| Margaret Burnett | Oregon State University, USA |
| Maria Francesca Costabile | University of Bari, Italy |
| Boris De Ruyter | Philips Research Europe, The Netherlands |
| Yvonne Dittrich | IT University of Copenhagen, Denmark |
| Gerhard Fischer | University of Colorado, USA |
| Anders Morch | University of Oslo, Norway |
| Antonio Piccinno | University of Bari, Italy |
| Volkmar Pipek | Siegen University, Germany |
| Mary Beth Rosson | Penn State University, USA |
| David Redmiles | University of California, USA |
| Gunnar Stevens | Siegen University, Germany |
| Volker Wulf | Siegen University, Germany |

## Organizing Committee

### Conference Chair

Panos Markopoulos — Eindhoven University of Technology, The Netherlands

### Program Chairs

| | |
|---|---|
| Fabio Paternò | Consiglio Nazionale delle Richerche – ISTI, Pisa, Italy |
| Simone Barbosa | Pontifical Catholic University of Rio de Janeiro, Brazil |

### Short Papers

| | |
|---|---|
| Stefano Valtolina | Università degli Studi di Milano, Italy |
| Simone Stumpf | City University of London, UK |

### Work in Progress

| | |
|---|---|
| Javed Vassilis Khan | Eindhoven University of Technology, The Netherlands |
| Iris Soute | Fontys University of Applied Sciences, Eindhoven, The Netherlands |

### EUD-Demonstrations

Barbara Rita Baricceli — Università degli Studi di Milano, Italy

### Industrial Liaison

Dima Aliakseyu — Philips Lighting, The Netherlands

**Workshops**

Andrea Bellucci                    Universidad Carlos III de Madrid, Spain

**Doctoral Consortium**

Antonella di Angeli                University of Trento, Italy
Antonio Piccino                    University of Bari, Italy

**Communications/Publicity**

Giulio Galesi                      Consiglio Nazionale delle Richerche – ISTI, Pisa, Italy
Nikos Batalas                      Eindhoven University of Technology, The Netherlands
Bruno Azevedo Chagas               Pontifical Catholic University of Rio de Janeiro, Brazil

**Local Arrangements**

Rosalinde Kennis                   Eindhoven University of Technology, The Netherlands
Jesus Muñoz                        Eindhoven University of Technology, The Netherlands

# Program Committee

Ignacio Aedo                       Universidad Carlos III de Madrid, Spain
Barbara Rita Barricelli            Università degli Studi di Milano, Italy
Andrea Bellucci                    Universidad Carlos III de Madrid, Spain
Giuseppe Desolda                   Università degli Studi di Bari Aldo Moro, Italy
Thomas Herrmann                    University of Bochum, Germany
Carlos Jensen                      Oregon State University, USA
Catherine Letondal                 ENAC, France
Thomas Ludwig                      University of Siegen, Germany
Monica Maceli                      Pratt Institute, USA
Alessio Malizia                    Brunel University, UK
Anders Morch                       University of Oslo, Norway
Antonio Piccinno                   University of Bari, Italy
Volkmar Pipek                      University of Siegen, Germany
David Redmiles                     University of California, Irvine, USA
Carmen Santoro                     ISTI-CNR, Italy
Carla Simone                       Università Milano Bicocca, Italy
Clarisse de Souza                  PUC-Rio, Brazie
Lucio Davide Spano                 ISTI-CNR, Italy
Simone Stumpf                      City University London, UK
Daniel Tetteroo                    Eindhoven University of Technology, The Netherlands
Volker Wulf                        University of Siegen, Germany
Tom Yeh                            University of Colorado Boulder, USA

# Contents

## Environments for EUD

Programming IoT Devices by Demonstration Using Mobile Apps . . . . . . . . .       3
  Toby Jia-Jun Li, Yuanchun Li, Fanglin Chen, and Brad A. Myers

Personalizing a Student Home Behaviour . . . . . . . . . . . . . . . . . . . . . . .       18
  Luca Corcella, Marco Manca, and Fabio Paternò

GURaaS: An End-User Platform for Embedding Research Instruments
into Games . . . . . . . . . . . . . . . . . . . . . . . . . . . . . . . . . . . . . . . . . .       34
  Carlos Pereira Santos, Jeroen van de Haterd, Kevin Hutchinson,
  Vassilis-Javed Khan, and Panos Markopoulos

Tools of the Trade: A Survey of Technologies in End-User
Development Literature . . . . . . . . . . . . . . . . . . . . . . . . . . . . . . . . .       49
  Monica G. Maceli

What Ails End-User Composition: A Cross-Domain Qualitative Study . . . . . .       66
  Vishal Dwivedi, James D. Herbsleb, and David Garlan

Semi-automatic Extraction of Cross-Table Data from
a Set of Spreadsheets . . . . . . . . . . . . . . . . . . . . . . . . . . . . . . . . . .       84
  Alaaeddin Swidan and Felienne Hermans

Quando: Enabling Museum and Art Gallery Practitioners to Develop
Interactive Digital Exhibits . . . . . . . . . . . . . . . . . . . . . . . . . . . . . .      100
  Andrew Stratton, Chris Bates, and Andy Dearden

Specification of Complex Logical Expressions for Task Automation:
An EUD Approach . . . . . . . . . . . . . . . . . . . . . . . . . . . . . . . . . . . .      108
  Giuseppe Desolda, Carmelo Ardito, and Maristella Matera

## The User in EUD

Public Staff Empowerment in e-Government: A Human Work Interaction
Design Approach . . . . . . . . . . . . . . . . . . . . . . . . . . . . . . . . . . . . .      119
  Stefano Valtolina, Barbara Rita Barricelli, Daniela Fogli,
  Sergio Colosio, and Chiara Testa

End User Comprehension of Privacy Policy Representations . . . . . . . . . . . .      135
  Sophia Kununka, Nikolay Mehandjiev, Pedro Sampaio,
  and Konstantina Vassilopoulou

An Integration of Empirical Study Participants into the Mobile Data
Analysis Through Information Visualization . . . . . . . . . . . . . . . . . . . . . . .     150
   Thomas Ludwig, Kevin Schneider, and Volkmar Pipek

The Participatory Design Process of Tangibles for Children's
Socio-Emotional Learning . . . . . . . . . . . . . . . . . . . . . . . . . . . . . . . . .     167
   Rosella Gennari, Alessandra Melonio, and Mehdi Rizvi

Potential Financial Payoffs to End-User Developers . . . . . . . . . . . . . . . . .     183
   Christopher Scaffidi

**Author Index** . . . . . . . . . . . . . . . . . . . . . . . . . . . . . . . . . . . . . . . .     191

# Environments for EUD

# Programming IoT Devices by Demonstration Using Mobile Apps

Toby Jia-Jun Li[1](✉), Yuanchun Li[2], Fanglin Chen[1], and Brad A. Myers[1](✉)

[1] Human-Computer Interaction Institute, Carnegie Mellon University, Pittsburgh, USA
{tobyli,bam}@cs.cmu.edu, fanglin@cmu.edu
[2] School of Electronics Engineering and Computer Science, Peking University, Beijing, China
yuanchun.li@pku.edu.cn

**Abstract.** The revolutionary advances of Internet of Things (IoT) devices and applications have helped IoT emerge as an increasingly important domain for end-user development (EUD). Past research has shown that end users desire to create various customized automations, which would often utilize multiple IoT devices. Many solutions exist to support EUD across multiple IoT devices, but they are limited to devices from the same manufacturer, within the same "eco-system" or supporting a common API. We present EPIDOSITE, a mobile programming-by-demonstration system that addresses this limitation by leveraging the smartphone as a hub for IoT automation. It enables the creation of automations for most consumer IoT devices on smartphones by demonstrating the desired behaviors through directly manipulating the corresponding smartphone app for each IoT device. EPIDOSITE also supports using the smartphone app usage context and external web services as triggers and data for automations, enabling the creation of highly context-aware IoT applications.

**Keywords:** Internet of Things · Programming by demonstration · End user development

## 1 Introduction

In the recent years, the rapid growth of Internet of Things (IoT) has surrounded users with various smart appliances, sensors and devices. Through their connections, these smart objects can understand and react to their environment, enabling novel computing applications [39]. A past study has shown that users have highly diverse and personalized desired behaviors for their smart home automation, and, as a result, they need end-user tools to enable them to program their environment [42]. Especially with the growing number of devices, the complexity of the systems, and their importance in everyday life, it is increasingly important to enable end users to create the programs themselves for those devices to achieve the desired user experience [33, 40].

Many manufacturers of smart devices have provided their customers with tools for creating their own automations. For example, LG has the SmartThinQ[1] app, where the

---

[1] https://us.smartthinq.com/.

© Springer International Publishing AG 2017
S. Barbosa et al. (Eds.): IS-EUD 2017, LNCS 10303, pp. 3–17, 2017.
DOI: 10.1007/978-3-319-58735-6_1

user can author schedules and rules for their supported LG smart appliances such as fridges, washers and ovens. Similar software is also provided by companies like Samsung (SmartThings), Home Depot (Wink) and WeMo. However, a major limitation for all of these is the lack of interoperability and compatibility with devices from other manufacturers. They all only support the limited set of devices manufactured by their own companies or their partners. Therefore, users are restricted to creating automations using devices within the same "ecosystem" and are unable to, for instance, create an automation to adjust the setting of an LG air conditioner based on the reading from a Samsung sensor.

Some platforms partially address this problem. For example, IFTTT (ifttt.com) is a popular service that enables end users to program in the form of "if *trigger*, then *action*" for hundreds of popular web services, apps, and IoT devices. With the help of IFTTT, the user can create automations across supported devices like a GE dishwasher, a WeMo coffeemaker and a Fitbit fitness tracker. However, the applicability of IFTTT is still limited to devices and services offered by its partners, or those that provide open APIs which can connect to IFTTT. Even for the supported devices and services, often only a subset of the most commonly used functions is made available due to the required engineering effort. Other platforms like Apple HomeKit and Google Home also suffer from the same limitations. Because of the lack of a standard interface or a standard protocol, many existing tools and systems cannot support the heterogeneity of IoT devices [17, 21]. While generalized architectures for programming IoT devices and higher-level representations of IoT automation rules and scripts have been proposed (e.g., [15, 16, 20, 21, 37]), they have not yet been widely adopted in the most popular commercial IoT products, and there is some reason for pessimism that such an agreement will ever happen.

To solve these problems, we create a new system named EPIDOSITE,[2] which is an end-user development (EUD) tool that enables the creation of automations for IoT devices from different ecosystems by demonstration though manipulating their corresponding mobile apps. Our system particularly targets the development of automation scripts for consumer IoT devices in the smart home environment by end users with little or no programming expertise. Thanks to the ubiquity of smartphones, for the majority of consumer IoT devices, there are corresponding smartphone apps available for remote controlling them, and these apps often have access to the full capabilities of the devices. A smartphone loaded with these apps is an ideal universal interface for monitoring and controlling the smart home environment [46]. Thus, by leveraging the smartphone as a hub, we can both read the status of the IoT sensors by scraping information from the user interfaces of their apps, and control the IoT actuators by manipulating their apps. To our knowledge, ours is the first EUD system for IoT devices using this approach.

---

[2] EPIDOSITE is a type of rock. Here, the name stands for "Enabling Programming of IoT Devices On Smartphone Interfaces for The End-users".

## 1.1 Advantages

Our approach has the following three major advantages:

**Compatibility:** Unlike other EUD tools for consumer IoT devices, which can only support programming devices from the same company, within the same ecosystem, or which provide open access to their APIs, EPIDOSITE can support programming for most of the available consumer IoT devices if they provide Android apps for remote control. For selected phones with IR blasters (e.g., LG G5, Samsung Galaxy S6, HTC One) and the corresponding IR remote apps, EPIDOSITE can even control "non-smart" appliances such as TVs, DVRs, home theaters and air conditioners that support IR remote control (but this obviously only works when the phone is aimed at the device).

**Interoperability:** EPIDOSITE can support creating automation across *multiple* IoT devices, even if they are from different manufacturers. Besides IoT devices, EPIDOSITE can also support the incorporation of arbitrary third-party mobile apps and hundreds of external web services into the scripts. The exchange of information between devices is also supported by demonstration. The user can extract values of the readings and status of IoT devices using gestures on one mobile app, and use the values later as input for other apps. This approach addresses the challenge of supporting *impromptu interoperability* [14], a vision that devices acquired at different times, from different vendors and created under different design constraints and considerations should interconnect with no advance planning or implementation.

**Usability:** We believe that EPIDOSITE should be easy to use, even for end users with little or no prior programming experience. Since the users are already familiar with how to use the mobile apps to monitor and to control IoT devices, EPIDOSITE minimizes the learning barrier by enabling users to use those familiar app interfaces to develop automations by demonstrating the procedures to control the IoT devices to perform the desired behaviors. A major advantage of PBD is that it can empower users while minimizing learning of programming concepts [30, 35]. The evaluation of the SUGILITE system [29], which shares the same demonstrational interface as EPIDOSITE, also suggests that most end users can successfully automate their tasks by demonstration using mobile apps on smartphones.

## 2 Related Work

Supporting end user development activities in the Internet of Things era has been identified as a particularly important and promising research direction [3]. Due to the dynamic nature of context, it is difficult or even impossible for a developer or a designer to enumerate all of the possible contextual states and the appropriate action to take from each state [19]. To solve this problem, the end users should play a central role in deciding how elements in the IoT ecosystem should interact with people and with other devices, and the end-users should be empowered to program the system behavior [3, 44]. The longitudinal study by Coutaz and Crowley [7] reported that families liked EUD for IoT devices in the smart home environment because it provides convenience and personalization. Much prior work has focused on enabling end users to configure, extend and customize the behaviors of their IoT devices with various approaches. However, we believe EPIDOSITE is the first to enable the users to create automations for IoT devices by demonstration using the devices' corresponding mobile apps.

In the specific area of EUD for developing home automation scripts across IoT devices, rule-based systems like HomeRules [10], IFTTT (ifttt.com) and Altooma (www.atooma.com) use a trigger-action model to allow users to create automation rules for supported web services and IoT devices. Compared with EPIDOSITE, those services can only support much a smaller set of devices. Smart home solution providers like Samsung, LG and Apple also provide software kits for end user development with their products, but unlike EPIDOSITE, they can only support devices within their own "ecosystems". Some generalized architectures and standardized models for programming IoT devices and higher-level representations of IoT automation rules and scripts have been proposed (e.g., [15, 16, 20, 21, 37]), but none have been widely adopted. In a field study for home automation systems [11], interoperability was shown to be important for the users. The same study showed that, although expert users reported that they facilitated communication between devices and services utilizing HTTP requests, this set-up would be difficult to configure for end users with limited technical background [11].

Visual programming tools such as Midgar [17], Jigsaw [22], Puzzle [9], Yahoo Pipes (http://pipes.yahoo.com/pipes) and Bipio (https://bip.io) enable the users to create programs, data pipelines and mashup applications between supported devices, services and APIs. AppsGate [7] provides a syntax-driven editor that empowers the users to program their smart home devices using a pseudo-natural language. Kubitza and Schmidt [25] proposed a web-based IDE that allows users to mash-up heterogeneous sets of devices using a common scripting language. However, the above approaches require the user to work with a visual programming language interface, a scripting language, or a domain-specific programming language (DSL), which is challenging for non-expert end users with little or no programming knowledge.

Some prior PBD systems such as motionEAP (www.motioneap.de) [40], Backpacks [38] and prior work in robot programming by demonstration (e.g., [1, 4]) enable users to program their desired behaviors by directly manipulating the physical objects (e.g., grabbing tools on an assembly line, or manipulating the arms of a robot). The *a CAPpella* system [12] empowers the user to specify a contextual situation by demonstration using data from multiple sensors in a smart environment. A major advantage of PBD is that it is easy to learn for end users with limited programming knowledge, as it allows users to program in the same environment in which they perform the actions [8, 30, 36]. However, these systems require the presence of extensive sensors on the devices and objects being programmed, or in the environment, which is costly and unavailable for most existing smart home devices and environments. As a comparison, EPIDOSITE shares these systems' advantages in usability and low learning barrier, but can work with most current IoT devices with available remote control Android apps without requiring extra sensors.

There are also PBD systems focusing on automating tasks on other domains, such as file management [34], photo manipulation [18] and web-based tasks [27]. The most relevant prior system to this work is SUGILITE [29], which is a PBD system for automating tasks on smartphones. Our EPIDOSITE system leverages the PBD engine from SUGILITE, extending its capabilities to support programming for IoT devices and provides new features specifically for smart home automation.

## 3   Example Usage Scenario

In this section, we use an example scenario to illustrate the procedure of creating an EPIDOSITE automation. For the scenario, we will create a script that turns on the TV set top box and turns off the light when someone enters the TV room. We will use a Verizon TV set-top box, a Philips Hue Go light and a D-Link DCH-S150 Wi-Fi motion sensor in this script. To our best knowledge, there exists no other EUD solution that can support all the above three devices.

First, the user starts EPIDOSITE (Fig. 1a), creates a new script and gives it a name. The phone then switches back to the home screen, and prompts the user to start demonstrating. The user now starts demonstrating how to turn off the light using the Philips Hue app – tapping on the Philips Hue icon on the home screen, choosing "Living Room", clicking on the "SCENES" tab, and selecting "OFF", which are the exactly same steps as when the user turns off the light manually using the same app. After each action, the user can see a confirmation dialog from EPIDOSITE (Fig. 1b). Running in the background as an Android accessibility service, the EPIDOSITE PBD engine can automatically detect the user's action and determine the features to use to identify the element using a set of heuristics (see [29] for more details), but the user can also manually edit the details of each recorded action in an editing panel (Fig. 1c). Figure 2a shows the textual

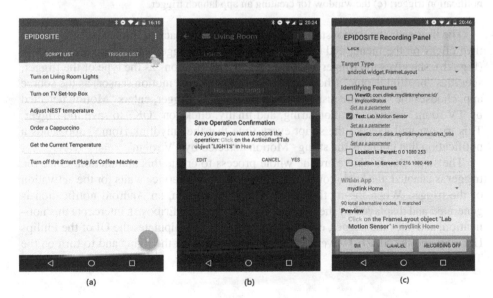

(a)                                (b)                                (c)

**Fig. 1.** Screenshots of EPIDOSITE: (a) the main screen of EPIDOSITE showing a list of available scripts; (b) the confirmation dialog for an operation; (c) the editing panel for one operation.

representation of the EPIDOSITE script created for turning off the light. Next, the user demonstrates turning on the TV set-top box using the SURE Universal Remote app on the phone (or other IR remote apps that support the Verizon TV set-top box), and EPIDOSITE records the procedure for that as well.

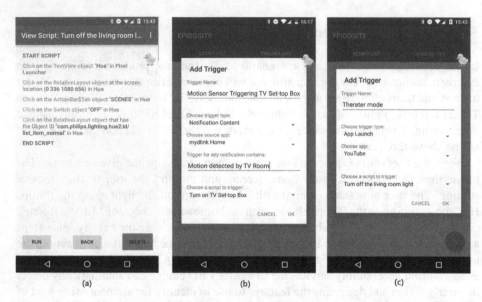

**Fig. 2.** Screenshots of EPIDOSITE's script view and trigger creation interfaces: (a) the script view showing the script from the example usage scenario; (b) the window for creating an app notification trigger; (c) the window for creating an app launch trigger.

The user ends the demonstration recording and goes back to the EPIDOSITE app. She then clicks on the menu, and chooses "Add a Script Trigger". In the pop-up window (Fig. 2b), she gives the trigger a name, selects "Notification" as the type of the trigger, specifies "mydlink Home" (the mobile app for the D-Link motion sensor) as the source app, chooses the script she just created as the script to trigger, enters "Motion detected by TV room" as the activation string, and finally, clicks on "OK" to save the trigger. This trigger will execute the script every time that the "mydlink Home" app sends a notification that contains the string "Motion detected by TV room".

The steps shown above are the whole process to create this automation. Once the trigger is enabled, the background Android accessibility service waits for the activation of the trigger. When the motion sensor detects a motion, an Android notification is generated and displayed by the mydlink Home app. Then EPIDOSITE intercepts this notification, activates the trigger, executes the script, and manipulates the UI of the Philips Hue app and the SURE Universal Remote app to turn off the lights and to turn on the TV set-top box.

# 4 System Design and Implementation

## 4.1 Implementation

The client component of EPIDOSITE is an Android application written in Java. It does not require root access to the Android system, and should work on any smartphone with Android 4.4 or above. The client component is standalone. There is also an optional add-on server application available for supporting automation triggered by external web services through IFTTT. The server application is implemented in Java with Jersey[3] and Grizzly[4].

The mobile programming by demonstration engine used in EPIDOSITE extends the prior mobile PBD system SUGILITE [29]. SUGILITE uses Android's accessibility API to support automating tasks in Android apps. During the demonstration, all of the user's interactions with the phone, together with the relevant UI elements on the screen, are recorded by a background recording handler through the accessibility API. SUGILITE then processes the recording and generates a reusable script for performing the task. SUGILITE also generalizes the script from the demonstrated example by analyzing the user interface structures of the apps used in the demonstration. For instance, if the user demonstrates how to turn on the living room light using the Philips Hue app, SUGILITE will detect "living room" as a parameter of this script, and automatically generalizes the script so it can be used to turn on other available Philips Hue lights by providing a different string when the script is invoked. With SUGILITE, the user can record an automation by demonstrating the procedure of performing the task using the user interfaces of any third-party Android app (with some exceptions noted in [29]), and then run the automation through a multi-modal interface, invoked through the GUI or using speech. SUGILITE also supports the viewing and editing of the scripts. Details about SUGILITE can be found in the earlier paper [29].

On top of SUGILITE, EPIDOSITE adds new features and mechanisms to support the programming of IoT devices in the smart home setting, including new ways for triggering scripts, new ways for scripts to trigger external services and devices, and new mechanisms for sharing information among devices. To better meet the needs of developing for IoT devices, EPIDOSITE also supports programming for different devices in separated subscripts, and reusing the subscripts in new scripts. For example, the user can demonstrate the two scripts for "turning off the light" and "turning on the TV", and then create a new script of "if …, turn off the light and turn on the TV") without having to demonstrate the procedures for performing the two tasks again.

## 4.2 Key Features

### Notification and App Launch Triggers

The most common context-aware applications in the smart home are naturally described using rule-based conditions in the model of trigger-action programming, where a *trigger*

---

[3] https://jersey.java.net/.
[4] https://grizzly.java.net/.

describes a condition, an event or a scenario, and an *action* specifies the desired behavior when its associated trigger is activated [13, 42]. In EPIDOSITE, scripts can be triggered by the content of Android notifications, or as a result of the launch of a specified app on the phone.

EPIDOSITE keeps a background Android accessibility service running at all times. Through the Android accessibility API, the service intercepts system notifications and app launches. If the content of a new notification contains the activation string of a stored notification trigger (as shown in the example usage scenario), or an app associated with an app launch trigger has just launched, the corresponding automation script for the trigger will be executed. Figure 2c shows the interface with which the user can create an automation that turns off the light when the YouTube app launches, after first creating the "Turn off the living room light" script by demonstration.

These features allow scripts to be triggered not only by mobile apps for IoT devices, as shown in the example usage scenario, but also by other third-party Android apps. Prior research has shown that the usage of smartphone apps is highly contextual [6, 23] and also varies [45] for different groups of users. By allowing the launching of apps and the notifications from apps to trigger IoT scripts, the user can create highly context-aware automation with EPIDOSITE, for example, to change the color of the ambient lighting when the Music Player is launched, to adjust the thermostat when the Sleep Monitor app is launched, or even to warm up the car when the Alarm app rings (and sends the notification) on winter mornings.

Using the above two types of triggers, along with the external service trigger introduced in the next section, user-demonstrated scripts for smartphone apps can also be triggered by readings and status of IoT sensors and devices. As shown in [29], many common tasks can be automated using PBD on smartphone apps. Some examples are ordering a coffee (using the Starbucks app), requesting cabs (Uber app), sending emails, etc. EPIDOSITE empowers users to integrate IoT smart devices with available smartphone apps to create context-aware and responsive automations.

### External Service Triggers

To expand the capabilities of EPIDOSITE to leverage all of the available resources, we implemented a server application that allows EPIDOSITE to integrate with the popular

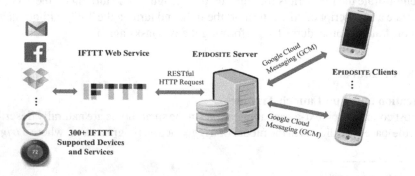

**Fig. 3.** The architecture of the EPIDOSITE external service trigger mechanism.

automation service IFTTT. Through this integration, an EPIDOSITE script can be triggered by over 360 web services supported by IFTTT, including social networks (e.g., Facebook, Twitter), news (e.g., ESPN, Feedly), email, calendar management, weather and supported devices like smart hubs (e.g., Google Home, Amazon Echo), smart appliances, fitness trackers, home monitors, and smart speakers. An EPIDOSITE script can also be used to trigger actions for IFTTT-supported services. Figure 3 shows the overall architecture for supporting external service triggers, consisting of the client side, the server side, the IFTTT service and how they communicate.

An IFTTT applet consists of two parts: a trigger and an action, in which either part can be an EPIDOSITE script. If an EPIDOSITE script is used as the trigger, then an HTTP request will be sent out to IFTTT via the EPIDOSITE server to execute the corresponding IFTTT action when the trigger is activated. Similarly, if an EPIDOSITE script is used as the action, then it will be executed on the corresponding client smartphone upon the client application receiving a Google Cloud Messaging (GCM) message sent by the EPIDOSITE server when the associated IFTTT trigger is activated. The EPIDOSITE server communicates with IFTTT through the IFTTT Maker channel, which can receive and make RESTful HTTP web requests. The EPIDOSITE server side application is also highly scalable and can handle multiple clients at the same time.

To create an IFTTT triggered script, the user first creates an EPIDOSITE script for the "action" part by demonstration, where the user records the procedure of performing the desired task by manipulating the phone apps. Then, the user goes to IFTTT, chooses "New Applet," and chooses a trigger for the script. After this, the user chooses the Maker channel as the action. For the address for the web request, the EPIDOSITE app on the phone will automatically generate a URL which the user can just paste into this field. The auto-generated URL is in the format of:

http://[SERVER_ADDRESS]/client=[CLIENT_NAME]&scriptname=[SCRIPT_NAME]

where *[SERVER ADDRESS]* is the address of the EPIDOSITE server, *[CLIENT_NAME]* is the name of the EPIDOSITE client (which by default is the combination of the phone owner's name and the phone model. e.g., "Amy's Nexus 6") and *[SCRIPT_NAME]* is the name of the EPIDOSITE script to trigger. The user can just paste this URL into the IFTTT field (see Fig. 4).

The procedure to create an EPIDOSITE-triggered IFTTT applet is similar, except that the user needs to add "trigger an IFTTT applet" as an operation when demonstrating the EPIDOSITE script, and then use the Maker channel as the trigger.

**Cross-app Interoperability**
Interoperability among IoT devices has been an long-time important challenge [14]. Sharing data across devices from different "ecosystems" often requires the user to manually setup the connection using techniques like HTTP requests, which require carefully planning and extensive technical expertise [11]. Middleware like Bezirk[5] and [5, 16, 24, 41] supports IoT interoperation and provides a high-level representation

---

[5] http://developer.bezirk.com/.

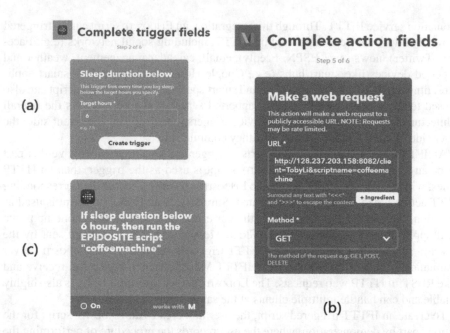

**Fig. 4.** Creating an IFTTT applet that triggers an EPIDOSITE script: (a) creating the trigger condition "sleep duration below 6 h" using the Fitbit activity tracker; (b) creating the action of running the EPIDOSITE script "coffeemachine" using the URL generated by EPIDOSITE; (c) the IFTTT applet created.

model for common IoT devices, but these also require the user to have sophisticated programming skills.

EPIDOSITE supports the user in extracting the value of a TextView object in the user interface of the an app by using a gesture during the demonstration, storing the value in a variables and then using the values saved in these variables later in the script. All the user needs to do to save a value is to click on the "Get a Text Element on the Screen" option from the recording menu while demonstrating, circle the desired element on the screen using a finger gesture (the yellow stroke in Fig. 5), and select the element in a pop-up menu (see Fig. 5). Later when the user needs to enter a string in a script, the user can instead choose to use the value from a previously created variable.

When a script is executed that contains a value extraction operation, EPIDOSITE will automatically navigate as demonstrated to the user interface where the desired value is located, and then will dynamically extract the value based on the resource ID and the location of the corresponding TextView object. This approach does not require the involved app to have any API or other data export mechanism. As long as the desired value is displayed as a text string in the app, the value can be extracted and used in other parts of the script.

Currently, EPIDOSITE only supports using the extracted values in later operations exactly as they were displayed. As future work, we plan to support the reformatting and transformation of the variable values, as well as common arithmetic and string operations on the values.

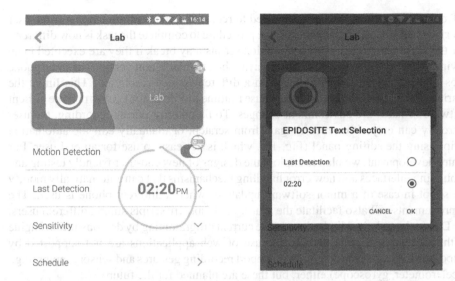

**Fig. 5.** Extracting the time of the last detection from a D-link motion sensor in the Mydlink Home app using a circle gesture in EPIDOSITE (Color figure online)

## 5   Limitations and Future Work

The current version of EPIDOSITE has several limitations. First, for executing an automation, the phone must be powered on and concurrently connected to all the devices involved in the automation. If the phone is powered off, or disconnected from the involved IoT devices, the automation will fail to execute. This limitation will particularly affect EPIDOSITE's applicability for devices that are connected to the phone via a local network or through a short-range wireless communication technology (e.g., Bluetooth, ZigBee, IR), since with these devices, the phone is restricted to be connected to the local network, or physically within range of the wireless connection for the automation to work. Second, EPIDOSITE automations need to run in the foreground on the main UI thread of the phone. Thus, if an automation is triggered when the user is actively operating the phone at the same time (e.g., if the user is on a phone call), then the user's interaction with the phone will be interrupted. The automation execution may also fail if it is interrupted by a phone event (e.g., an incoming phone call) or by the user's action.

For some of the above limitations, an approach is to use a separate phone as the hub for IoT automation, and to run EPIDOSITE on that phone instead of using the user's primary smartphone. By doing this, the separate phone can be consistently plugged in and stay connected with the IoT devices to ensure that the automations can be triggered and executed properly. Currently, a compatible Android phone can be purchased for less than $50, which makes this solution affordable.

Further limitations include that the current version of EPIDOSITE provides little assistance in testing and debugging. When an automation uses a trigger that cannot be activated manually (e.g., at a future time, or due to a weather condition), the user may not be able to demonstrate or test this automation. In the case that the controlling app of an

IoT device is updated, the user may need to record the demonstration again if the user interface of the app has changed, or if the procedure to complete the task is now different. For the same reason, EPIDOSITE automation scripts may break if they are executed in an environment with different IoT devices available, with different versions of smartphone apps running, or on a smartphone with a different screen resolution. This limits the sharing of EPIDOSITE scripts, and may cause runtime problems for EPIDOSITE if the current software or hardware environment changes. To fix an error during recording, the user currently can only either record again from scratch, or manually edit the automation script using the editing panel (Fig. 1c), which is not easy to use for an end user. For future development, we plan to explore the designs of new end-user friendly testing and debugging interfaces and new error handling mechanisms that can automatically modify the script in case of a minor software update or when a different phone is used. The improvements will also facilitate the sharing of EPIDOSITE scripts among different users.

Due to the technical limitations in the current programming by demonstration engine in the system, tasks that involve the use of web applications are not supported by EPIDOSITE. EPIDOSITE also does not yet support recording gestures and sensory inputs (e.g., accelerometer, gyroscope) either, but these are planned for the future.

In this work, we enabled the user to trigger automations for IoT devices based on the usage context of smartphones by providing the notification and app launch triggers. For future work, we plan to generalize these capabilities, to design usable and easily understandable ways for the end users to create automations combining the contents displayed by various apps, the inputs from the available phone sensors, and the available personal data on the phone. For example, using the location sensor of the phone, one could enable different automation scripts for the same trigger depending on where the user was. Existing context-aware computing research have contributed many technical solutions for transforming the smartphone usage and sensor data into more meaningful behavioral-centric personal data [43]. EPIDOSITE offers opportunities to connect user-centric behaviors on smartphones and users' smart home environments. We hope this will empower the end users to create more intelligent and useful context-aware applications.

We also plan to explore how to make it easier for end users to create more complex automations with control structures such as compound conditionals and loops. AppsGate [7] supports creating control structures in a syntax-driven editor using a pseudo-natural language, which was shown to be easy for creating simple rules, but difficult for creating compound conditionals. SmartFit [2] introduces an interactive graphical editor with which end users can create conditionals using IoT sensor data for rule-based EUD systems. However, it still remains a major design challenge to make it easier for end users to express the logic and the control structures in programming by demonstration systems. Gamut [31, 32] is a PBD system that can infer programming logic from multiple examples from the user, but it has been shown to be hard for non-expert end users to provide meaningful and helpful additional examples for inferring programming logics [26, 31, 32]. We are currently investigating the approach of having the users talk about their intentions using speech during the demonstration, and inferring the programming logic using techniques from AI and natural language processing [28].

# 6    Conclusion

In this work, we introduce EPIDOSITE, a new programming by demonstration system that makes it possible for end users to create automations for consumer IoT devices on their smartphones. It supports programming across multiple IoT devices and exchanging information among them without requiring the devices to be of the same brand or within the same "ecosystem". The programming by demonstration approach minimizes the necessity to learn programming concepts. EPIDOSITE also supports using arbitrary third-party Android mobile apps and hundreds of available web services in the scripts to create highly context-aware and responsive automations.

**Acknowledgement.**    This work was supported in part by the Yahoo! InMind project.

# References

1. Argall, B.D., et al.: A survey of robot learning from demonstration. Robot. Auton. Syst. **57**(5), 469–483 (2009)
2. Barricelli, B.R., Valtolina, S.: A visual language and interactive system for end-user development of internet of things ecosystems. J. Vis. Lang. Comput. (2017, in press)
3. Barricelli, B.R., Valtolina, S.: Designing for end-user development in the Internet of Things. In: Díaz, P., Pipek, V., Ardito, C., Jensen, C., Aedo, I., Boden, A. (eds.) IS-EUD 2015. LNCS, vol. 9083, pp. 9–24. Springer, Cham (2015). doi:10.1007/978-3-319-18425-8_2
4. Billard, A., et al.: Robot programming by demonstration. In: Siciliano, B., Khatib, O. (eds.) Springer Handbook of Robotics, pp. 1371–1394. Springer, Heidelberg (2008)
5. Blackstock, M., Lea, R.: IoT interoperability: a hub-based approach. In: 2014 International Conference on the Internet of Things (IOT), pp. 79–84. IEEE (2014)
6. Böhmer, M., et al.: What's in the apps for context? Extending a sensor for studying app usage to informing context-awareness. In: Proceedings of the 2013 ACM Conference on Pervasive and Ubiquitous Computing Adjunct Publication, pp. 1423–1426. ACM, New York (2013)
7. Coutaz, J., Crowley, J.L.: A first-person experience with end-user development for smart homes. IEEE Pervasive Comput. **15**(2), 26–39 (2016)
8. Cypher, A., Halbert, D.C.: Watch What I Do: Programming by Demonstration. MIT Press, Cambridge (1993)
9. Danado, J., Paternò, F.: Puzzle: a visual-based environment for end user development in touch-based mobile phones. In: Winckler, M., Forbrig, P., Bernhaupt, R. (eds.) HCSE 2012. LNCS, vol. 7623, pp. 199–216. Springer, Heidelberg (2012). doi:10.1007/978-3-642-34347-6_12
10. De Russis, L., Corno, F.: HomeRules: a tangible end-user programming interface for smart homes. In: Proceedings of the 33rd Annual ACM Conference Extended Abstracts on Human Factors in Computing Systems, pp. 2109–2114. ACM, New York (2015)
11. Demeure, A., Caffiau, S., Elias, E., Roux, C.: Building and using home automation systems: a field study. In: Díaz, P., Pipek, V., Ardito, C., Jensen, C., Aedo, I., Boden, A. (eds.) IS-EUD 2015. LNCS, vol. 9083, pp. 125–140. Springer, Cham (2015). doi: 10.1007/978-3-319-18425-8_9
12. Dey, A.K., et al.: A CAPpella: programming by demonstration of context-aware applications. In: Proceedings of the SIGCHI Conference on Human Factors in Computing Systems, pp. 33–40. ACM (2004)

13. Dey, A.K., et al.: iCAP: interactive prototyping of context-aware applications. In: Fishkin, K.P., et al. (eds.) Pervasive Computing, pp. 254–271. Springer, Berlin Heidelberg (2006)

14. Edwards, W.K., Grinter, R.E.: At home with ubiquitous computing: seven challenges. In: Abowd, Gregory D., Brumitt, B., Shafer, S. (eds.) UbiComp 2001. LNCS, vol. 2201, pp. 256–272. Springer, Heidelberg (2001). doi:10.1007/3-540-45427-6_22

15. Fox, A., et al.: Integrating information appliances into an interactive workspace. IEEE Comput. Graph. Appl. **20**(3), 54–65 (2000)

16. Gama, K., et al.: Combining heterogeneous service technologies for building an Internet of Things middleware. Comput. Commun. **35**(4), 405–417 (2012)

17. González García, C., et al.: Midgar: generation of heterogeneous objects interconnecting applications. a domain specific language proposal for Internet of Things scenarios. Comput. Netw. **64**, 143–158 (2014)

18. Grabler, F., et al.: Generating photo manipulation tutorials by demonstration. In: ACM SIGGRAPH 2009 Papers. pp. 66:1–66:9. ACM, New York (2009)

19. Greenberg, S.: Context as a dynamic construct. Hum.-Comput. Interact. **16**(2), 257–268 (2001)

20. Guinard, D., et al.: Towards physical mashups in the web of things. In: 2009 Sixth International Conference on Networked Sensing Systems (INSS), pp. 1–4. IEEE (2009)

21. Guinard, D., Trifa, V.: Towards the web of things: web mashups for embedded devices. In: Workshop on Mashups, Enterprise Mashups and Lightweight Composition on the Web (MEM 2009), in Proceedings of WWW (International World Wide Web Conferences), Madrid, Spain (2009)

22. Humble, J., Crabtree, A., Hemmings, T., Åkesson, K.-P., Koleva, B., Rodden, T., Hansson, P.: "Playing with the bits" user-configuration of ubiquitous domestic environments. In: Dey, Anind K., Schmidt, A., McCarthy, Joseph F. (eds.) UbiComp 2003. LNCS, vol. 2864, pp. 256–263. Springer, Heidelberg (2003). doi:10.1007/978-3-540-39653-6_20

23. Jesdabodi, C., Maalej, W.: Understanding usage states on mobile devices. In: Proceedings of the 2015 ACM International Joint Conference on Pervasive and Ubiquitous Computing, pp. 1221–1225. ACM, New York (2015)

24. Katasonov, A., et al.: Smart semantic middleware for the Internet of Things. ICINCO-ICSO **8**, 169–178 (2008)

25. Kubitza, T., Schmidt, A.: Towards a toolkit for the rapid creation of smart environments. In: Díaz, P., Pipek, V., Ardito, C., Jensen, C., Aedo, I., Boden, A. (eds.) IS-EUD 2015. LNCS, vol. 9083, pp. 230–235. Springer, Cham (2015). doi:10.1007/978-3-319-18425-8_21

26. Lee, T.Y., et al.: Towards understanding human mistakes of programming by example: an online user study. In: Proceedings of the 22nd International Conference on Intelligent User Interfaces, pp. 257–261. ACM, New York (2017)

27. Leshed, G., et al.: CoScripter: automating and sharing how-to knowledge in the enterprise. In: Proceedings of the SIGCHI Conference on Human Factors in Computing Systems, pp. 1719–1728. ACM, New York (2008)

28. Li, T.J.-J., et al.: Designing a conversational interface for a multimodal smartphone programming-by-demonstration agent. In: Conversational UX Design CHI 2017 Workshop, Denver, CO (2017, in press)

29. Li, T.J.-J., et al.: SUGILITE: creating multimodal smartphone automation by demonstration. In: Proceedings of the 2017 CHI Conference on Human Factors in Computing Systems. ACM, Denver (2017, in press)

30. Lieberman, H.: Your Wish is My Command: Programming by Example. Morgan Kaufmann, San Francisco (2001)

31. McDaniel, R.G., Myers, B.A.: Gamut: demonstrating whole applications. In: Proceedings of the 10th Annual ACM Symposium on User Interface Software and Technology, pp. 81–82 ACM, New York (1997)
32. McDaniel, R.G., Myers, B.A.: Getting more out of programming-by-demonstration. In: Proceedings of the SIGCHI Conference on Human Factors in Computing Systems, pp. 442–449 ACM, New York (1999)
33. Mennicken, S., et al.: From today's augmented houses to tomorrow's smart homes: new directions for home automation research. In: Proceedings of the 2014 ACM International Joint Conference on Pervasive and Ubiquitous Computing, pp. 105–115. ACM, New York (2014)
34. Modugno, F., Myers, B.A.: Pursuit: graphically representing programs in a demonstrational visual shell. In: Conference Companion on Human Factors in Computing Systems, pp. 455–456. ACM, New York (1994)
35. Myers, B.A.: Demonstrational interfaces: a step beyond direct manipulation. Computer **25**(8), 61–73 (1992)
36. Myers, B.A.: Visual programming, programming by example, and program visualization: a taxonomy. In: Proceedings of the SIGCHI Conference on Human Factors in Computing Systems, pp. 59–66. ACM, New York (1986)
37. Pintus, A., et al.: The anatomy of a large scale social web for internet enabled objects. In: Proceedings of the Second International Workshop on Web of Things. pp. 6:1–6:6. ACM, New York (2011)
38. Raffle, H., et al.: Beyond record and play: backpacks: tangible modulators for kinetic behavior. In: Proceedings of the SIGCHI Conference on Human Factors in Computing Systems, pp. 681–690. ACM, New York (2006)
39. Ricquebourg, V., et al.: The smart home concept: our immediate future. In: 2006 1st IEEE International Conference on E-Learning in Industrial Electronics, pp. 23–28 (2006)
40. Schmidt, A.: Programming ubiquitous computing environments. In: Díaz, P., Pipek, V., Ardito, C., Jensen, C., Aedo, I., Boden, A. (eds.) IS-EUD 2015. LNCS, vol. 9083, pp. 3–6. Springer, Cham (2015). doi:10.1007/978-3-319-18425-8_1
41. Song, Z., et al.: Semantic middleware for the Internet of Things. In: 2010 Internet of Things (IOT), pp. 1–8 (2010)
42. Ur, B., et al.: Practical trigger-action programming in the smart home. In: Proceedings of the SIGCHI Conference on Human Factors in Computing Systems, pp. 803–812. ACM, New York (2014)
43. Wiese, J.S.: Evolving the Ecosystem of Personal Behavioral Data (2015)
44. Zhang, T., Brügge, B.: Empowering the user to build smart home applications. In: Proceedings of 2nd International Conference on Smart Homes and Health Telematics (ICOST2004), Singapore (2004)
45. Zhao, S., et al.: Discovering different kinds of smartphone users through their application usage behaviors. In: Proceedings of the 2016 ACM International Joint Conference on Pervasive and Ubiquitous Computing, pp. 498–509. ACM, New York (2016)
46. Zhong, Y., et al.: Smart home on smart phone. In: Proceedings of the 13th International Conference on Ubiquitous Computing, pp. 467–468. ACM, New York (2011)

# Personalizing a Student Home Behaviour

Luca Corcella, Marco Manca[(✉)], and Fabio Paternò

HIIS Laboratory, CNR-ISTI, Via Moruzzi 1, 56124 Pisa, Italy
{luca.corcella,marco.manca,fabio.paterno}@isti.cnr.it

**Abstract.** Trigger-Action programming is emerging as an expressive and effective approach when customizing services and applications that have to react to several dynamic events. Recent research efforts aim to overcome some limitations of existing commercial tools in supporting editing of personalization rules. However, they have often been applied and assessed in laboratories. In this work we report on how a personalization platform has been applied to an application controlling the home of a group of students. The home has been equipped with various appliances and sensors accessible through an Arduino board. The personalization platform has been customized to integrate with the home application through a context manager middleware. The resulting personalization tool and the home application have been used and assessed by the students living in the home and various colleagues and friends without programming experience.

**Keywords:** End-User Development for home applications · Trigger-action programming · Context-aware applications

## 1 Introduction

Major recent technological trends have seen the advent of mobile and Internet of Things technologies. This has implied that we live in more and more variegated contexts of use characterised by the dynamic association of people, devices, things, and services. Many types of dynamic events are generated in such rich contexts of use. At the same time the number of users accessing applications and interested in their potential customization is increasing. Such users have variegated needs and interests, which often are not well supported by existing applications. Thus, it becomes fundamental to provide users without programming experience with tools that allow them to personalize the context-dependent behaviour of their applications [1]. A typical domain in which such issues often arise is the home. Indeed, various sensors and appliances are being introduced to make our homes more intelligent for security, heating, and other aspects. However, different people may have different views about the most suitable way to exploit such technologies, and it is difficult to find applications able to satisfy all the possible needs.

In recent years such issues have stimulated the interest of various researchers [2] in finding novel solutions to ease the use and customization of context-dependent applications. The goal is to obtain intelligent environments in which both devices and users are able to interact in a context-dependent manner. In this perspective End-User Development (EUD) [3] tools can play an important role in transforming users from passive

S. Barbosa et al. (Eds.): IS-EUD 2017, LNCS 10303, pp. 18–33, 2017.
DOI: 10.1007/978-3-319-58735-6_2

consumers of existing applications into active producers in determining the behaviour of intelligent environments. Various apps for customizing the behaviour of existing applications in mobile devices or Web services have been introduced, such as Atooma[1], Tasker[2], IFTTT[3]. In general, they adopt the trigger-action programming paradigm in which some events and/or conditions determine the performance of some actions. However, such approaches present difficulties to find a good trade-off between usability and expressiveness (the ability to specify the many possible types of triggers and actions) [4].

One tool that aims to overcome such limitations is TARE (Trigger-Action Rule Editor) [5], an editor for specifying trigger-action personalization rules that can be applied to Web applications. In the corresponding personalization platform it is integrated with a context manager that is able to connect to a variety of sensors and devices, and provide logical descriptions of the events and conditions that are verified. However, its evaluation has been carried out in a laboratory, and we deemed it interesting to investigate its use in realistic environments. Thus, we have equipped a students' home with a number of sensors and devices with the support of an Arduino board. The home is a typical environment suitable for the deployment of sensors and actuator representative of the Internet of Things possibilities. We chose a students' home because they showed interest and enthusiasm in participating in the experiment, in addition, they share common rooms in the house, and this can highlight particular situations that can hardly occur in other homes. We have customized the context manager for accessing the sensors and devices in the considered home, and a responsive Web application has been developed to provide users with easy access to the appliances' state and control it. Then, the Web application has been integrated with TARE in order to allow users to define personalization rules and check the effects of their performance. We have then carried out a usability test to assess the effectiveness and usefulness of the resulting personalization environment and its application, and gathered feedback from the students after use over long time. To summarize, the contributions of this work are:

- Demonstrate how a general personalization platform can be integrated in a real context of use (with specific sensors, devices, and appliances) and an associated application;
- Report on the usability of the integrated personalization platform and application assessed through a user test carried out in the actual context of use, and trials carried out, still in the real context, over a one month period.

In the paper after discussing related work, we present some background information on TARE, next we describe the home application developed and the students home equipped with various sensors and devices. Then, we illustrate how they have been integrated with TARE and the associated personalization platform, and report on the usability test and discuss its results along with the experiences of the home inhabitants. Lastly, we draw some conclusions and provide indications for future work.

---

[1] https://play.google.com/store/apps/details?id=com.atooma.
[2] http://tasker.dinglisch.net.
[3] https://ifttt.com/.

## 2   Related Work

In recent years various apps have been introduced to support some level of person-alization. They have different features and complexity. Tasker requires some tech-nical knowledge, while Spacebrew[4] users should have some knowledge in Java-Script programming. Atooma and IFTTT are free tools and more intuitive in terms of use, but still with some limitations. However, such tools do not provide imme-diate support for home personalization. In this perspective an interesting contribu-tion is AppGate [6]. It is composed of a set of tools that support the specification of rules, which are described through a subset of natural language by an editor that aims to support their specification taking into account the actual state of the home context. A first test of this tool has been carried out in the home of the researchers who designed it and some volunteers. The users specified some rules, indicating 3–5 that on average can be useful in their daily life.

IFTTT is an environment that allows users to connect existing Web applications (such as Gmail, Twitter, Facebook) and devices (such as Philips HUE, Nike+ , Ther-moSmart, Samsung HUB). Each rule can contain only one trigger and one action. Its limitations are that it does not support rules with trigger compositions and the list of applications that can be connected is not easy to manage and understand. A recent study [7] indicated that users can quickly learn rules with multiple triggers and actions. Atooma is an Android app that allows users to specify rules, with also the possibility to include up to five elements in the triggers and actions. The possible triggers and actions are grouped in categories in order to facilitate their identification and access, even if they are less than those supported by IFTTT. A study [8] reported a user test with these two applications with some qualitative and quantitative results. They seem to indicate that users liked more Atooma than IFTTT, the rule-based approach has been appreciated, also because it allows them to easily automatize and personalize some daily activities.

Overall, the studies that have addressed usability of trigger-action programming tools have often been carried out in laboratories (for example [8]), far from realistic contexts of use where to immediately perceive the results of their execution. One excep-tion is AppGate, which was tested by the authors in their home. In this work we present a study that assess in a real context of use the usability of a rule-based personalization platform, which can be applied not only to the home but also in other environments such as shops, hospitals, and data warehouses.

## 3   Home Application

In order to test the personalization environment a responsive Web home application has been developed, which allows users to customize and control the home appliances and sensors and check their status (Fig. 1). The sensors are able to detect the temperature, humidity, gas and smoke presence, and the motion; moreover, in the house there are

---

[4] http://docs.spacebrew.cc/.

some appliances that can be remotely controlled (tv, radio, fan and the entrance, kitchen and living room lights).

**Fig. 1.** Home application (mobile version)

In order to read the sensors values we used an Arduino board equipped with an Ethernet interface to connect it to the router; moreover, we connected the Arduino board to a series of sensors (such as Kookye Smart Home Sensor Kit for Arduino and Raspberry Pi[5]). Thus, in this case, Arduino acted as an hub, and for this purpose we implemented a RESTful web service, which provides the application with a JSON object containing the values read from the sensors. The backend of the home application has been developed with Node.js[6], an open-source, cross-platform JavaScript runtime environment with an event-driven architecture capable of asynchronous input/output processing. Moreover, the application backend is able also to communicate with the smart objects that are installed in the home (e.g. the Philips HUE lamps) in order to change their state. The user interface is presented as a dashboard and users can immediately interact with the home appliances and visualize the data read from the sensors. Sensors and appliances are organized in a grid layout and represented through the Card component of Material Design. The grid layout along with the Card component facilitate the visualization of the user interface in small devices such as smartphones, where the cards are displayed one below the other.

The user interface updates the sensor values through asynchronous AJAX request to the backend part. The application also integrates a vocal interface to interact with appliances and sensors implemented with the JavaScript library Artyom.js. In addition to the

---

[5] http://kookye.com/2016/08/01/smart-home-sensor-kit-for-arduinoraspberry-pi/.

[6] https://nodejs.org.

management and control of smart devices, the application handles some external services, such as Weather and Calendar Events.

## 4    The Personalization Approach

TARE has been developed in such a way that users can customize and adapt applications belonging to different domains, such as smart retail, ambient-assisted living, smart homes. Its main goal is to allow users without programming skills to be able to combine, configure, monitor and customize various aspects of an application depending on the context of use. Some characterising features are the possibility of combining multiple triggers and actions; natural language feedback; support of a meta-design approach; and trigger-action rules management.

The editor utilizes a context-model that is supported by the Context-Manager, a middleware component which integrates all the contextual information from the various sensors. The Context Manager is composed of a server and various delegates installed on the available devices. The context model is structured along four dimensions (user, environment, technology and social relationship) which aim to describe the relevant aspects that can affect interactive context-dependent applications. The User dimension describes all the information related to the user such as personal data, education, preferences, position, etc. The Environment dimension defines all the characteristics of the space where the application is executed or where the user acts. The Technology dimension considers all the attributes of the devices, sensors and appliances that are present in the considered context of use. Finally, the Social dimension concerns the social relationships that can exist between people that are present in the context of use.

Our starting point was a general context model that had to be customized in order to create a more specific one to consider all the relevant aspects in the target home. For this purpose, we identified the sensors installed in the home and the available objects and devices in the home. A new Context Model Editor has been developed in order to facilitate the refinement of the generic context model. It is an interactive software able to graphically show the generic context model in a tree-like representation and support its editing. The root is the context node which is decomposed into 4 categories representing the four main dimensions. Each node in the tree represents a context category which is further decomposed into other categories or entities. Three different colours have been used: blue for dimension nodes, green for the categories and pink for the context entities (Fig. 2). The context model editor does not require any programming knowledge. It should be used by some domain expert that is able to clearly indicate the relevant contextual aspects.

When all the changes on the generic context model are done, it is possible to generate automatically an XML schema with the description of the specific context model. Such schema can be loaded and interpreted by the Trigger-Action Rule Editor (TARE), which will present all the corresponding triggers that can be useful to define the personalization rules. In order to create a TARE instance specific for the target context of use it is also necessary to indicate the smart objects, devices and appliances that exist in it.

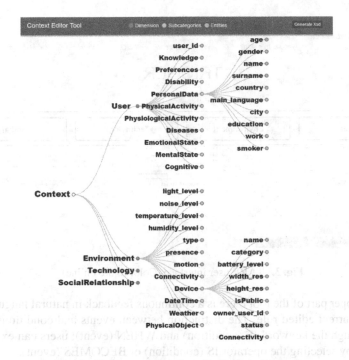

**Fig. 2.** Context-model editor (Color figure online)

## The Trigger Action Rule Editor (TARE)

TARE is a Web tool that helps users without programming experience to create personalization rules in order to customize the behaviour of devices and applications. Users can start creating rules either by triggers or by actions and it is possible to reuse existing rules as a starting point to create new ones. Rules are composed of two parts: trigger and actions and the basic structure is as follows:

*IF/WHEN <trigger_expression> DO <action_expression>*

The *trigger_expression* part describes the events or the conditions that trigger the rule execution, while the *action_expression* defines the actions that should be executed. Each expression can be composed of one or more triggers/actions: triggers can be combined through the AND/OR operators, while actions are executed sequentially.

During the rule editing, triggers are defined by navigating through the hierarchy described in the context model defined through the Context Model editor: each contextual dimension is traversed passing through a number of conceptual levels until a context entity is reached (the context entities are the basic elements of the context model). In order to show only the relevant elements, the contextual levels are presented in an interactive way: the editor only shows the children of the selected element. Figure 3 shows the TARE interface representing the editing of a context entity, the yellow rectangles represent the path to reach the selected entity: Environment -> Physical Object -> hue lamp 1 entrance -> State.

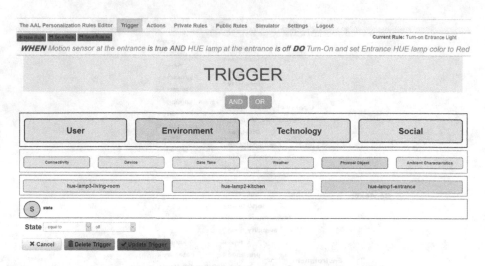

**Fig. 3.** TARE user interface (Color figure online)

In the upper part of the tool there is a continuous feedback in natural language indicating the current edited rule. The distinction between events and conditions is highlighted through the keyword IF (condition) and WHEN (event); users can express this distinction by selecting the operator IS (condition) or BECOMES (event).

When the Authoring tool is configured users can start to edit the rules for the target context of use. Rules are saved in JSON format and then sent to the Adaptation Engine module. When the application is deployed it subscribes to this module (Adaptation Engine), which is in charge of subscribing to the context manager in order that it be informed of the occurrence of the events and conditions defined in the rules. Then, when a trigger is verified the application receives, interprets and applies the actions of the rules indicating how to modify the state of the involved devices and appliances.

## 5    Integration of the Home App and Personalization Platform

As a first step, the house environment was studied in order to understand which sensors can be useful, where to put them and how to access them. A students' home was chosen to bring the personalization environment out of the laboratory and evaluate it in a real case. The selected house is composed of 4 bedrooms, a living room, a kitchen and a bathroom; it is occupied by 4 people including 3 university students (not computer experts and without programming experience).

The people living in the house chose to install sensors only in common areas, which are: kitchen, entrance and living room. The goal of the home application was to increase the home comfort; the level of security within the home; entertainment; and monitor the domestic consumption. An Arduino board was used to connect with the sensors, and it was expanded with an Ethernet interface in order to connect it to the router and then to the internet in order to provide data to the application which was located in an external server. Figure 4 shows where the sensors were installed within the house: at the entrance it was positioned the motion, noise and light sensors and a Philips hue lamp; the Arduino and Philips bridges were connected to the router installed at the entrance. The Philips Bridge was able to communicate with the three Hue Lamps installed in the house through the ZigBee protocol.

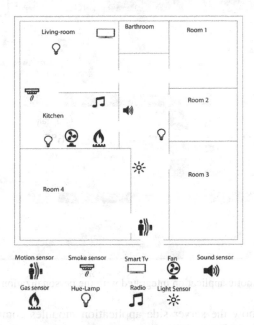

**Fig. 4.** Map of the student house with sensors and devices

The kitchen was equipped with the smoke and gas sensors, a Hue lamp, and two electric smart sockets to which the fan and the radio devices were connected. These smart sockets were connected with Arduino, which is able to provide the electric power when needed. The television and a Hue lamp were installed in the living room.

In the domotic domain, users personalize and control their devices though applications which are able to manage some objects and visualize the data originated by the sensors. Usually such applications provide a limited set of customizations, and they are not able to react to various events that can occur in the context of use. The personalization platform can be integrated with the applications in order to provide more extended support for this purpose. Thus, the home application described has been integrated with the Personalization Platform in order to allow users to further personalize the application so that it can dynamically reacts to a broader set of contextual changes according to the users' indications expressed with the trigger-action rules.

For implementing the integration, the application has been extended with a script able to interpret and visualize the personalization rules created with TARE. Thus, the home application can receive the list of rules associated with it and subscribe to the Adaptation Engine in order to receive the corresponding actions when a relevant rule is triggered. These rules can be visualized in a panel added on the right sidebar (Fig. 5 shows an example where one rule is visualized in the top-right part).

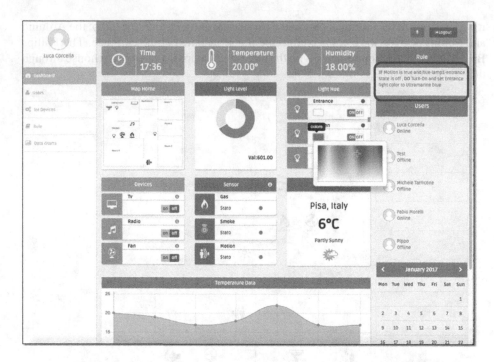

**Fig. 5.** Domotic application integrated with the personalization platform

Figure 6 shows how the server side application modules communicate with the Personalization Platform. First of all, when the home application is deployed the server side module (*Subscription Module*) subscribes to the Adaptation Engine indicating its name and the application end point through a REST service. The application end point is the URL of an application service that will receive the actions to perform from the Adaptation Engine. Then, if a user specified a rule such as: "When the light level in the kitchen is less than 50 then turn-on the kitchen light" and the light level actually goes below this threshold, then the Adaptation Engine will send the action to the application end point specified during the subscription. In order to trigger a rule, the Context manager should be informed every time a sensor, a device or an appliance change their values: e.g. when a flat mate turns on a light (through the application or through a physical switch) or when motion sensor detects a movement then the IoT manager sends these updates to the context manager. The Context manager exposes a RESTful web service for each context entity that should be updated. There is a module (*IoT Manager*) on the application server side part in charge of monitoring the IoT sensors installed in the house. Each time a sensor or an appliance changes its state, this module will update the Context server through the corresponding REST service.

Finally, there is the module (*Actions Receiver*), which corresponds to the end-point specified during the subscription. This module receives the actions when a rule is triggered, interprets them and communicates with the IoT manager in order to change the state of the appliances involved in the actions. There can be two different types of actions: Update, which will update the state of a home device, thus the Action Receiver module

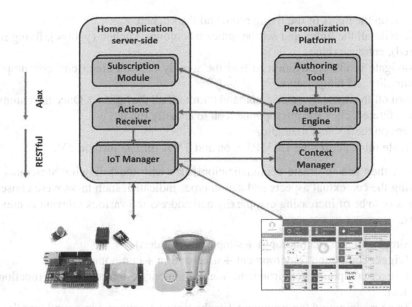

**Fig. 6.** Integration between domotic application and personalization platform

will call the corresponding function, implemented in the IoT Manager module, specifying the involved device, the action type (change state, change colour, etc.) and the new value (e.g. state = on, colour = red); Invoke Function, this action specifies which function the application should invoke, examples are: sending a notification or a SMS, or displaying the charts of the temperature, humidity or power consumption.

## 6   Usability Evaluation

We report on the use of the application and the personalization tool in a specific test and over a one month trial period. For the test, a number of additional users were invited in the students' home in order to receive feedback from a broader audience still in the same real context where the actual effects of their personalization could be observed. We think that this type of feedback is more meaningful than that obtainable in a laboratory because in this case users can have a better and immediate understanding of the actual effects of the rules that they specify.

**Usability Test**
The test was carried out by twenty users (12 males), aged between 20 and 28. They had some familiarity with technologies, in particular Web technologies, but not experience in programming. In order to access the various features of the application, the tasks they had to perform were:

(1) Turn on the lights of the living room and the kitchen.
(2) Turn on all the lights and set the indicated colours: kitchen (yellow), living room (red), entrance (blue).
(3) Navigate in the application to find the weekly data on electricity consumption, humidity and temperature.
(4) Turn off the lights by voice command ("turn off all the lights"). Once the command was uttered, click the microphone icon to actually run it.
(5) Turn on the TV and the radio.
(6) Create this rule: IF hue-LAMP3 is on and TV is off DO turn on TV.

Then, they had to create personalization rules with the following structures and involving the contextual aspects and action types indicated, such tasks were chosen in such a way to be of increasing complexity and address the various relevant contextual aspects:

(7) Simple Trigger (technology) + simple action (alert).
(8) Trigger compound (environment + user) action + compound (alert).
(9) Trigger compound (environment + environment) + simple action (functionalities).
(10) Trigger compound (environment + technology) + actions compound (appliances, functionality).
(11) Trigger compound (user) + action compound (appliances, reminders).
(12) Trigger compound (user environment + technology) + simple action (appliance).
(13) Create a new rule from a rule created earlier.

Participants received an introduction to the motivations and goals of the test, and a high level description of the application, TARE, and the structure and possible content of the rules. The users were observed by one of the authors during the test in order to annotate particular comments and emotional states, their sessions were also logged with Camtasia.

Figure 7 shows a box-and-whisker plot reporting the average task performance time along with minimum, maximum and quartiles. Users seemed able to interact comfortably with the sensors and appliances, easily understanding how they were represented in the application user interface. The task performance with the personalization tool (tasks 6 to 13) was variable. Most users seemed to perform better over time. Simple rules required less time. Task 8 took relatively long, probably because it was the first example where they had to compose two triggers. Some users encountered some difficulties in understanding the use of the logical operators to compose triggers and tried to avoid their use. Some users thought that they could use the logical operators even in the action specifications. The data indicate that users became more familiar with editing the rules over time and became more efficient. Indeed, if we consider the rule associated with task 12, it involved three triggers and one action with an average time of 2'24", while trigger 8, which required only one trigger and one action took on average 2'36".

Regarding the application, task 3 and 4 presented some problems for some users. Task 3 was intended to verify whether the search for information regarding weekly electricity consumption, the house temperature and humidity. Its box plot indicates that a few users encountered some problems in finding the requested data: they did not notice the link to access them, and thus navigated across the application for a while before finding them. Task 4 related to the use of voice commands to interact with the sensors. The command to activate voice input was not well positioned in the user interface, and therefore many users sometimes took some time to find it and often asked for help from the evaluator.

We found three types of errors: wrong selections of the elements defining the triggers or the actions; wrong ways to compose triggers and actions or use the logical operators; wrong selections in the application, for example in selecting the page where the electrical consumption or the temperature are reported. Some errors were performed also in the use of the vocal commands because some users did not understand that it had to be explicitly activated.

In order to perform tasks 7 to 12 users specified 120 rules. The rules after the specification were executed so that users could see their effects in the home.

We can notice (Table 1) that 88 were correctly specified and executed. In the analysis of the errors we have classified them into two categories: moderate and serious errors. Moderate errors refer to wrong values in a trigger definition or a wrong parameter in action definition. The resulting rules can still work but the specified behaviour is not exactly the desired one. They happened in 26 cases (row three in Table 1). For example, a user specified a rule "IF temperature = 14 DO send a message "too cold" to 3281234567". While the correct condition should have been "IF temperature <= 14". Serious errors lead to rules that do not produce any meaningful effect (they happened in 6 cases). An example is "IF there is someone at home and lights are on then turn on the lights".

**Table 1.**  Types of error occurred during the test

|  | Simple rule | Complex rules |
|---|---|---|
| Executable | 17 | 71 |
| Not executable | 1 | 5 |
| Not correctly executable | 2 | 24 |

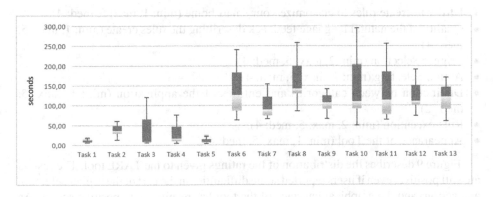

**Fig. 7.**  Task completion time

The users also had to rate some aspects of the application and the personalization tool through a 1–5 Likert Scale, where 5 was the highest ranking. For the application they rated:

- User interface consistency in the sensors' description (min: 3, max: 5, med: 4).
- Usefulness of voice commands (min: 2, max: 5, med: 4).
- Usefulness of the map representing the sensors in the house (min: 2, max: 5, med: 4).
- Usefulness of sensor monitoring and intelligent devices control through the application (min: 3, max: 5, med: 4)
- Quality of sensor integration with the Home application, and their control (min: 4, max: 5, med: 4).

The diagram below (Fig. 8) shows the distribution of the ratings. It is possible to note that none of the aspects was rated 1, and there were few 2s and 3s. The vocal interaction was the aspect that raised more concerns, probably because users were not used to it.

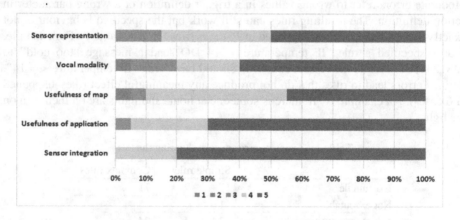

**Fig. 8.** Application ratings

For the personalization tool the aspects they had to rate were:

- Utility to create rules to customize your smart home (min: 1, max: 5, med: 4).
- Quality of the natural language feedback describing the rules create (min: 1, max: 5, med: 4).
- Trigger Selection (min: 2, max: 5, med: 4).
- Action Selecting (min: 2, max: 5, med: 4).
- Distinction between categories and entities of the application (min: 1, max: 5, med: 2).
- Rule execution (min: 2, max: 5, med: 4).
- Appearance of the Tool (min: 1, max: 5, med: 4).

Figure 9 describes the distribution of the ratings given to the TARE tool. The results are still positive, even if users reported some difficulties in the part of the trigger selection and actions and the graphical interface of the tool has received less positive scores. As for the problems in finding the trigger attributes, we observed that the majority of users started to look for the desired attribute following a path that made sense for them, that is, choosing a dimension (for example, user), and then continue exploring the trigger structure. The users who were not able to quickly find the desired attribute can be divided into two categories: the curious, that iteratively explored all the possible triggers with the goal of finding at a certain point the desired one; and those who repeatedly tried under the wrong dimension the desired intermediate nodes. In order to complete the task, the evaluator had to ensure that users considered all trigger types required by the rule structure specified in the proposed task. One useful option for those users who tend to "give up" after a couple of fruitless searching could be to provide some automatic support. For example, the ability to specify a keyword (for example the name of an attribute) on a search engine to obtain the path to the corresponding attribute in the contextual triggers structure.

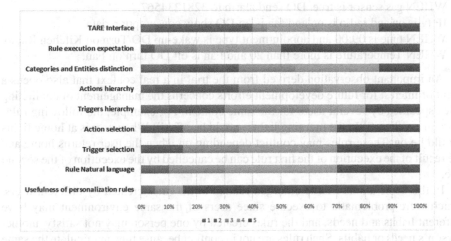

**Fig. 9.** TARE ratings

In conclusion, the participants also expressed suggestions and observations by answering some open questions. Regarding further application functionality, they suggested to integrate further home appliances such as heaters, washing machines, dishwashers, etc. In terms of suggestions for the application they indicated a preference for including support for other languages, and to better integrate voice commands, they would have liked that the voice assistant be always active. Regarding the personalization tool, a user suggested the possibility to introduce the ability to create rules by using a form, since he found that the current organization of the triggers and actions is uncomfortable because of the continuous page scrolling that users have to carry out. In addition, some participants suggested to integrate a search engine for triggers and actions. Others suggested the possibility of including a map of entities and categories so that users can quickly orient themselves when searching them.

**Trial Report**

In addition to this user test we have also collected the results of the experience of the students living in the home who used the application and the personalization tool for a long period of time. One of the authors was able to briefly talk to them and observe their use of the personalized application almost daily for one month. Three of them had no programming experience. In the beginning they were not convinced of the utility of the approach while over time they appreciated it and used it with some satisfaction. They preferred to use the mobile version of the responsive application. After some days of trials with the application they were requested to write some personalization rules that they deemed useful. Examples of the rules provided are:

- WHEN light-level less than 10 and time is 22:00 and entrance light is off DO Turn on Entrance Light.
- WHEN time is 22:00 and tv is off and motion is true, DO turn on living room tv.
- WHEN gas sensor is true, DO send alarm to 3281234567.
- IF tv is on and radio is on and fan is on DO show consumption data.
- WHEN time is 09:00 and appointment type is wake-up DO Turn on Kitchen Radio.
- WHEN Temperature is more than 20 and Fan is off DO turn on Fan.

An important observation derived from the trial in a real context that also opens a point of interest for future development efforts concerns the management of conflicting rules specified by several users for the same context. For example, the following rules were in conflict: (i) In the morning lights should be off; (ii) When user is at home lights should be on. These rules may conflict depending on when the user returns home and the result of the execution of the first rule can be cancelled by the execution of the second one.

In the home another issue emerged related to the rules created by different users, which were problematic to execute since users of the same environment may have different habits and needs, and the rules created by one person may not satisfy another person's needs or habits. Such rules are not in conflict because they manipulate the same resources (as the previous example with the lights) but they should not be performed since they do not meet the needs of all inhabitants. For example, it happened that a flatmate specified a rule whose execution created problems because it conflicted with the needs of the other housemates. This situation occurred with the following rule: - WHEN time is 8:30 AM DO Turn-on radio.

In this case the radio would wake up the housemates who want to continue to sleep at that time, while the user specified this rule in order to listen to the radio, which is located in the kitchen, during breakfast.

# 7    Conclusions and Future Work

In this paper a solution that allows end-users to customize applications taking into account the context of use by specifying trigger-action rules has been presented. In order to assess the effectiveness of this approach, the TARE tool and the corresponding plat-form have been customized to a specific home context of use. A home application has been developed and has been integrated with the personalization platform in order to test this environment in a real context.

The performed user tests indicate that people without programming experience are able to define personalization rules through the TARE tool with limited effort, and can learn how to use it in short time. The reported experience consisting in customizing and deploying the personalization platform for a students' home highlighted the usefulness of the proposed approach in a real context. It also indicated some issues that were not considered sufficiently before: sometimes the execution of the rules can produce effects that may not match the needs of all the users in the considered context. Future work will be dedicated to improving the TARE tool in order to better reasoning about rules performance in multi-users environments.

## References

1. Bellucci, A., Vianello, A., Florack, Y., Jacucci, G.: Supporting the serendipitous use of domestic technologies. IEEE Pervasive Comput. **15**(2), 16–25 (2016)
2. Desolda, G., Ardito, C., Matera, M.: End-user development for the Internet of Things: EFESTO and the 5 W composition paradigm. In: Daniel, F., Gaedke, M. (eds.) Rapid Mashup Development Tools: Second International Rapid Mashup Challenge, RMC 2016, Lugano, Switzerland, 6 June 2016, Revised Selected Papers, pp. 74–93. Springer, Cham (2017)
3. Lieberman, H., Paternò, F., Klann, M., Wulf, V.: End-user development: an emerging paradigm. In: Lieberman, H., Paternò, F., Wulf, V. (eds.) End-User Development. Human-Computer Interaction Series, vol. 9, pp. 1–8. Springer, Dordrecht (2006). doi: 10.1007/1-4020-5386-X_1
4. Lucci, G., Paternò, F.: Understanding end-user development of context-dependent applications in smartphones. In: Sauer, S., Bogdan, C., Forbrig, P., Bernhaupt, R., Winckler, M. (eds.) HCSE 2014. LNCS, vol. 8742, pp. 182–198. Springer, Heidelberg (2014). doi: 10.1007/978-3-662-44811-3_11
5. Ghiani, G., Manca, M., Paternò, F., Santoro, C.: Personalization of context-dependent applications through trigger-action rules. ACM Trans. Comput.-Hum. Interact. **24**(2), Article No. 14 (2017)
6. Coutaz, J., Crowley, J.L.: A first-person experience with end-user development for smart homes. IEEE Pervasive Comput. **15**(2), 26–39 (2016). doi:10.1109/MPRV.2016.24
7. Ur, B., McManus, E., Ho, M.P.Y., Littman, M.L.: Practical trigger-action programming in the smart home. In: Proceedings of the SIGCHI Conference on Human Factors in Computing Systems (CHI 2014), pp. 803–812. ACM, New York. doi:10.1145/2556288.2557420
8. Cabitza, F., Fogli, D., Lanzilotti, R., Piccinno, A.: Rule-Based Tools for the Configuration of Ambient Intelligence Systems: A Comparative User Study. Springer Science+Business Media, New York (2016). doi:10.1007/s11042-016-3511-2

# GURaaS: An End-User Platform for Embedding Research Instruments into Games

Carlos Pereira Santos[1,2(✉)], Jeroen van de Haterd[1], Kevin Hutchinson[1], Vassilis-Javed Khan[2], and Panos Markopoulos[2]

[1] NHTV Breda University of Applied Sciences, Monseigneur Hopmansstraat 1, 4817 JT Breda, Netherlands
{santos.c,140066,hutchinson.k}@nhtv.nl
[2] Eindhoven University of Technology, 5612 AZ Eindhoven, Netherlands
{c.a.pereira.santos,v.j.khan,p.markopoulos}@tue.nl

**Abstract.** In this paper, we detail a software platform that enables game developers to expose aspects of their games to researchers who are not necessarily familiar with game development, providing them the possibility to customize game content for behavioral user research, and more specifically to embed survey items in a game context. With this platform we introduce the concept of Games User Research as a Service (GURaaS). This articled describes the process we followed to design GURaaS, its high level architecture and its application in a case study. We envision that GURaaS will assist researchers and organizations by helping them expand their reach in finding participants and in collecting survey data reducing the tedium for survey participants.

**Keywords:** Game User Research · System architecture · End user

## 1 Introduction

There is a growing number of research studies in utilizing games for a research purpose; well-known examples include quantifying malaria parasites [1], creating accurate protein structure models [2], or tagging images to support the semantic web [3].

As in all aforementioned cases, the general approach researchers follow is to design a purpose-specific game, which are point-solutions that are not aimed to address broader research needs. Although such an approach can be very effective, it does require a considerable investment by behavioral researchers in game development which is typically neither their expertise nor their interest. In addition, this process does not easily scale up: first, because only well-resourced projects and ventures will be able to develop such games, and second, this approach fails to make good use of existing games that could be adapted for research purposes.

In practice, such an approach is restrictive in terms of resource requirements: a research team would either need to have a game development background or be able to outsource this task. It is obvious that not every research group would have the people or the budget required in order to develop such a game.

© Springer International Publishing AG 2017
S. Barbosa et al. (Eds.): IS-EUD 2017, LNCS 10303, pp. 34–48, 2017.
DOI: 10.1007/978-3-319-58735-6_3

In addition, designing a game that would be fun to play and become popular is an extra challenge. We argue that for a variety of purposes scalability could be achieved if researchers are allowed to add their content (research instruments) into existing games. To realize that vision, a platform that interfaces existing games with researchers is required, that enables them to re-use game software and facilitates them in adapting it for their research purpose.

Although there is a clear benefit for the researchers, one may question the added value for game developers of such a platform. Game developers are already using game telemetry techniques to improve their own development procedures, like remote debugging, target audience analysis and revenue tracking. However, the rapid development cycles of casual games combined with low development budgets create a complex development context, such that game developers are always looking for easy integration tools to support their work.

An easy to use, well documented platform which allows developers to automate the remote logging and to conduct proper Games User Research [4] to assess user experiences would be an added value for game developers [5]. In addition, it can be used as an alternative revenue stream for game developers by allowing their games to become a research platform, in a fashion similar to how Apple ResearchKit[1] is used and the way it exposes mobile data to researchers.

Our vision is to provide Games User Research as a Service (GURaaS). Specifically we aim to support this vision through a cloud-based platform that uses games as a dissemination tool, and collects large amounts of data by logging in-game player behavior, and which empowers researchers (including game researchers) to integrate and conduct studies among the player population. The GURaaS platform was designed and developed based on a stakeholder-centered analysis of the needs and requirements of each stakeholder (players, researchers and game developers). In this paper, we present in detail the findings of our process; the multi-tier high-level architecture; and how the online platform works. We conclude by explaining the setup of a case study and the next steps for future research.

## 2 GURaaS Design

At a conceptual level there are already several frameworks for developing serious games [6]. Such frameworks identify on an abstract level which components are important in a serious game. However, what is currently lacking is a practical implementation of such frameworks in the form of a platform that helps to match games with research needs. The platform have two main features: *(F1)* an in-game recording system and, *(F2)* a set of customizable player research activities.

**F1: In-game Recording System.** The platform contains a game and player behavior data recording system, which allows developers and researchers to collect and analyze detailed player data. This feature is common in todays' game development processes to

---

[1] http://www.apple.com/lae/researchkit/.

support game designers to use data-driven design and researchers to use quantitative and statistical research methods to analyze players' in-game behavior.

This data is also valuable for the player; a Player Dossier is a data-driven reporting tool which allow players to track, analyze and share their own in-game performance [7]. Player Dossiers are frequently available and are normally available on supporting online platforms linked to a specific game.

**F2: Player Research Activities.** This feature allows researchers to dynamically add the option to embed in the games explicit activity requests to players. In detail, a research activity is defined as a task that researchers can request to collect evidence from players that is relevant for their study. Such a request can be as simple as answering a Yes/No question.

Although, researchers could potentially have access to detailed player data *(F1)*, it is difficult to understand the player's experience based solely on the player in-game data, and so a more explicit protocol would be required to obtain more information from the players.

**Feature Analysis.** Both features F1 and F2 are valuable for both researchers and developers. The *In-game recording* (F1) is common practice in today's game develop-ment practices, but the *Player research activities* is pioneering by allowing researchers and practitioners to customize the collection of evidence. The combination of both features can help obtain complementary enriched data sets, which allows developers and researchers to gain a deeper understanding of the player. In the sections below we report the findings of our design approach, where we analyze in detail the system features by studying each actor's main motivation and needs, namely: *(i)* Players; *(ii)* Developers; and *(iii)* Researchers.

## 2.1  Players

Although players don't have an active role on deciding the game content, they have an active role in selecting the games they are playing, so it is essential to understand player motivations and how those may clash with the platform features (F1 and F2).

The in-game recordings (F1) has the essential role of facilitating the logging of player interaction, but for players this is completely transparent and therefore there is no need for a detailed analysis. On the other hand, the players are not used to engaging in research activities (F2), therefore we need to consider whether are player motivations are affected.

There is substantial literature that documents the video-game industry's focus in the players' engagement with their products; engagement is what addresses players' moti-vations and translates into notable user experiences which keep players involved with the product, brand or sequels [8–10].

A lesson to be drawn from the past, especially from serious games which do not solely focus on entertaining players and which may consequently fail to do so suffi-ciently, is to maintain player motivation. Charsky [11] clearly describes and justifies that the failure to address player motivation is the main factor that differentiates between Serious Games, Simulations and Edutainment; if players do not have an extrinsic motivation to engage with simulations and edutainment products, then those products are fated to fail. When the simulations and edutainment provide intrinsic motivations they become serious games.

For the purpose of our platform, it is essential to understanding player motivations and to assure the motivation is not deflected by the introduction of the games user research elements.

**Games.** Games reflect a fast rule based simulation, easy to achieve, which is a simplification of life. There are multiple theories that may explain why people play games e.g. the Maslow's Need Hierarchy Theory [12]. Although entertainment and games are definitely linked, there is a difference between both; Crawford [13] defines games by subdividing entertainment into multiple categories (illustrated in Fig. 1).

**Fig. 1.** Illustration of Crawford classification of entertainment products.

Entertainment can be an inert activity, like reading a book or watching TV, but also may involve interactivity. If an interactive entertainment product does not have a goal it is considered a toy, otherwise it is considered a challenge. Interactive challenges can be defined as individual (puzzles) or collective. A collective interactive challenge that does not allow people to react/confront each other is considered a competition (like a race), while an interactive entertainment challenge that allows conflict between participants defines a game.

Video-games can be clearly defined as interactive entertainment products which use game mechanics to challenge players and provide immediate feedback on their performance, fitting Crawford taxonomy [13]. Today's video games are quite adept in keeping the player's focus in small tangible tasks, and provide rewards when those tasks are completed successfully (e.g. new level, experience points, in-game currency, etc.). Such game mechanics support different types of fun to keep the players motivated [14].

**Fun.** Understanding what attracts players and supplying them the right keys/types of fun is extremely relevant. Lazzaro [15] describes the four keys to fun, which are able to identify game genres but also, to identify player motivation:

- Easy fun: curiosity from exploration, role play, and creativity;
- Hard fun: challenge, winning, achieving of a difficult goal;
- People fun: amusement from social interaction, competition and cooperation;
- Serious fun: excitement from educating or changing the player and their world.

Normally game designers, determine their target audience and identify their main motivations. By utilizing those fun keys while designing a game, they encourage increased player engagement.

Thoughtlessly adding research activities into game environments may disrupt the gameplay, meaning that using and disrupting in-game player behavior may confront the player and reduce the entertaining value (fun). Still, some games provide intermittent external stimuli to players by introducing advertisements in their game context, in the form of interactive audio-video and graphic representations, which require the player's action to either engage or dismiss the advertisement (see Fig. 2).

**Fig. 2.** Examples of in-game advertisements.

**Free to Play Games.** A study with over two thousand developers and players took a closer look into in-game advertisements [16]. The data showed that in-game advertisements in mobile games are popular with today's developer community. The reason is simple: the number of players who are actually willing to pay for the games is rather low. Thus it leaves game studios with a single monetizing option: that of advertisements. The same study makes clear that players understand the need of in-game advertisement. In fact, 54% of the players selected rewarded videos as their preferred way to pay for mobile in-game content. Rewarded videos are advertisements in video format that reward the player after viewing them, by providing some sort of virtual goods (e.g. virtual coins).

**Player Rewards.** Known game design patterns use rewards as a positive feedback for players [17]. Most player rewards are purely virtual game goods, like access to new in-game content, but other rewards like prizes, merchandising, services or even the players own data (player dossier), have been used to reward players.

Furthermore, player rewards have been used to stimulate and/or persuade player behavior in real life; for example Berkovsky [18] uses in-game virtual goods to stimulate real physical player activity. Another example was described above, where the acceptance and satisfaction of player towards in-game advertisement can be improved by providing in-game rewards [16].

**Rewarding Research Activities.** Presenting unsolicited research activities to players, might cause some distrust and annoyance. In addition, the nature of research activities requires researchers to request specific and sometimes personal questions like personality traits, and performance metrics that might create privacy concerns. To increase players' compliance it is important to (optionally) offer rewards like in-game content (e.g. currency, new levels, outfits, perks). Note that a balance between the activity (time, effort and interference) and the reward is important; this might mean the need to phase the rewards for example through a point system.

## 2.2 Game Developers

For the context of this report we define game developers as institutions or single developers that contribute to the development and publication of a game.

In todays' video-game context there are three major target platforms (PC, Console and Mobile) and all have multiple well known online stores that allow game developers to self-publish their games. This led to a shift in the industry that allows more independent groups and companies to self-production. Although the market is large it is dominated by the online stores and their ranking. The large majority of the published games have to fight for market share in order for the game to be profitable [19].

In terms of tools, developers already make use of a large and diverse set: game engines, modeling software, bug tracking, source control systems, management, documentation, analytics and/or publishing. Most of those decentralized online systems, which allow different people to take the responsibility over different aspects of the development process.

Additionally, developers are accustomed to integrating external libraries in their products like analytic tools, in-game advertisements or links to social network systems [20].

**Game Developer Motivations.** For professional developers games are a business which needs to be profitable. The investment in the integration of a platform in the game needs to be compensated by incentivizing the developer. Therefore for developers, they need to see benefits of using it which can be measured in multiple ways, like: development effort or time reduction, increased user base, better product or larger profits.

A tangible benefit for game developers is *In-game recording* (F1) which allows remote tracking, especially during the final stages of the development cycle where the pressure to launch the game increases and player experience needs to be measured accurately. Added value can be provided to developers if extra features, like a remote logging system, is present which directly supports the game development and which is similar in scope and implementation procedures.

Creating a space for using the same platform that is used by the game developers and allowing external parties to conduct research using the player base, might open new revenue streams which is really important in the current market setting.

**Games User Research.** Game User Research (GUR) is a research area that focuses on methodologies to measure and interpret player behavior. Game companies are increasingly using Games User Research in their development process since it has been shown to be extremely valuable to measure user experiences [4, 21]. Although there are already known methodologies that are applied regularly, each company has their own GUR data collection and analysis tools. For new companies that want to start this process, it is a large investment to learn these research techniques, develop an internal tool and only then be able to apply them [5]. It is clear that at this point there is a need for a proper player behavior collection *(F1)* and user experience measurement tool *(F2)*.

## 2.3 Researcher

Many researchers around the world have difficulties gathering research participants to perform all sorts of experiments and pilots for studies that require human subjects. Crowdsourcing platforms have recently emerged as attractive alternative to recruit participants for the purposes of collecting data and they have proven to be as good or better than other recruiting methods like sampling university students [22]. In addition, crowdsourcing can provide a more ethnically diverse and more work-experienced sample.

Although crowdsourcing platforms seem to be efficient data collection tool, they are viewed as labor portals which are not clear in terms of ethical guidelines and labor regulations in some regions [23]. For example, collecting data from children using crowdsourcing may be unethical or even illegal. In other cases, attaching a reward to participation in the study may conflict with the research goals and be incompatible with the sampling strategy of the researcher.

This work does not propose to replace Crowdsourcing platforms but it rather provides an alternative which allows researchers to reach specific target groups, for example by focusing on groups that play specific game genres, but also are able to have more control over the tasks of the participants, by allowing them to directly embed studies within the games and gather data to perform statistical analyses.

*Research activities* (F2) are requested to be performed by a set of selected and curated players depending on their profile, and past research activities reducing problems with bias and quality of the result, they also can be flagged for untrusted wordy results and being avoided in future studies.

**Researcher's Goal.** We believe a researcher's motivation for using a tool like this is to have access to research participants. Games allow them to reach specific target populations and have control over the task the player is required to perform. This can be complemented by the ability to access in-game data (through F1), but also, query players about their experiences and motivations (through F2).

Moreover, we believe that this platform will create a good opportunity for games to be used as personality measuring tools. Player Modeling is a research field that analyses a player's in-game behavior and attempt to produce models that explain or predict the player's behavior.

The main goal is to use the player models to improve gameplay or develop business models of games [24]. As of late, player modeling as also been used to profile player personalities like the Big Five Personality Traits [25], HEXACO [26], Need for Cognition [27] and Self-Esteem [28]. Through games personality traits tests can be made without potential biases, such as awareness of the study objectives, because players are having fun.

**Enabling Research through Games.** The platform allows researchers to embed research instruments directly within games and in that way be able to collect self-report or behavioral data form players. These two features will allow researchers to target specific target audiences, and complement the results with in-game player behavior data gathered by the system.

## 3   Architecture

In this section we describe the architecture that focuses on gathering in-game player behavior in large scale.

To consider a platform that is able to intake a constant influx of in-game log data, for multiple games and each might have thousands of simultaneous players, we have to consider a highly available and highly scalable cloud-based system.

We choose to prioritize service availability and resilience, in detriment to data loss and consistency. It is most important to not impact the game's performance, even if a few logs are lost, and note that, the selection of the data that is sent is directly dependent on the bindings the game developers add to the game.

Bellow we describe in detail the main components of the platform (see Fig. 3):

- Game User Research Kit;
- Game User Research Server; and
- Game User Research Portal.

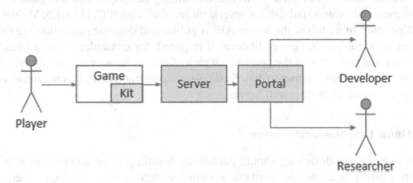

**Fig. 3.** Main architecture components depicting a software kit which will be embedded in the game, and which sends game information to a server, which is then visualized through a portal for both developers and researchers alike.

### 3.1   Game User Research Kit

The Game User Research Kit aims to be a compact extension library that will be incorporated into the main game built. This would work as a plugin system directly available from the game engines' asset store.

The Game User Research Kit is focused on the following principles:

- Performance: such a library needs to have minimal impact on the game performance, and used resources that may interfere with the game experience (e.g. bandwidth, memory, CPU).
- Adjustable: most games try to innovate; the player's in-game behavior logs need to be flexible and tied to custom data schemas.
- Availability: ready to be used within most game engines, use off-the-shelve or be easy to develop, and also supports software debugging and testing processes.
- Well-documented: support the developers' learning curve, by providing simple and clear instructions with code samples, tutorials and/or online support.

**Embedding Game User Research Kit in a Game.** Like described above, developers have access to a programming library which provides access to most GURaaS required functionality.

For the in-game recording system (*F1*) it requires the direct involvement of game developers in the sense that each game it is unique and requires different elements to be tracked/logged; it is up to the game developer to explicit identify the relevant elements that require to be recorded. The library takes the responsibility to competently and with minimum performance loss to store this information locally and push it through the online API.

Customizable player research activities (*F2*) are simplified by requiring from developers to only identify the space (canvas) where the research activities are going to be displayed. GURaaS takes the responsibility to obtain, display, collect and store player responses for the research activities.

Since the Game User Research Kit is automatically integrated with the game engine environment, it is able to publish for several target platforms (PC, HTML5, Mobile and even Console). In addition, the server API is public and documented, allowing developers to build their own custom libraries if required, for example, create a library in JavaScript and make use of the open API which allows to register events directly from webpages, or even use iframes to directly display research activities that are made available by the Game User Research Server.

### 3.2   Game User Research Server

The system we are designing should potentially handling large amounts of data. To support a highly scalable and available system the micro-services design pattern was used to support a scalability [29]. We envision that the system should be able to grow and evolve by adding new services as user needs shift. On the other hand, we also need to understand the main complications of using micro-services: the system will have dozens of different services, therefore the information and overall system state is distributed, meaning it requires a set of tools to support its indexing and management of the resources.

All external APIs made available follow RESTful protocols over HTTP to encourage third party entities to create their own libraries and sub-systems to connect to it. Since there are no sensitive data –such as medical records- involved, security is not a priority, but, there are secure protocols to improve and keep safe sensitive data if required in the future. The most relevant services of the server are presented in Fig. 4. The main data entry point is the Game Recording Gateway, and since it uses HTTP, the overall system availability can be maintained by the number of deployed instances and an effective load balancer.

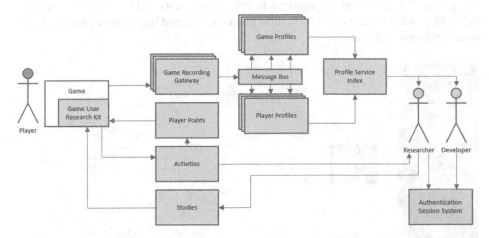

**Fig. 4.** Detailed chart of the most relevant services and communication channels of the Game User Research Server.

The Game Recording Gateway service maintains a temporary copy of the delivered records and periodically pushes the records into a Message Bus. The Message Bus will allow an easy and scalable way to share records amongst specialized Profiling Services. When required to integrate new Profile Services, they will only require to be linked with the Message Bus, and without requiring to alter any of the existing systems.

Game and Player Profiling Services perform parallel and specialized actions over the same data, some examples would be: store player game sessions, analyze log issues, create indexed heat maps, or create player models. Although the Profiling Services may vary in nature, they essentially have a common goal: process in-game data and provide outcomes through an external API.

We highlight that not all data need to be processed by all services. Services will selectively and through an accumulative process enrich their knowledge base and make information available to external entities. Moreover, services can filter and provide data information to other services, hence creating more compelling and complex information systems.

A simple example of a profiling service is a heat-map, which accumulatively populates 2D level information about specific game player events (movement, deaths, or missed jumps). The only in-game records that are processed are the ones containing relevant information for heat-maps, the others are simply discarded by the service.

The Game User Research Kit allows Developers to embed Research Activities directly in their games, like depicted in Fig. 4. Those studies can optionally award a set of points/coins that the player can then trade for in-game content. The services Player Points, Activities and Studies are responsible for those features that are available to researchers through the Game User Research Portal.

### 3.3  Game User Research Portal

The portal (Fig. 5) acts as the interface to both Researchers and Developers to access the GUR profiled game content, like: most played games and levels, gameplay, user and target audience profiling.

**Fig. 5.** Game User Research portal, depicting the wizard screen where researchers can define a study. In this case, the Nanobots game is displayed. Researchers can choose this game to embed their research instruments (e.g. a questionnaire)

Most of the data will be readily available to be imported into appropriate software such as SPSS or R. Even though a raw format is provided, specific profiling services might have an intermediary service to translate into a HTML/or another readable format for most users.

## 4 Case Study

*Runner*[2] (Fig. 6) is a game designed and developed to be a data-gathering tool that was and will be used for multiple research projects. Runner is a platformer game where the goal is to reach the end of the level as fast as possible. The only actions the player can take are moving left, right, jumping and grabbing (also known as wall jumping). The game is controlled with the keyboard keys: W, A and D, or the arrow keys and Space, which are common for platformer games.

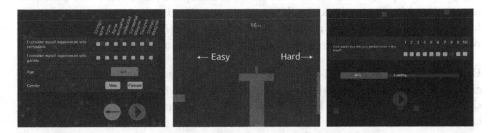

**Fig. 6.** Screen captures of *Runner,* a platform game using the GURAAS platform which logs player behavior and includes dynamic questionnaires. (**Left**) Dynamic questionnaire which requests player demographics before the game. (**Center**) Game screen where the player is faced with a choice of paths. (**Right**) A post-game questionnaire is shown while the next level loads. (Color figure online)

The game was purposely designed to be a barren 2D platformer with negligible narrative, which only exposes players to the core game mechanics. This means aspects that could affect the player's interaction with these core mechanics, like plot, character-self representation and graphics, were avoided or kept to a minimum. An example of this abstraction is the player's avatar: the simple red rectangle that can be seen in the center image of Fig. 6.

By avoiding the influence of these aspects the chance that results of studies performed on the game are specific to this game are minimized. Additionally, by not relying on specific narratives or graphics in the core gameplay these elements could also easily be replaced if required for a future experiment. However, it must be noted that by avoiding these influences certain other assumptions are made. An experimenter should therefore always look for the most suitable game and a game shall not be suitable for all types of experiments.

The game has two tutorial levels in which the controls are explained and the player can practice the basic game mechanics. After the tutorials the game has eight levels of increasing difficulty. Overall the game is tuned to have a high difficulty, as games that require dexterity and hand-eye coordination often do well catering to Lazarro's Hard Fun category [15].

---

[2] Free online game http://kaocean.com/runner/.

**Using GURaaS in Runner.** Runner was developed in Unity[3] and published in HTML5 to be easily available and accessible. The Game User Research Kit was embedded into the development environment allowing the developers to have access to methods that could benefit from GURaaS features.

Since the specific game was developed to have a high degree of difficulty, the developers mainly collected information about player key performance indicators, namely: *(i)* time of the first successful attempt to reach the end of a level, *(ii)* the total time a player spent in a level, including all the failed attempts, and *(iii)* the number of attempts required to complete a level. Other variables pertaining the player behavior were also recorded namely: *(i)* player pace, and *(ii)* path choices. The developers also created space for researchers to introduced research activities, namely: *(i)* when the game starts, *(ii)* when the game ends, *(iii)* before a level starts, and *(iv)* after a level ends.

**Using Runner to Study Self-Esteem.** The first study that was performed on Runner aimed to test whether self-esteem correlates with player behavior in games. Results showed a positive correlation between self-esteem and the players' post-level self-evaluation [28].

Researchers were able to define research activities to be performed by the players through the GURaaS portal. Specifically, when the game starts the players answer a simple demographic questionnaire followed by the Rosenberg Self-Esteem Scale [30]. In addition, after a player successfully completes a level, he/she answers also a Self-Evaluation questionnaire while the next level is loading (see Fig. 7). Although

**Fig. 7.** GURaaS Portal demonstration of how a researcher can create or modify an in-game research task. In this case, it is demonstrating a section of the interface which is defines the in-game questionnaire which can be seen at Fig. 6 (left).

---

[3]  https://unity3d.com/.

developers defined two other spaces for research activities, they were not used in this study.

All player data related to in-game behavior, performance and answers to the research activities, were accessible through the GURaaS portal and easily downloadable and then analyzed by 3rd party statistic tools, where all recorded variables were studied, namely: questionnaire answers, performance indicators and player behavior.

A future study is planned that examines the correlation between game difficulty and user experience. Gameplay data will be used to determine a player's performance in a level and the results thereof can be compared to a questionnaire that evaluates user experience after the level. A similar analysis can be done for the overall game by looking at a player's overall performance and user experience.

## 5 Conclusion

This paper has introduced the concept of Game User Research as a Service, and demonstrated its feasibility by the development of the GURaaS platform which allows researchers to easily implement games for a research purpose. This paper has described the software architecture of GURaaS that we envision will align researchers' and game developers' agendas. Researchers wish to utilize games for their studies more and more often. Game developers look for new revenue streams and tools to improve the experience of their players. The proposed platform helps both parties by opening the wealth of player data and willingness to play already successful games to a much broader group.

The paper has described a case of using GURaaS to develop a game that measures player's self-esteem by logging their in-game behavior. This case was conducted with the involvement of the developers of GURaaS. Future studies, will examine how third parties may be able to develop games with a research purpose without the direct involvement of GURaaS developers. The platform is finalizing its development and it is in the testing phase, after which it will be released publicly.

Future studies will focus on improving and measuring the usability of the platform from the stakeholder's point of view. We hope this becomes an open platform that will enable both game and researchers to cooperate in knowledge development, but also to bring those two communities closer together.

## References

1. Luengo-Oroz, M.A., Arranz, A., Frean, J.: Crowdsourcing malaria parasite quantification: an online game for analyzing images of infected thick blood smears. J. Med. Internet Res. **14**, e167 (2012)
2. Khatib, F., Cooper, S., Tyka, M.D., Xu, K., Makedon, I., Popovic, Z., Baker, D., Players, F.: From the Cover: Algorithm discovery by protein folding game players (2011)
3. von Ahn, L., Dabbish, L.: Labeling images with a computer game. In: ACM Conference on Human Factors in Computing Systems, pp. 319–326 (2004)
4. Mirza-Babaei, P., Zammitto, V., Niesenhaus, J., Sangin, M., Nacke, L.: Games user research. In: CHI 2013 Extended Abstracts on Human Factors in Computing Systems - CHI EA 2013, p. 3219 (2013)

5. Nacke, L., Moser, C., Drachen, A., Mirza-Babaei, P., Abney, A., Zhenyu, Z.: (Cole) lightweight games user research for indies and non-profit organizations. In: CHI Extended Abstracts on Human Factors in Computing Systems, pp. 3597–3603 (2016)
6. Yusoff, A., Crowder, R., Gilbert, L., Wills, G.: A conceptual framework for serious games. In: Proceedings - 2009 9th IEEE International Conference on Advanced Learning Technologies, ICALT 2009, pp. 21–23 (2009)
7. Medler, B.: Player dossiers: Analyzing gameplay data as a reward. Game Stud. 11 (2011)
8. Learning, D.G.: Fun, Play and Games: What Makes Games Engaging. Scientist, 1–31 (2001)
9. Hoffman, B., Nadelson, L.: Motivational engagement and video gaming: a mixed methods study (2010)
10. Sharritt, M.J., Sharritt, M.A.: User-experience game research? In: Games + Learning + Society (GLS) 6.0 (2010)
11. Charsky, D.: From Edutainment to Serious Games: A Change in the Use of Game Characteristics (2010)
12. Maslow, A.H.: A Theory of Human Motivation (1970)
13. Crawford, C.: The art game design. Epilepsy Res. **49**, 512 (2008)
14. Schell, J.: The Art of Game Design: A Book of Lenses. Morgan Kaufmann, Burlington (2008)
15. Lazzaro, N.: Why We Play Games: Four Keys to More Emotion Without Story (2004)
16. In-game advertising the right way: Monetize, engage, retain (2016)
17. Björk, S., Holopainen, J.: Patterns in Game Design (2005)
18. Berkovsky, S., Coombe, M., Freyne, J., Bhandari, D., Baghaei, N.: Physical activity motivating games: virtual rewards for real activity. In: CHI 2010 Games Play, pp. 243–252 (2010)
19. Geraldus Galehantomo, P.S.: Platform Comparison Between Games Console, Mobile Games And PC Games (2015). http://journal.unika.ac.id/index.php/sisforma/article/view/407
20. Mehm, F., Reuter, C., Göbel, S., Steinmetz, R.: Future trends in game authoring tools. In: Herrlich, M., Malaka, R., Masuch, M. (eds.) ICEC 2012. LNCS, vol. 7522, pp. 536–541. Springer, Heidelberg (2012). doi:10.1007/978-3-642-33542-6_70
21. Nacke, L.E., Drachen, A., Kuikkaniemi, K., De Kort, Y.A.W.: Playability and player experience research. In: Proceedings of the IEEE, pp. 1–11 (2009)
22. Behrend, T.S., Sharek, D.J., Meade, A.W., Wiebe, E.N.: The viability of crowdsourcing for survey research. Behav. Res. Methods **43**, 800–813 (2011)
23. Dolmaya, J.M.: The Ethics of Crowdsourcing. Linguist. Antverp, pp. 97–110 (2011)
24. Yannakakis, G.N., Spronck, P., Loiacono, D., André, E.: Player modeling (2013). http://drops.dagstuhl.de/opus/volltexte/2013/4335/
25. van Lankveld, G., Spronck, P., van den Herik, J., Arntz, A.: Games as personality profiling tools. In: 2011 Conference on Computational Intelligence and Games, pp. 197–202 (2011)
26. Worth, N.C., Book, A.S.: Personality and behavior in a massively multiplayer online role-playing game. Comput. Human Behav. **38**, 322–330 (2014)
27. Pereira Santos, C., Khan, V.-J., Markopoulos, P.: Inferring a player's need for cognition from hints. In: ACM Intelligent User Interfaces 2016, pp. 76–79 (2016)
28. Pereira Santos, C., Hutchinson, K., Khan, V.J., Markopoulos, P.: Measuring self-esteem with games. In: ACM Intelligent User Interfaces 2017, pp. 95–106 (2017)
29. Namiot, D., Sneps-Sneppe, M.: On Micro-services Architecture (2014). http://injoit.org/index.php/j1/article/view/139
30. Rosenberg, M.: Rosenberg self-esteem scale (RSE). Accept. Commit. Ther. **52** (1965)

# Tools of the Trade: A Survey of Technologies in End-User Development Literature

Monica G. Maceli[✉]

Pratt Institute, School of Information, New York, NY, USA
mmaceli@pratt.edu

**Abstract.** The fundamental ideas core to the field of end-user development (EUD) emerged in the early 1990s with influential authors advocating for the need for modifiable software that could be crafted by the end user. The modern technology landscape that emerged in the intervening years is vastly different – with technology interwoven into every aspect of our lives and becoming increasingly malleable. In pursuit of building our understanding of what technology tools currently demonstrate EUD concepts and how this has changed over time, this work reports on the results of an assessment of 73 research articles from EUD publication venues, from 2004 to 2016, which emphasize the original development or extension of a technology tool. The technology tools largely fell into the categories of programming environments and frameworks, web and information authoring tools, mashup-creation and spreadsheet tools, with a diverse range of relatively infrequent tool types observed as well.

**Keywords:** End-user development · Technology tools · Literature survey

## 1 Introduction

The field of end-user development (EUD), positioned within the richly complex intersection of humans and computers, has historically drawn from a broad set of both humanistic and technological perspectives. Researchers have engaged in both studying and constructing the technology systems that bring the underlying vision – that of end-users contributing to system design and development – to life. Early researchers in the field, several decades ago, could only imagine the modern technologies that would enrich individuals' lives and become flexible in a myriad of ways. At that time, now nearly three decades ago, researchers and practitioners were confronted with technologies far more rigid than we have today and such technologies were largely confined within the boundaries of the workplace.

The evolution of technology tools introduced new possibilities for end-users to customize, program, contribute content, and generally shape systems in use. In tandem with technological changes, socio-cultural shifts yielded an increased desire on the part of users to craft, create, and otherwise modify our tools and environments, technological and otherwise. This move, from consumer to creator, paired with the necessarily flexible software and hardware, has set the stage for the increasing realization of EUD concepts in practice. In light of such changes, a closer look at the technology tools

© Springer International Publishing AG 2017
S. Barbosa et al. (Eds.): IS-EUD 2017, LNCS 10303, pp. 49–65, 2017.
DOI: 10.1007/978-3-319-58735-6_4

emphasized in EUD research over the past years, can illustrate how the field, and its possibilities, have evolved.

Little research has explored the shape of the field through the lens of the technology tools currently embodying EUD concepts, by looking broadly across literature in the field. The aim of this work is therefore to explore: what types of technology tools are considered currently representative of EUD? How have these changed in recent years? What opportunities for expansion in the range of tools studied, if any, exist? Qualitative data analysis and text mining techniques were used to identify commonalities among such technology tools, changes over time, and to suggest areas for future growth in EUD technologies research.

## 2  Background

End-user development emerged several decades ago as a potential solution to the key challenge of design: the separation, both in time and space, between the setting of design and the ultimate setting of use. This yielded a need to *design-in-use*, explored early on by Hendersen and Kyng [1] among others, defining the needs for systems that could be shaped in the hands of their end users, in use. Design, in their view, should address: changing situations of use, the complexity and unpredictability of the real world, and the need to design for many different situations of use. This would be achieved through designing for *tailorability*. Tailorability emphasized building technology and architecture to support user-driven modification during the design process, and ultimately throughout the life of the system. Three activities which characterize modifiable software were identified: (1) choosing between alternative anticipated and designed-for behaviors, (2) constructing new behaviors from existing pieces or smaller parts, and (3) altering the artifact itself (the most radical sort of change) [1]. Early research further drew a distinction between *adaptable* and *adaptive* systems; the former being flexible such that the use may change the behavior of its parts, the latter dynamically adapting itself to the user's needs [2]. Significant difficulties were inherent to all proposed approaches, however, including problems ranging from the need for increased development efforts to the potential unwillingness of end users to contribute as system designers.

The challenge of creating modifiable software was beginning to be realized through systems emerging from EUD-related research in the 1980s and 1990s. For example, Trigg et al. in 1987 explored adapting and tailoring a hypertext system [3]; Fischer proposed the Seeding, Evolutionary Growth, and Reseeding (SER) Model wherein a system "seed" is co-designed, allowed to grow naturally through use, then re-seeded to reorganize as necessary [4], as well as constructed knowledge-based design environments (DODEs) which provided a constantly evolving space in which users shaped the system [5]. During this time, there were significant changes in technology and the approach taken in studying its design, construction, and use. Notable researchers in human-computer interaction (HCI) identified these "waves" of change as driving a need to reassess the focus of design activities as the context of use and tools themselves evolved (summarized in Table 1, below).

**Table 1.** Phases of human-computer interaction [6, 7]

| | Phases of the Field of Human-Computer Interaction (HCI) | | |
|---|---|---|---|
| | 1st Wave | 2nd Wave | 3rd Wave |
| Focus of design activities | Efficiently matching workers to machine interfaces | End users as active contributors to design activities and needs | End users begin to be empowered to mold technology in use |
| Context of design | Known and constrained work environments | Discretionary use contexts – from the office to the home and daily life | Technology used in ubiquitous and rapidly changing contexts |
| Technological focus | Desktop, workplace computing | Personal computing | Ubiquitous and mobile computing |

The "3rd wave" [7] trend, of end users becoming empowered to shape technology in use, was bolstered by both increasingly flexible, lightweight technology tools as well as in a growing culture of participation in which end users were motivated to seek a deeper, hands-on relationship with their tools. Though increased involvement by end users introduced its own set of challenges, environments allowing for rich end-user interactions and fostering cultures of participation were emerging in a variety of technological contexts, including: patient support, technology education, general and domain-specific encyclopedias, citizen journalism, and others [8].

Given the broadening nature of EUD work and its applications, Lieberman et al. [9] posed a definition of end-user development as "a set of methods, techniques, and tools that allow users of software systems, who are acting as non-professional software developers, at some point to create, modify, or extend a software artifact", with potential end-user activities consisting of parameterization/customization of existing features or novel program creation and modification. The end users themselves within EUD tools were typically beginning users desiring to extend their systems in an unsupported way or domain experts in fields other than computer science desiring computer automation to assist in achieving their goals [10]. As the interest in involving end-users in design and development activities grew, distinct areas of foci emerged. End-user programming (EUP) emphasized the construction of programs and writing of code to support personal goals by end users with a broad range of programming expertise, while end-user software engineering (EUSE) explores the need for technologies to assist end user programmers in improving their software quality by engaging in engineering activities surrounding construction, e.g. determining requirements, testing, or debugging [11]. EUP activities have been well-represented across "educational simulation builders, web authoring systems, multimedia authoring systems, e-mail filtering rule systems, CAD systems, scientific visualization systems, and spreadsheets" [12] among others. EUSE research aims to understand and support end-user programmers in software engineering activities, and many of the systems studied are similar to those in EUP and EUD, such as spreadsheet tools.

End-user development expands the research lens to include a wide range of activities involving end users throughout systems design and development, including significant attention to organizational and socio-cultural aspects. Going further longitudinally, meta-design [13] advocates for end user involvement as co-designers in system development throughout the entire life of the system, requiring modifiable EUD features in technology tools to realize this vision. Though a wide variety of modern systems can be considered to demonstrate EUD-like characteristics and technological features, Stav et al. [14] noted that the EUD community had a historic focus largely on the perspective and needs of the end-user with a lack of focus on technical realization of EUD tools. However, looking backwards, Tetteroo and Markopoulos [15] found that engineering as applied research was the most common method and purpose employed by researchers within EUD, in their survey of research from 2004 to 2013.

## 3  Research Methods

Tetteroo and Markopoulos [15], in their 2015 survey of EUD literature, identified a sub-set of research work focused on engineering – aimed at the original development of a tool or technology – and re-engineering – focused on the engineering of modifications or extensions to an existing tool or technology. A deeper analysis of papers within these two categories formed the basis for this study, in pursuit of the research questions posed earlier. A total of 73 papers ranging in publication date from 2004 to 2016 were collected and assessed (Appendix A), all of which emphasized the novel development or iterative improvement of technology tool(s).

Publication venues that were used to generate the list of relevant papers included EUD-related conference proceedings (CHI, AVI, UIST and IS-EUD) and related journals (Visual Languages and Human Centered Computing, Journal of Visual Languages and Computing, International Journal on Human Computer Studies, Interacting with Computers, and Transactions on Computer Human Interaction). Papers chosen included author keywords of End User Development, End User Programming, End User Software Engineering and/or meta-design and covered the original development or iterative improvement of a specific technology tool. The final corpus consisted of 48 papers identified as engineering or re-engineering-focused in the prior survey of EUD literature conducted by Tetteroo and Markopoulos [15], with the addition of 25 similarly relevant articles published in the same venues in the intervening years of 2013 to 2016, for a final total of 73 papers.

After identification and collection, papers were independently assessed by the author and a graduate assistant to identify the overall purpose of the work, the technology tool being studied, the general category of the tool, and the means of tool evaluation, if any. Inductive qualitative analysis was used to code text describing the technology tools and to identify common themes to be used to categorize the tools. Lastly, a plain text version of each paper was created to be used for text mining techniques with the tm [16] package in R [17]. Texting mining techniques were used to explore commonly correlated terms, as well as to perform topic modeling [18] to identify common themes within the corpus.

## 4   Results

The 73 papers assessed (Appendix A), focused on the novel creation or extension of an EUD technology tool over the period of 2004 through 2016. There was a general increase in volume of publication over time, with notable peaks in publication aligned with conferences, such as IS-EUD, that occur biennially (Fig. 1, below).

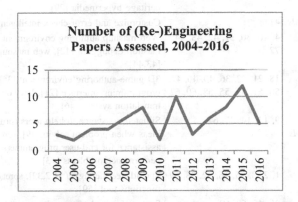

**Fig. 1.** Number of papers assessed, from the period of 2004 through 2016

The results of the qualitative coding to identify broad categories of the technology tools are presented in Table 2 (below), including selected representative examples within each category.

**Table 2.** Categorized technology tools in papers studied (all bracketed numbers reference citations in Appendix A)

| EUD Technology Tools | Related Papers | Examples |
|---|---|---|
| Assistive technology tools | 11, 65 | Mobile meta-design tool for cognitively disabled [11] |
| Co-design tools | 7, 23 | Extreme co-design tool for quickly deploying and evaluating prototypes [7], software that facilitates co-design by collecting and organizing outcomes from different techniques [23] |
| Collaboration tools | 27, 63, 73 | Collaborative web mapping application [27], meta-design environment for co-located meeting support [73] |
| Consumer product tools | 5 | Product configuration tool [5] |
| Data management tools | 33, 53, 70 | Data transformation tool [33], tailorable quality assessment service for social media data [53] |
| Domain-specific tools | 12, 19, 24, 26, 29, 34, 61, 67 | Business process modeling environment [24], gesture-based language drawing tool for music composition [67], customization tools for cultural heritage hypermedia [29] |
| Intelligent agent tools | 41 | Customize and error-check intelligent agents [41] |
| Mashup tools | 4, 10, 30, 31, 42, 43, 44, 72 | Web mashup authoring environment [4,10,30], web mashup debugging [42], web mashup versioning [43,44] |
| Programming environments and frameworks | 18, 21, 22, 36, 40, 46, 47, 50, 51, 52, 55, 58, 60, 62 | 3D game-authoring environment [36], database programming interface [21], keywords to code translation system [46] |
| Programming problem-solving tools | 9, 13, 14, 37, 64 | Situated assistance to help users form and develop ideas when problem solving [9], semi-automatic assistance for end-user programmers to fix performance problems [13] |
| Spreadsheet tools | 1, 2, 8, 15, 16, 32, 38, 59 | Spreadsheet debugger [1,2,32], spreadsheet-defined functions tool [59] |
| Tangible and pervasive computing tools | 35, 45, 68, 69 | System for exploring environmental data through physical ambient visualizations [35], tool for creating intelligent sensors [45] |
| Web and information authoring tools | 3, 6, 17, 20, 25, 28, 39, 48, 49, 54, 56, 57, 66, 71 | Interactive web application builder for local and web service data [17], information awareness application customization tool [25] |

Thirteen categories of technology tools were identified, in total, with "programming environments and frameworks" and "web and information authoring tools" the most prevalent (Fig. 2, below). The remainder of the top 5 categories observed included mashup tools, spreadsheet tools, and domain-specific tools. Domain-specific tools were technology tools oriented around solving a problem particular to a distinct domain, e.g. e-government, music composition, or cultural heritage.

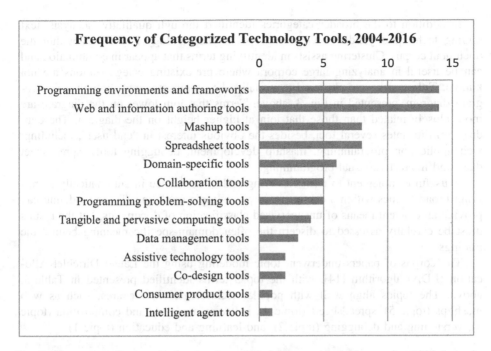

**Fig. 2.** Frequency of categorized technology tools in papers assessed, covering 2004 through 2016

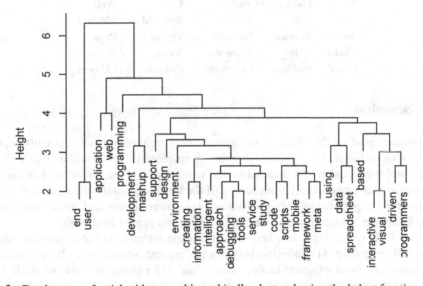

**Fig. 3.** Dendrogram of article title terms hierarchically clustered using the hclust function in R

In addition to the broader categories identified through qualitative analysis, text mining techniques yielded a view into specific terminology and topics within the document corpus. Clustering assists in identifying terms that appear in combination and can be useful in analyzing large corpora where pre-existing categorizations are not known. Title terms were clustered to visualize key topics covered through a dendrogram diagram, presented in Fig. 3, above. Terms that join lower on the diagram are more closely related than those that join at higher height on the diagram. The dendrogram illustrates several foci, besides the obvious interest in "end user", including: web application programming, mashup development, debugging tools, spreadsheet data, and interactive/visual programming.

A useful complement to term clustering and of assistance in automatically identifying broad themes within a document corpus is topic modeling. Topic modeling can provide an efficient means of unsupervised classification of documents, but the results must be carefully assessed to discern the often domain-specific meaning behind the findings.

The corpus of papers underwent topic modeling using the Latent Dirichlet Allocation (LDA) algorithm [14], with the top 5 terms identified presented in Table 3, above. The topics align well with popular technologies in the area, such as web mashups (topic 5), spreadsheets (topic 4), software modeling and composition (topic 3), versioning and debugging (topic 2), and learning and education (topic 1).

**Table 3.** Top 5 terms from LDA topic modeling of corpus of papers

| Topic 1 | Topic 2 | Topic 3 | Topic 4 | Topic 5 |
|---------|---------|---------|---------|---------|
| Script | Participant | Model | Cell | Web |
| Idea | Pipe | Service | Spreadsheet | Mashup |
| Student | Version | Domain | Figure | Page |
| Model | Debug | Software | Value | Widget |
| Learn | Problem | Composition | Column | Element |

## 5  Discussion

The primary goal of this work is to explore what technologies are currently representative of end-user development, drawing from research work within EUD, EUP, EUSE, and meta-design. As detailed in the results section earlier, several dominant areas of focus emerged clearly from review of the literature, from both a qualitative and quantitative perspective, including: programming environments and frameworks, web and information authoring tools, mashup-creation and spreadsheet tools.

Early EUD researchers identified several ways in which modifiable software might be shaped, including: (1) choosing between anticipated alternatives, (2) constructing new behaviors from existing/smaller pieces, and (3) altering the artifact itself [1]. Several of the most common technology tool types are focused on the second means of modification – constructing new behavior from parts – as evident by the popularity of web authoring, mashup, and spreadsheet tools, all of which provide functionality to extend and customize using existing features, e.g. existing web service APIs, macros, or web page content, as a basis. In contrast, many of the systems categorized as programming environments and frameworks, sought a deeper level of customization in building from the ground up, approaching the third possibility – of altering the artifact itself. However, this mechanism of more drastically shaping software appears to remain elusive and it becomes difficult to define boundaries between the various levels of modifiability, particularly as many systems typically support both anticipated and designed-for behaviors and end-user driven modifications.

It is interesting to note that many of the technologies facilitating these behaviors have longstanding use in the field, e.g. the web service APIs that facilitate the web and information authoring and mashup system have been a popular focus for EUD work dating back to the mid-2000s and realized in the emergence of popular systems such as Yahoo! Pipes (now defunct). Though clearly able to facilitate a great deal of end-user development activity, such technologies are not without their own challenges. For example, in the context of mashup makers, Grammel and Storey in 2008 identified a need for context-specific suggestions, mashup element finders, and testing/debugging tools to allow for effective end-user modification [19]. Many of the technology tools studied were indeed oriented around solving the challenges emerging from EUD activities, such as assisting with debugging, finding errors, identifying code for reuse, and tracking versions of changes over time. These issues were anticipated by earlier work, for example in Fischer's SER Model [4] which noted the need to re-formalize, restructure and reorganize the system as it evolved over time, likely in an unwieldy manner. The challenge of end-users maintaining systems over time has sparked research in maintenance-in-use (e.g. [20]); EUD researchers appear to have found a role in providing tools to make these activities more manageable, particularly in the EUSE realm.

Related closely to the tool itself is its intended end user(s); research in the EUD field, and its related subfields, created technology tools designed to support a particular type of end user. These intended end users were also used to define and articulate particular areas of focus, e.g. the end user that may contribute to a range of activities from co-design to coding over time within meta-design, or the end user programmer seeking to improve their software's quality within EUSE research. Lieberman et al. [9] suggest that EUD tools primarily support novice users with unsupported needs and/or domain experts desiring to extend their systems, while others (such as Ko, et al. [11]) note the broad range in motivations and roles of those engaging in EUD activities as end-users. Both of these perspectives were evident in the data collected, through the large number of tools designed for particular domains' users (as detailed in Table 2, above) and the sheer variety in end-users, from caregivers of the cognitively disabled to consumers customizing products to cultural heritage or art domain experts creating multi-media. As would be expected, many tools focused on the more general novice non-professional programmer, but these tools tended to be spreadsheet or mashup-based. The vast numbers of potential end users seem to have created a research environment with significant exploration of distinct domains' users but less attention to yielding more broadly generalizable findings across the field as a whole.

Furthermore, on the end-user side, establishing a culture of participation, allowing for reflection on practice, and promoting mutual learning are equally important in shaping such systems [21]. Though it was not the primary focus of this paper, the means of tool evaluation were also collected during the research process. Of the projects that reported conducting an evaluation process, most described quantitative measures, such as the errors detected or task time taken, or broader subjective participant experiences in case studies. Classic HCI measures, such as those associated with usability or usefulness, are of value in evaluating any designed system. Measures directed towards understanding the more elusive social dimensions of EUD could also benefit from greater focus.

This survey paper also attempted to identify changes in the types of technology tools studied over time. Although, as noted earlier, an overall increase in the number of publications moving towards the present was observed, the most popular topics did not show a clear pattern of increasing. As Table 4, below, illustrates, peaks of number of publications were observed, but largely driven by the various influential publication venue timelines.

**Table 4.** Frequency of publication within the most popular categories of technology tools

| | 2004 | 2005 | 2006 | 2007 | 2008 | 2009 | 2010 | 2011 | 2012 | 2013 | 2014 | 2015 | 2016 |
|---|---|---|---|---|---|---|---|---|---|---|---|---|---|
| Mashup tools | | | | 1 | | | | 3 | | 1 | 2 | | 1 |
| Programming environments and frameworks | 1 | 2 | 3 | 1 | | 2 | | 2 | | 1 | 1 | | 1 |
| Spreadsheet tools | | 2 | | 1 | | | 1 | | | 1 | 2 | | 1 |
| Web and information authoring tools | 1 | | | 1 | 4 | 2 | 1 | | 1 | | 3 | | 1 |

Many infrequently observed categories – e.g. tangible and pervasive computing, intelligent agents – appeared sporadically across the years studied and therefore make it difficult to identify trends. A few areas, notably those of collaboration and data management tools, though appearing in small numbers, have only emerged within the past 5 years. Revisiting research of this sort in the coming years can yield additional clarity and perspective on these trends. The findings do suggest that many of the types of EUD technology tools studied have not changed significantly over the past decade and can indicate potential areas of expansion and allied fields. Visual and graphical programming environments and long-standing areas of focus, such as mashup and spreadsheet tools, dominated. Mobile technology tools were observed to be well-integrated into a variety of projects studied, particularly as a delivery mechanism for the resulting information system. Relatively little work addressed newer user interface paradigms, such as tangible or voice interfaces, and social and crowdsourcing technologies were similarly less represented, though demonstrative of EUD behaviors (e.g. [22]), suggesting that EUD researchers are not directly contributing to the development of such tools in a significant fashion.

That is not to say, however, that research work highly relevance to EUD is not happening in these areas at all. Rather, the wider human-computer interaction (HCI) field has begun to study, create, and discuss end-user modifiable systems as they become more commonplace. These research communities publish in different venues, use different language to describe their work, and may have superficial or significant overlap with EUD work, e.g. in tangible computing research, social media, or cross-device interaction within the CHI community. This poses a great challenge (and limitation) to EUD-related survey work, such as is presented in this paper, around the identification and selection or omission of literature and publishing venues.

As technologies evolved, EUD features and functionality have become increasingly desired and expected by end-users. There likely exists research in other areas of HCI that aligns well with the EUD vision, challenges, and goals. This trend raises interesting questions for the EUD research community around its relationship to the wider HCI field. As end users continue to shape their increasingly malleable technologies, EUD may become a central concern of mainstream HCI work. This future potential suggests a need for EUD researchers to collaborate in identifying allied fields and forging new interdisciplinary relationships to both share our expertise and maintain our relevance and currency.

# 6 Conclusion

This research study reports on the results of a literature survey assessing the technology tools created and revised within current EUD research, with attention to the type of technology tool, the changes in tool types over time, and the potential for broadening study. Several clear areas of technology tool focus emerged: programming environments and frameworks, web and information authoring tools, mashup-creation and spreadsheet tools. Many of these foci have been common in the field for many years, and though a diverse range of additional tools were noted – for example, product configuration, intelligent agents, and assistive technologies – consistent growth in the more peripheral areas were not observed. This work can provide useful context for those working in the area of applied research in EUD, as well as suggest areas that the field may take on a more prominent role. Potential for applied researchers to expand on descriptive work with a significant technological focus exists as well.

# Appendix A – List of Papers Reviewed

1. Abraham, R., Erwig, M.: Goal-Directed Debugging of Spreadsheets. Proc. VL/HCC 2005. pp. 37–44 IEEE, Washington, DC, USA (2005)
2. Abraham, R., Erwig, M.: UCheck: A Spreadsheet Type Checker for End Users. J. Vis. Lang. Comput. 18, 1, 71–95 (2007)
3. Admire, J., Al Zawwad, A., Almorebah, A., Karve, S., Scaffidi, C.: Code You Can Use: Searching for web automation scripts based on reusability. Proc. VL/HCC 2014. pp. 81-88 IEEE, Melbourne, VIC (2014)

4. Aghaee, S., Pautasso, C.: End-user development of mashups with naturalmash. J. Vis. Lang. Comput. 25, 4, 414-432 (2014)
5. Ardito, C. et al.: An Ontology-Based Approach to Product Customization. In: Costabile, M.F. et al. (eds.) End-User Development. pp. 92–106 Springer Berlin Heidelberg (2011)
6. Ardito, C., Costabile, M.F., Desolda, G., Lanzilotti, R., Matera, M., Piccinno, A., Picozzi, M.: User-driven visual composition of service-based interactive spaces. J. Vis. Lang. Comput. 25, 4, 278-296 (2014)
7. Bellucci, A., Jacucci, G., Kotkavuori, V., Serim, B., Ahmed, I., Ylirisku, S.: Extreme Co-design: Prototyping with and by the User for Appropriation of Web-connected Tags. In: Díaz, P. et al. (eds.) End-User Development. pp. 109-124 Springer International Publishing (2015)
8. Benson, E., Zhang, A.X., Karger, D.R.: Spreadsheet driven web applications. Proc. UIST'14. pp. 97-106 ACM, New York, NY, USA (2014)
9. Cao, J., Fleming, S.D., Burnett, M., Scaffidi, C.: Idea Garden: Situated support for problem solving by end-user programmers. Interact. Comput. 27, 6, 640–660 (2015)
10. Cappiello, C. et al.: Enabling End User Development through Mashups: Requirements, Abstractions and Innovation Toolkits. In: Costabile, M.F. et al. (eds.) End-User Development. pp. 9–24 Springer Berlin Heidelberg (2011)
11. Carmien, S.P., Fischer, G.: Design, Adoption, and Assessment of a Socio-technical Environment Supporting Independence for Persons with Cognitive Disabilities. Proc. CHI'08. pp. 597–606 ACM, New York, NY, USA (2008)
12. Celentano, A., Maurizio, M.: An End-User Oriented Building Pattern for Interactive Art Guides. In: Costabile, M.F. et al. (eds.) End-User Development. pp. 187–202 Springer Berlin Heidelberg (2011)
13. Chambers, C., Scaffidi, C.: Impact and utility of smell-driven performance tuning for end-user programmers. J. Vis. Lang. Comput. 28, 176-194 (2015)
14. Chambers, C., Scaffidi, C.: Utility and accuracy of smell-driven performance analysis for end-user programmers. J. Vis. Lang. Comput. 26, 1-14 (2015)
15. Chang, K. S. P., Myers, B. A.: Using and Exploring Hierarchical Data in Spreadsheets. Proc. CHI'16. pp. 2497-2507 ACM, New York, NY, USA (2016)
16. Chang, K.S.P., Myers, B.A.: A spreadsheet model for using web service data. Proc. VL/HCC 2014. pp. 169-176 IEEE, Melbourne, VIC (2014)
17. Chang, K.S.P., Myers, B.A.: Creating interactive web data applications with spreadsheets. Proc. UIST'14. pp. 87-96 ACM, New York, NY, USA (2014)
18. Danado, J., Paternò, F.: Puzzle: A mobile application development environment using a jigsaw metaphor. J. Vis. Lang. Comput. 25, 4, 297-315 (2014)
19. Dax, J., Ludwig, T., Meurer, J., Pipek, V., Stein, M., Stevens, G.: FRAMES–A Framework for Adaptable Mobile Event-Contingent Self-report Studies. In: Díaz, P. et al. (eds.) End-User Development. pp. 141-155 Springer International Publishing (2015)
20. De Souza, C.S., Cypher, A.: Semiotic Engineering in Practice: Redesigning the CoScripter Interface. Proc. AVI'08. pp. 165–172 ACM, New York, NY, USA (2008)

21. Deng, Y. et al.: Designing a Framework for End User Applications. In: Costabile, M.F. et al. (eds.) End-User Development. pp. 67–75 Springer Berlin Heidelberg (2011)
22. Dey, A.K. et al.: A CAPpella: Programming by Demonstration of Context-aware Applications. Proc. CHI'04. pp. 33–40 ACM, New York, NY, USA (2004)
23. Díaz, P., Aedo, I., van der Vaart, M.: Engineering the Creative Co-design of Augmented Digital Experiences with Cultural Heritage. In: Díaz, P. et al. (eds.) End-User Development. pp. 42-57 Springer International Publishing (2015)
24. Dörner, C. et al.: Supporting business process experts in tailoring business processes. Interact. Comput. 23, 3, 226 – 238 (2011)
25. Eagan, J.R., Stasko, J.T.: The Buzz: Supporting User Tailorability in Awareness Applications. Proc. CHI'08. pp. 1729–1738 ACM, New York, NY, USA (2008)
26. Fogli, D., Parasiliti Provenza, L.: A Meta-design Approach to the Development of e-Government Services. J. Vis. Lang. Comput. 23, 2, 47–62 (2012)
27. Fogli, D.: Cultures of Participation in Community Informatics: A Case Study. In: Dittrich, Y. et al. (eds.) End-User Development. pp. 201–216 Springer Berlin Heidelberg (2013)
28. Fujima, J. et al.: Clip, Connect, Clone: Combining Application Elements to Build Custom Interfaces for Information Access. Proc. UIST'04. pp. 175–184 ACM, New York, NY, USA (2004)
29. Garzotto, F., Megale, L.: CHEF: A User Centered Perspective for Cultural Heritage Enterprise Frameworks. Proc. AVI'06. pp. 293–301 ACM, New York, NY, USA (2006)
30. Ghiani, G. et al.: Creating Mashups by Direct Manipulation of Existing Web Applications. In: Costabile, M.F. et al. (eds.) End-User Development. pp. 42–52 Springer Berlin Heidelberg (2011)
31. Ghiani, G., Paternò, F., Spano, L.D., Pintori, G.,: An environment for end-user development of web mashups. Int J Hum-Comput St. 87, 38-64 (2016)
32. Grigoreanu, V.I. et al.: A Strategy-centric Approach to the Design of End-user Debugging Tools. Proc. CHI'10. pp. 713–722 ACM, New York, NY, USA (2010)
33. Guo, P.J. et al.: Proactive Wrangling: Mixed-initiative End-user Programming of Data Transformation Scripts. Proc. UIST'11. pp. 65–74 ACM, New York, NY, USA (2011)
34. Hale, P. et al.: User-driven Modelling: Visualisation and Systematic Interaction for End-user Programming. J. Vis. Lang. Comput. 23, 6, 354–379 (2012)
35. Houben, S., Golsteijn, C., Gallacher, S., Johnson, R., Bakker, S., Marquardt, N., Capra, L., Rogers, Y.: Physikit: Data Engagement Through Physical Ambient Visualizations in the Home. Proc. CHI'16. pp. 1608-1619 ACM, New York, NY, USA (2016)
36. Ioannidou, A. et al.: AgentCubes: Incremental 3D End-user Development. J. Vis. Lang. Comput. 20, 4, 236–251 (2009)
37. Jernigan, W., Horvath, A., Lee, M., Burnett, M., Cuilty, T., Kuttal, S., Peters, A., Kwan, I., Bahmani, F., Ko, A: A principled evaluation for a principled idea garden. Proc. VL/HCC 2015. pp. 235-243 IEEE, Atlanta, GA, USA (2015)
38. Kandogan, E. et al.: A1: End-user Programming for Web-based System Administration. Proc. UIST'05. pp. 211–220 ACM, New York, NY, USA (2005)

39. Karger, D.R. et al.: The Web Page As a WYSIWYG End-user Customizable Database backed Information Management Application. Proc. UIST'09. pp. 257–260 ACM, New York, NY, USA (2009)
40. Ko, A.J., Myers, B.A.: Barista: An Implementation Framework for Enabling New Tools, Interaction Techniques and Views in Code Editors. Proc. CHI'06. pp. 387–396 ACM, New York, NY, USA (2006)
41. Kulesza, T. et al.: Where Are My Intelligent Assistant's Mistakes? A Systematic Testing Approach. In: Costabile, M.F. et al. (eds.) End-User Development. pp. 171–186 Springer Berlin Heidelberg (2011)
42. Kuttal, S.K. et al.: Debugging Support for End User Mashup Programming. Proc. CHI'13. pp. 1609–1618 ACM, New York, NY, USA (2013)
43. Kuttal, S.K. et al.: Versioning for Mashups – An Exploratory Study. In: Costabile, M.F. et al. (eds.) End-User Development. pp. 25–41 Springer Berlin Heidelberg (2011)
44. Kuttal, S.K., Sarma, A., Rothermel, G.: On the benefits of providing versioning support for end users: An empirical study. ACM Trans. Comput.-Hum. Interact. 21, 2, Article 9 (2014)
45. Laput, G., Lasecki, W.S., Wiese, J., Xiao, R., Bigham, J.P., Harrison, C.: Zensors: Adaptive, rapidly deployable, human-intelligent sensor feeds. Proc. CHI'15. pp. 1935-1944 ACM, New York, NY, USA (2015)
46. Little, G., Miller, R.C.: Translating Keyword Commands into Executable Code. Proc. UIST'06. pp. 135–144 ACM, New York, NY, USA (2006)
47. Lunzer, A., Hornbaek, K.: RecipeSheet: Creating, Combining and Controlling Information Processors. Proc. UIST'06. pp. 145–154 ACM, New York, NY, USA (2006)
48. Macías, J.A., Castells, P.: Providing end-user facilities to simplify ontology-driven web application authoring. Interact. Comput. 19, 4, 563–585 (2007)
49. Macías, J.A., Paternò, F.: Customization of Web applications through an intelligent environment exploiting logical interface descriptions. Interact. Comput. 20, 1, 29 – 47 (2008)
50. Neumann, C. et al.: End-user Strategy Programming. J. Vis. Lang. Comput. 20, 1, 16–29 (2009)
51. Prahofer, H. et al.: The Domain-Specific Language Monaco and Its Visual Inter-active Programming Environment. Proc. VL/HCC 2007. pp. 104–110 IEEE Computer Society, Washington, DC, USA (2007)
52. Repenning, A., Ioannidou, A.: Agent Warp Engine: Formula Based Shape Warping for Networked Applications. Proc. AVI'08. pp. 279–286 ACM, New York, NY, USA (2008) 0 (2005)
53. Reuter, C., Ludwig, T., Ritzkatis, M., Pipek, V.: Social-QAS: Tailorable Quality Assessment Service for Social Media Content. In: Díaz, P. et al. (eds.) End-User Development. pp. 156-170 Springer International Publishing (2015)
54. Rossen, B., Lok, B.: A crowdsourcing method to develop virtual human conver-sational agents. Int J Hum-Comput St. 70, 4, 301-319 (2012)
55. Ruthruff, J.R. et al.: Interactive, Visual Fault Localization Support for End-user Programmers. J. Vis. Lang. Comput. 16, 1, 3-40 (2005)

56. Scaffidi, C. et al.: Using Scenario-based Requirements to Direct Research on Web Macro Tools. J. Vis. Lang. Comput. 19, 4, 485–498 (2008)
57. Scaffidi, C. et al.: Using Traits of Web Macro Scripts to Predict Reuse. J. Vis. Lang. Comput. 21, 5, 277–291 (2010)
58. Scaffidi, C., Dove, A., Nabi, T.: LondonTube: Overcoming Hidden Dependencies in Cloud-Mobile-Web Programming. Proc. CHI'16. pp. 3498-3508 ACM, New York, NY, USA (2016)
59. Sestoft, P., Sørensen, J.Z.: Sheet-Defined Functions: Implementation and Initial Evaluation. In: Dittrich, Y. et al. (eds.) End-User Development. pp. 88–103 Springer Berlin Heidelberg (2013)
60. Souza, C.S. de et al.: Semiotic Traces of Computational Thinking Acquisition. In: Costabile, M.F. et al. (eds.) End-User Development. pp. 155–170 Springer Berlin Heidelberg (2011)
61. Spahn, M., Wulf, V.: End-User Development of Enterprise Widgets. In: Pipek, V. et al. (eds.) End-User Development. pp. 106–125 Springer Berlin Heidelberg (2009)
62. Stav, E. et al.: Using Meta-modelling for Construction of an End-User Development Framework. In: Dittrich, Y. et al. (eds.) End-User Development. pp. 72–87 Springer Berlin Heidelberg (2013)
63. Stevens, G. et al.: Appropriation Infrastructure: Supporting the Design of Usages. In: Pipek, V. et al. (eds.) End-User Development. pp. 50–69 Springer Berlin Heidelberg (2009)
64. Surisetty, S., Law, C., Scaffidi, C.: Behavior-based clustering of visual code. Proc. VL/HCC 2015. pp. 261-269 IEEE, Atlanta, GA, USA (2015)
65. Tetteroo, D., Vreugdenhil, P., Grisel, I., Michielsen, M., Kuppens, E., Vanmulken, D., Markopoulos, P.: Lessons Learnt from Deploying an End-User Development Platform for Physical Rehabilitation. Proc. CHI'15. pp. 4133-4142 ACM, New York, NY, USA (2015)
66. Toomim, M. et al.: Attaching UI Enhancements to Websites with End Users. Proc. CHI'09. pp. 1859–1868 ACM, New York, NY, USA (2009)
67. Tsandilas, T. et al.: Musink: Composing Music Through Augmented Drawing. Proc. CHI'09. pp. 819–828 ACM, New York, NY, USA (2009)
68. Turchi, T., Malizia, A., Dix, A.: Fostering the adoption of Pervasive Displays in public spaces using tangible End-User Programming. Proc. VL/HCC 2015. pp. 169-176 IEEE, Atlanta, GA, USA (2015)
69. Van Herk, R. et al.: ESPranto SDK: An Adaptive Programming Environment for Tangible Applications. Proc. CHI'09. pp. 849–858 ACM, New York, NY, USA (2009)
70. Velasco-Elizondo, P. et al.: Resolving Data Mismatches in End-User Compositions. In: Dittrich, Y. et al. (eds.) End-User Development. pp. 120–136 Springer Berlin Heidelberg (2013)
71. Verou, L., Zhang, A.X., Karger, D.R.: Mavo: Creating Interactive Data-Driven Web Applications by Authoring HTML. Proc. UIST'16. pp. 483-496 ACM, New York, NY, USA (2016)

72. Wong, J., Hong, J.I.: Making Mashups with Marmite: Towards End-user Programming for the Web. Proc. CHI'07. pp. 1435–1444 ACM, New York, NY, USA (2007)
73. Zhu, L., Herrmann, T.: Meta-design in Co-located Meetings. In: Dittrich, Y. et al. (eds.) End-User Development. pp. 169–184 Springer Berlin Heidelberg (2013)

# References

1. Henderson, A., Kyng, M.: There's no place like home: continuing design in use. In: Greenbaum, J., Kyng, M. (eds.) Design At Work: Cooperative Design of Computer Systems, pp. 219–240. L. Erlbaum Associates, Hillsdale (1991)
2. Fischer, G.: Shared knowledge in cooperative problem-solving systems - integrating adaptive and adaptable components. In: Schneider-Hufschmidt, M. et al. (eds.) Adaptive User Interfaces - Principles and Practice, pp. 49-68. Elsevier Science Publishers (1993)
3. Trigg, R.H., Moran, T.P., Halasz, F.G.: Adaptability and tailorability in NoteCards. In: Proceedings of the Presented at Interact 1987 (1987)
4. Fischer, G., McCall, R., Ostwald, J., Reeves, B., Shipman, F.: Seeding, evolutionary growth and reseeding: supporting the incremental development of design environments. In: Proceedings of the CHI 1994, pp. 292–298. ACM, New York (1994)
5. Fischer, G.: Domain-oriented design environments. Autom. Softw. Eng. **1**, 177–203 (1994)
6. Bannon, L.J.: From human factors to human actors: the role of psychology and human-computer interaction studies in system design. In: Greenbaum, J., et al. (eds.) Design At Work: Cooperative Design of Computer Systems, pp. 25–44. L. Erlbaum Associates (1991)
7. Bødker, S.: When second wave HCI meets third wave challenges. In: Proceedings of the CHI 2006, pp. 1–8. ACM, New York (2006)
8. Fischer, G.: Understanding, fostering, and supporting cultures of participation. Interactions **18**(3), 42–53 (2011)
9. Lieberman, H., Paternò, F., Klann, M., Wulf, V.: End-user development: an emerging paradigm. In: Lieberman, H., Paternò, F., Wulf, V. (eds.) End-User Development, pp. 1–8. Springer, The Netherlands (2006)
10. Lieberman, H., Paternò, F., Wulf, V. (eds.): End User Development. Springer, Heidelberg (2006)
11. Ko, A.J., et al.: The state of the art in end-user software engineering. ACM Comput. Surv. **43**(3), 1–44 (2011)
12. Ruthruff, J.R., et al.: Interactive, visual fault localization support for end-user programmers. J. Vis. Lang. Comput. **16**(1), 3–40 (2005)
13. Fischer, G., et al.: Meta-design: a manifesto for end-user development. Commun. ACM **47**(9), 33–37 (2004)
14. Stav, E., Floch, J., Khan, M.U., Sætre, R.: Using meta-modelling for construction of an end-user development framework. In: Dittrich, Y., Burnett, M., Mørch, A., Redmiles, D. (eds.) IS-EUD 2013. LNCS, vol. 7897, pp. 72–87. Springer, Heidelberg (2013). doi:10.1007/978-3-642-38706-7_7
15. Tetteroo, D., Markopoulos, P.: A review of research methods in end user development. In: Díaz, P., Pipek, V., Ardito, C., Jensen, C., Aedo, I., Boden, A. (eds.) IS-EUD 2015. LNCS, vol. 9083, pp. 58–75. Springer, Cham (2015). doi:10.1007/978-3-319-18425-8_5

16. Feinerer, I., Hornik, K., Meyer, D.: Text mining infrastructure in R. J. Stat. Softw. **25**(5), 1–54 (2008)
17. R Core Team: R: A language and environment for statistical computing. https://www.r-project.org/about.html
18. Grün, B., Hornik, K.: Topicmodels: an R package for fitting topic models. J. Stat. Softw. **40**(13), 1–30 (2011)
19. Grammel, L., Storey, M.A.: An end user perspective on mashup makers. University of Victoria Technical report DCS-324-IR (2008)
20. Marcolin, M., D'Andrea, V., Hakken, D.: Participatory maintenance-in-use: users' role in keeping systems alive. In: Proceedings of the PDC 2012, pp. 57–60. ACM, New York (2012)
21. Fischer, G., Herrmann, T.: Socio-technical systems: a meta-design perspective. Int. J. Sociotechnology Knowl. Dev. **3**(1), 1–33 (2011)
22. Maceli, M.: Co-design in the wild: a case study on meme creation tools. In: Proceedings of the PDC 2016, pp. 161–170. ACM, New York (2016)

# What Ails End-User Composition: A Cross-Domain Qualitative Study

Vishal Dwivedi(✉), James D. Herbsleb, and David Garlan

School of Computer Science, Carnegie Mellon University,
5000 Forbes Avenue, Pittsburgh, USA
{vdwivedi,jdh,garlan}@cs.cmu.edu

**Abstract.** Across many domains, end-users need to compose computational elements into novel configurations to perform their day-to-day tasks. End-user composition is a common programming activity performed by such end-users to accomplish this composition task. While there have been many studies on end-user programming, we still need a better understanding of activities involved in end-user composition and environments to support them. In this paper we report a qualitative study of four popular composition environments belonging to diverse application domains, including: Taverna workflow environment for life sciences, Loni Pipeline for brain imaging, SimMan3G for medical simulations and Kepler for scientific simulations. We interview end-users of these environments to explore their experiences while performing common compositions tasks. We use "Content Analysis" technique to analyze these interviews to explore what are the barriers to end-user composition in these domains. Furthermore, our findings show that there are some unique differences in the requirements of naive end-users vs. expert programmers. We believe that not only are these findings useful to improve the quality of end-user composition environments, but they can also help towards development of better end-user composition frameworks.

## 1 Introduction

Increasingly, end-users rely on computations to support their professional activities. Although in some cases turnkey applications and services are sufficient to carry out computational tasks, there are many situations where users must adapt computing to their specific needs. These adaptations can take many forms: from setting preferences in applications, to "programming" spreadsheets, to creating orchestrations of services in support of some business process. This situation has given rise to an interest in end-user programming [13], and, more generally, end-user software engineering [7] or end-user computing [6]. This emerging field attempts to find ways to better support users who, unlike professional programmers, do not have deep technical knowledge, but must somehow find ways to harness the power of computation to support their tasks.

One important subclass of end-user computation arises in domains where end-users must compose existing computational elements into novel configurations. In these domains end-users typically have access to a large number of

© Springer International Publishing AG 2017
S. Barbosa et al. (Eds.): IS-EUD 2017, LNCS 10303, pp. 66–83, 2017.
DOI: 10.1007/978-3-319-58735-6_5

**Table 1.** Example composition environments across different domains

| Type | Compositions |
|---|---|
| *Astronomy* | Electromagnetic image processing tasks [1] |
| *Bioinformatics* | Biological data-analysis services [9] |
| *Digital music production* | Audio sequencing and editing [10] |
| *Environmental Science* | Spatio-temporal experiments [17] |
| *Geospatial Analysis* | Interactive visualization of geographical data [12] |
| *Home Automation* | Home devices and services [8] |
| *Neuroscience* | Brain-image processing libraries [2] |
| *Scientific computing* | Transformational workflows [16] |
| *Socio-technical Analysis* | Dynamic network creation, analysis, reporting and simulation [15] |

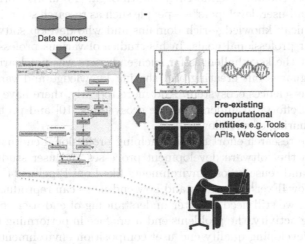

**Fig. 1.** Compositions using Taverna environment.

existing applications and data sets, which must be composed in novel ways to perform various domain-specific tasks besides generate reports and miscellaneous research findings. Table 1 lists examples of some of these domains and the types of compositions end-users build.

Innovative research in these domains often requires scientists to compose a large number of tools and apply them to data sets to perform experiments and diagnose problems. Figure 1 illustrates Taverna - a popular composition environment that is used to create compositions by combining existing web-services discovered through various service registries.

Unfortunately, assembling such elements into coherent compositions is a non-trivial matter. In many cases users must have detailed low-level knowledge of things like application parameter settings, application invocation idiosyncrasies, ordering restrictions, and scripting languages. Further, it may be difficult for end-users to determine whether a set of components can be composed at all, and, if not, what to do about it. For example, differences in data encodings may make direct component composition infeasible without the inclusion of one or more format converters. Even when a legal composition can be achieved, it may not have the performance (or other quality attributes) critical to the needs of the end-users. Across many domains, such problems with end-user composition has led to a large number of a large number of composition environments, out of which only few are successfully adopted by these communities.

The above factors have spurred a number of research projects aimed at understanding of end-user programming and improving the usability of the programming environments. Andrew Ko et al [7] surveyed the software engineering challenges faced by end-users, including a framework for handling requirements, as well as making decisions about design, reuse, integration, testing, and debugging for end-user software engineering. Judith Segal [16] in his work has studied "professional end-user developers" — people such as research scientists who work in highly technical, knowledge-rich domains and who develop software in order to further their professional goals. In his studies of various professionals, Segal discovered that the key challenges for such end-users was not learning the programming languages but creating and sharing knowledge and various cultural aspects of the e-sciences ecosystem. And more recently, there have been a number of research efforts to understand the ecosystems [10] and problems related to reuse and sharing of workflows [4].

Much of the research effort towards helping professional end-user developers has focused on the software development processes and user studies to understand sharing and reuse across environments like Loni Pipeline [4] and projects such as Workflow4Ever[1] to understand how end-users can reproduce their workflows. However, we still need a better understanding of end-user composition as a programming activity, the problems end-users face in performing that, and the challenges in developing quality end-user composition environments.

In previous research, we have developed a technique called "end user architecting" and a software framework to support end-user composition [5]. As a part of this work, we formed some initial hypotheses about key critical barriers to end-user composition — something that we identified through exploratory studies and system implementation in three domains: dynamic network analysis, brain imaging, and geospatial analysis. However, for much of this work, we were the developers of these environments. A confirmation of these hypotheses required a principled study of end-users, perhaps of different composition environments.

To do this, we designed a qualitative study where we interviewed users of some carefully selected composition environments across very different domains. We asked the end-users about their experiences in creating compositions, the challenges they faced and the characteristics of composition environments that support or inhibit composition tasks.

---

[1] https://www.force11.org/node/4708.

Specifically, we have had the following four research questions:

**Q1.** *For what purposes do end-users use composition environments?*
We wanted to see for what activities did end-users used their composition environments. Was it merely drawing and execution or were there more types of tasks involved?

**Q2.** *What composition tasks do end-users perform and what difficulties they face in those tasks?*
Through open questions based on a sample composition the end-users drew, we wanted to understand the types of composition activities and the general difficulties end-users faced in creating compositions.

**Q3.** *What key quality features do end-users want in their composition environments, and what is the relative importance of these features?*
We had some assumptions about the quality problems and we wanted to test if these were indeed true.

**Q4.** *Does "skill level determine relative importance of the environment features and the quality problems?*
We wanted to determine if expertise with composition environments played any role in the kinds of problems end-users faced. To quantify skill-level, we assumed experts were people who had more than one year experience using their composition environments while anyone with less than 1 year experience was considered a beginner.

This paper presents the results from our study focusing specifically on these questions. In Sect. 2, we describe our initial hypothesis about barriers to end-user composition. In Sect. 3, we describe the research design of our study. In Sect. 4, we present the key five findings of our study. Finally, we have a discussion about the possible implications of these findings and some recommendations for composition environment developers to build quality end-user composition environments.

## 2    Barriers to End-User Composition

As noted above, a large number of domains depend on composing computational elements to accomplish some domain specific tasks. A number of research and practitioner-based efforts have produced platforms that provide end-user tools for composition, reuse and execution within these domains. Furthermore, there exists a large number of component repositories and environments that support computational models, such as workflow execution, widget composition, data exploration or music synthesis and composition.

While many of these platforms have been successful, there are others that have failed to make a mark. In our previous work [5] we hypothesized that the following quality barriers impact the adoption of end-user composition environments:

1. **Excessive technical detail:** Creating compositions currently often requires knowledge of myriad low-level technical details, such as data formats, parameter settings, file locations, ordering constraints, execution conventions, scripting languages, etc. As Fig. 2 illustrates, brain imaging research using FSL

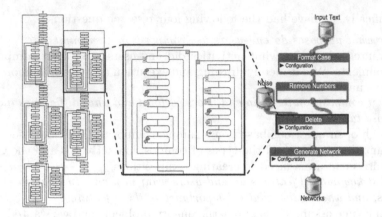

**Fig. 2.** An example end-user composition mapped to a BPEL language script

toolsuite[2] requires a user to understand and create detailed execution scripts that specify how to configure each of the constituent tools, which may have dozens of configuration parameters. As another example, in the domain of intelligence analysis a typical composition that involves two logical steps, but is executed in the context of a service-oriented architecture (SOA), requires the end-user to specify a Business Processing Event Language (BPEL) script shown in Fig. 2 [15]. The script requires the user to explicitly specify low-level details that handle control flow, variable assignment, exception handling, and other programming constructs.

2. **Inappropriate computational models:** The computational models provided by typical execution platforms, such as SOA, may require end-users to map their tasks into a computational vocabulary that is quite different from the natural way of decomposing the task in that domain. For example, tasks that are logically represented in the end-user's mind as a workflow may have to be translated into the very-different vocabulary of service invocations executing on a SOA, as illustrated in Fig. 2.

3. **Inability to analyze compositions:** There may be many restrictions on legal ways to combine elements, dictated by things like format compatibility, domain-specific processing requirements, ordering constraints, and access rights to data and applications. Currently, discovering whether a composition satisfies these restrictions is largely a matter of trial and error, since there are few tools to automate such checks. Moreover, even when a composition does satisfy the composition constraints, its extra-functional properties — or quality attributes — may be uncertain.

4. **Lack of support for reuse:** An important requirement in many communities is the ability for professionals to share their compositions with others in those communities. For instance, brain researchers may want to replicate the analyses of others, or to adapt an existing analysis to a different setting (e.g.,

---

[2] www.fmrib.ox.ac.uk/fsl.

executed on different data sets). Packaging such compositions in a reusable and adaptable form is difficult, given the low-level nature of their encodings, and the brittleness of the specifications.

5. **Impoverished support for execution.** The execution environment for compositions is often impoverished. Compared to the capabilities of modern programming environments, end-users have relatively few tools for things like compilation into efficient deployments, interactive testing and debugging (e.g., setting breakpoints, monitoring intermediate results, etc.), history tracking, and graceful handling of run-time errors. This follows in part from the fact that in many cases compositions are executed in a distributed environment using middleware that is not geared towards interactive use and exploration by technically naive users.

These quality barriers were identified based on our exploratory studies in three domains: dynamic network analysis, brain imaging, and geospatial analysis [5]. In theory, we believed that these would hold for other domains too. Our multiple-case study is designed to evaluate if this is indeed true. We were also interested in discovering whether any other important quality dimensions or important observations would help in the design of successful end-user composition environments.

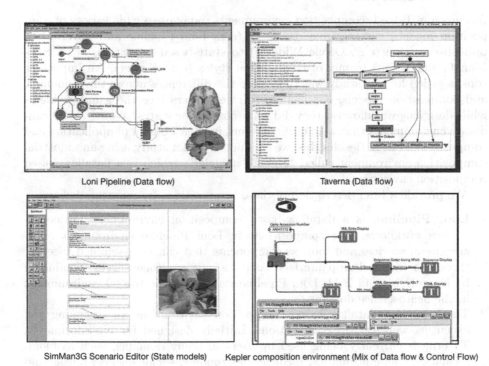

Loni Pipeline (Data flow)  Taverna (Data flow)

SimMan3G Scenario Editor (State models)  Kepler composition environment (Mix of Data flow & Control Flow)

**Fig. 3.** Composition environments under study.

In the next section, we describe our qualitative study of the four composition environments (Fig. 3).

# 3    A Qualitative Study to Investigate Problems Faced by End-Users in Designing Compositions

We chose an exploratory, qualitative research method that aims to understand how end-users used their composition environments across different domains and problems faced by them. Our method consists of three main phases:

- The case selection and protocol design phase, in which we developed the research protocol and identified a diverse set of composition environments with different composition styles and application domains.
- The interview phase, wherein we elicited responses from the selected end-users.
- The qualitative data analysis phase, in which we coded the interview transcripts and systematically drew inferences from the data.

Next, we describe the 3 phases of our study.

## 3.1    Case Selection

As shown in Table 1, composition environments today use a wide variety of composition models, varying from dataflows (e.g., Loni Pipeline and Taverna) to publish-subscribe (e.g., Ozone Widgets) to state-based transitions (e.g., SimMan3G simulation) to mix of composition styles (e.g., Kepler). An important consideration for our study was to explore the differences across these domains and composition models. For instance, did end-users face the same problems while designing workflows as they did while composing states? We selected 4 candidate environments that were quite different in their domain of application and composition models. Besides this, we conducted a pilot study using an industrial composition environment called "Appian modeler", which is a dataflow based composition environment.

We provide a brief description of these composition environments below:

1. **Loni Pipeline:** is a dataflow-based composition environment for neuroscience workflows. The compositions in Loni Pipeline environment reference data, services and tools as components that can be assembled together through a drag and drop interface. As per a software usage survey[3] conducted by NeuroDebian in 2011, Loni Pipeline was one of the top 20 environments in the neuroscience domain.
2. **Taverna:** is a dataflow-based composition environment for designing and executing web-services compositions. Initially designed for bio-informatics, Taverna is currently being used by users in many domains, such as bioinformatics, cheminformatics, medicine, astronomy, social science, music, and digital preservation.

---

[3] http://neuro.debian.net/survey/2011/results.html.

Table 2. Study participants.

| Tool | Participant | Expertise level |
|------|-------------|-----------------|
| Appian modeler | P0 (Pilot) | Beginner |
| Taverna | P1 | Beginner |
| Taverna | P3 | Expert |
| Taverna | P4 | Expert |
| SimMan3G | P5 | Beginner |
| SimMan3G | P6 | Expert |
| SimMan3G | P7 | Beginner |
| Kepler | P8 | Beginner |
| Kepler | P9 | Expert |
| Loni Pipeline | P10 | Beginner |
| Loni Pipeline | P11 | Expert |

3. **SimMan3G:** is a state-based patient simulation system that facilitates health-care training by simulating real-life medical scenarios such as a cardiac arrest, breathing complications and change of vital signs on the high-fidelity manikins. Medical training professionals can combine a sequence of such activities to create a medical scenario (such as an asthma attack) and the complications that go along with it. These activities can be currently programmed in a composition and automatically executed on a manikin or a simulator.

4. **Kepler:** Kepler is a composition environment for designing and executing scientific workflows that uses a mix of dataflow and control flow semantics. Using Kepler's graphical user interface, users can compose various analytic components and data sources to create a scientific workflow. The Kepler software helps users share and reuse data, workflows, and components developed by the scientific community to address common needs.

For the composition environments described above, we recruited 10 participants (plus one additional for the pilot) who had a different degree of expertise in using the composition environment. The average total interview time per participant for each interview was about 35 min. Our participants consist of a mix of beginners (with less than a year experience) and experts (who had been using their composition environment for many years). Table 2 shows the list of participants for the study. It is to be noted that our "expertise level" criteria was fairly subjective and was reinforced during the interview through direct questions about the participants background and the level of their experience and expertise using their composition environments.

## 3.2    Semi-structured Interviews

For our qualitative study, we followed a semi-structured interviewing discipline [3], which means that although the interviews were guided by an explicit interview protocol that defined the general topics that the interviews would examine, we were free to devise new questions to further probe interviewees on specific subjects.

All subjects were asked to either draw a composition (as a homework task), or reproduce an existing composition they had previously drawn. During the interview, all participants were asked to open up their composition and they were interviewed about their experience writing that composition. The general technique used was to start with open-ended questions such as "What problems did you face in creating this composition?", and then ask detailed questions about specific types of problems.

Our interviews consisted of an introductory script to secure informed consent followed by a series of topics to be covered including the following:

- Questions about a participant's role and background and expertise
- Questions about a recently drawn composition (before the interview) that participants needed to open up and use as a recall mechanism
- Questions about features used to create that composition
- Questions about problems faced and quality issues of the environment
- Ratings of quality issues
- Suggestions: how can limitations be addressed?

We instructed participants to speak out loud and explain their actions while working with the composition environments. The recorded audio statements of participants were further transcribed and analyzed.

## 3.3    Data Analysis and Interpretation

Given the exploratory nature of our research questions, "Content Analysis" [11] is the main analytic method used in our study. The content analysis technique allows building an understanding of underlying reasons and motivations of participants while using unstructured or semi-structured data (such as interviews).

We recorded all participant interviews and used Amazon Turks to transcribe the audio into text, which needed some post processing. We used coding theory [14] to link the findings about end-user preferences to the interview dataset and validate whether our observations were consistent. In particular, we employed a two-cycle coding method: in the first cycle, we applied the "hypothesis coding method to our dataset using the predefined code list. In the second cycle, we applied axial/pattern coding to discover patterns from the dataset [14].

A selection of sample 1st cycle codes is listed in Table 3. As a second-cycle coding activity, we identified patterns and selective heuristics that led to some of the key findings for the study that we discuss in the Findings section.

**Table 3.** Sample (first-level) codes for the study.

| 1st cycle codes | |
|---|---|
| 1. Composition motives (mot)<br>• Simulation (mot:simulation)<br>• Experimentation (mot:experiment)<br>• Teaching (mot:teaching)<br>• Automation (mot:automation)<br>• Other (mot:other) | 4. Resolution of problems (res)<br>• Analysis tools (res: tools)<br>• Intuition (res: intuition)<br>• Execution (res: execution)<br>• Reference Documentation (res: docs)<br>• Other (res: other) |
| 2. Nature of Composition (nat)<br>• Computation model (nat: compModel)<br>• Abstraction level (nat: abstractionLevel)<br>• Other (nat: other) | 5. Desired Feature (des)<br>• General Purpose (des: general)<br>• Tool-specific feature (des: specific) |
| 3. Quality issues with composition environments (issue)<br>• Technical detail (issue: techDetail)<br>• Reuse support (issue: reuseSup)<br>• Execution support (issue: execSup)<br>• Analysis support (issue: analysis)<br>• Computation model mismatch (issue: compMismatch)<br>• Other (issue: oth) | 6. Skill level of end user (skill)<br>• Beginner (skill: beginner)<br>• Expert (skill: expert)<br>• Unknown (skill: Unknown)<br>7. Rating (rating)<br>• Highly important (rating: highImp)<br>• Low importance (rating: lowImp)<br>• Unknown (rating: Unknown) |
| Other codes... | |

## 4   Findings

In this section we revisit the research questions we identified in Sect. 1 and how content analysis helped us to find answers to those questions. As an outcome of our analysis, we discuss 5 key findings that provide some insight into how end-users use composition environments and what problems they face. We believe, these could be a basis for further research and improvements to composition environments.

### 4.1   Finding 1: Goals of End-User Composition — End-users Use Composition Environments Not only to Perform composition Tasks, but They Also Serve as Experimentation And learning Tools

To address *ResearchQuestion1* ("For what purposes do end-users use composition environments?"), we evaluated the first-cycle attribute codes, where participant responses point to a number of "Composition Motives". While the frequency of codes varied across environments, the general finding was that participants used the environments as learning and experimentation tools. Table 4 lists the breakdown of general composition motives for the participants.

While the frequency of occurrences of codes was not the most interesting observation, what was more relevant was "how" end-users performed the

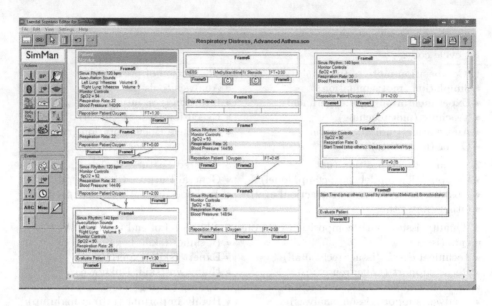

**Fig. 4.** A respiratory distress scenario using SimMan3G (Participant P6)

**Table 4.** General layout of composition motives.

|  | Frequency (Coding Units) | Frequency (Interviews) | Frequency (Participants) | Examples |
|---|---|---|---|---|
| *mot: simulation* | 12 | 10 | 7 | Medical Simulation, Workflow simulations, etc. |
| *mot: experiment* | 22 | 10 | 10 | Tutorials, Adapt compositions, etc. |
| *mot: teaching* | 4 | 10 | 1 | Medical Simulation teaching |
| *mot: automation* | 14 | 10 | 10 | Workflow automation |
| *mot: other* | 32 | 10 | 4 | Exploration, Debug, Reuse, Learning, etc |

composition tasks and the qualitative reasoning in doing them. As an example, Fig. 4 shows a composition on SimMan3G simulator for an advanced asthma attack scenario simulated on a high-fidelity manikin. The typical problem in such composition scenarios is fine-tuning the properties about the medicine dosage, oxygen levels etc. Much of the composition activity for this composition environment involved going to-and-fro between composition and execution to understand the individual components. While drawing a composition may be important, much of the effort was spent in interactive learning and exploration.

To exemplify how important is this exploration and experimentation activity, here are some statements collected during the interviews:

- "Before we begin simulation, we follow a worksheet to organize our thoughts and we constantly refer to that to find out who the patient is, what kind of position they are in [properties] .... we go to-and-fro between this worksheet, drawing, and execution to learn more..." [Participant P5 about Medical Simulation scenario]
- "The biggest problem is not connecting everything together but to understand what's going on" [Participant P1, Taverna]
- "...Sometimes there is a need to take a different model and use a different controller, but that means manually figuring out all the signals and even look at code to find what's going on..." [Participant P8, Kepler]

For many participants the composition environments were a mechanism to quickly test some components, or explore an existing composition to learn a concept. This aspect is often missed in many composition environments. Composition environments can further support learning and cognition by providing tutorials, integrating repositories with composition environments (like myExperiment in Taverna).

## 4.2 Finding 2: Types of End-User Tasks — End-User Composition Involves Multiple Phases, Including: (i) Search and Exploration (ii) Reuse (iii) Construction (iv) Analysis (v) Execution, and (vi) Debugging

To address *ResearchQuestion2* ("What composition tasks do end-users perform and what difficulties they face in writing compositions?"), we evaluated the first-cycle attribute codes, where participant responses point to a number of "Composition Tasks" and "Composition Problems". While first cycle codes provided us instances of tasks such as search, reuse, construction, analysis, execution and debugging (not necessarily in that order), what was more interesting was to find pattern codes such as:

[task: search→task: construct→task: execution→tasks: analysis→task: debugging] for each composition environment. The ordering and membership of such patterns varied, but such patterns were common across all the four environments under study.

Analysis of our interview data showed that end-user composition activity is not a monolithic drawing and execution activity. In fact, the composition activity started with search (on online forums, desktops, component repositories) followed by some level of reuse, experimentation and debugging. External reuse (other people's composition) was rare, and used primarily for learning purposes. But even while drawing everything from scratch, end-users flipped through these phases for a better understanding of the compositions.

While this may seem a not-so-novel finding at first, we can't stress the importance of these phases any lesser. We found almost all the participants going

**Table 5.** End-user ratings for quality features (Low Importance:1 - High Importance:10)

| Tool | Appian | Taverna | | | SimMan3G | | | Kepler | | Loni Pipeline | | Average Score |
|---|---|---|---|---|---|---|---|---|---|---|---|---|
| Participant | P0 | P1 | P2 | P3 | P4 | P5 | P6 | P7 | P8 | P9 | P10 | |
| Skill-level | Beginner | Beginner | Expert | Expert | Beginner | Expert | Beginner | Beginner | Expert | Beginner | Expert | |
| Technical detail | 6 | 2 | 2 | 2 | 2 | 2 | 6 | 1 | 2 | 4 | 2 | 2.5 |
| Reuse support | 4 | 8 | 9 | 8 | 5 | 2 | 5 | 8 | 4 | 4 | 5 | 5.8 |
| Execution support | 4 | 10 | 10 | 8 | 8 | 10 | 8 | 6 | 8 | 8 | 8 | 8.4 |
| Analysis support | 9 | 10 | 9 | 8 | 9 | 8 | 10 | 6 | 7 | 10 | 7 | 8.4 |
| Computation model mismatch | 8 | 2 | 3 | 2 | 9 | 4 | 8 | 6.5 | 10 | 2 | 2 | 4.85 |

**High importance:** Analysis Support, Execution Support
**Some importance:** Reuse Support, Computational model mismatch
**Low Importance:** Technical detail

through these phases during their composition activity and they struggled when tool-support was missing for any phase. While some environments had better support for all these phases (e.g., Taverna) and others had limited support for some of these phases (e.g., SimMan3G, which had limited search and exploration capability), in which case end-users resorted to external artifacts like using checklists online forums etc. Not only was it important to support all the phases, but it was also important to allow easy switch between them. Providing support for all these phases is an engineering challenge but it greatly helps the composition activity.

### 4.3 Finding 3: End-Users Face Some Common Problems Across Different Composition Styles and Domains

To address *ResearchQuestion3* ("What key quality features do end-users want in their composition environments, and what is the relative importance of these features?"), we evaluated the first-cycle attribute codes for the code (quality) issue. While in Sect. 2, we had hypothesized about the key critical barriers for end user composition. We found these to be generally true for all composition environments. As shown in Table 5[4], Analysis and Execution Support were the most important features for end-users as they not only helped in debugging but also learning about compositions. Computation model mismatch played an important role for environments that had a computation style that was very different from composition mechanism. An example was SimMan3G editor, where people thought in terms of sequences and dataflows but had to program events, which was not an easy cognitive switch. Support for reuse was also an important requirement to address composition problems. However, the form of reuse varied across environments. "Self-reuse" was the primary form of reuse. "External

---

[4] Note that ratings used in Table 5 are not absolute. In this qualitative study, their main role was to help the end-users easily express their preferences.

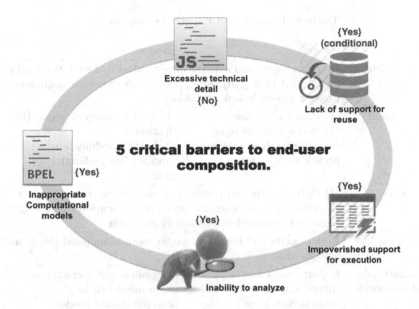

**Fig. 5.** Our initial hypotheses about end-user composition quality problems.

reuse" via repositories was used mainly used for experimentation and learning. This was not a very surprising result as prior studies have found similar observations [4]. It was slightly surprising that end-users rarely faced any difficulty with the technical vocabulary of the environments. As long as the composition environments provided support for exploration and debugging, the participants were fairly comfortable with the detailed technical vocabulary for all the environments under study (Fig. 5).

## 4.4  Finding 4: The Skill Level and Purpose Determines the Quality Features Needed by End-Users

To address *ResearchQuestion4* ("Does" skill-level determine relative importance of the environment features and the quality problems?), we looked at patterns of occurrences of [Skills→Quality]. Analysis of our interview data showed some very interesting differences in the preferences of experts and beginners (Summarized in Table 6). We were slightly surprised that beginners were less troubled by the technical details. Perhaps, this had more to do with a visual vocabulary of all the environments. But even in environments like Kepler where some coding knowledge was required, the end-users were comfortable in understanding, if not writing the code. As long as their composition environment allowed them to explore and debug, they did not rate language-constructs and technical details as a barrier to composition tasks. However, in retrospect, this finding is corroborated by similar studies by Judith Segal [16], where he found that programming language complexity was not the key challenge for most professional end-user developers.

**Table 6.** Preference of Experts vs. Beginners

|  | Experts | Beginners |
|---|---|---|
| Technical detail | Both beginners and experts were comfortable with the level of technical details (Surprising, because we expected beginners to prefer a less-technical vocabulary) | |
| Reuse support | (1) Prefer self-reuse (2) When there were no repositories there was low preference for reuse | 1. Prefer external reuse (for learning) 2. Costly modification implied low preference for reuse |
| Execution support | (1) Both experts and beginners preferred execution support (2) While experts relied on interactive execution (for debugging), beginners preferred more turnkey execution | |
| Analysis support | Both experts and beginners prefer more automated checks and custom analysis | |
| Computational model mismatch | Experts don't find computational model mismatch as issue | Beginners are overwhelmed by a mismatch in computational model |

One major difference was the level of reuse for both types of end-users. External reuse was rare, and mainly used for educational purposes. In fact, the most common form of reuse was self-reuse where end-users preferred to use their prior compositions. However, presence of curated repositories changed some of this behavior to some extent. For experts, the bigger concern was not only time spent in learning and exploration, but also trust issues with external compositions.

Here are some statements to describe the nature of reuse being currently practiced:

- "Do you generally reuse your own components or some repository".... "Mostly my own. A vast majority of trends are located in ... folder, I have created over 9 and I have re-purposed them for various scenarios" [Participant P6, an expert SimMan3G end-user describing a self-reuse scenario]
- "I used the myExperiment repository. It helped me a lot to design examples before I could design my own workflows" [Participant P1, an end-user (who had little prior-experience with Taverna) describing an external-reuse scenario for learning purposes]

## 4.5 Finding 5: When Composition Model is Misaligned with Computation Model, it Leads to Difficulties in Composition

Another observation that we realized through our interviews was that end-users struggled when visual composition vocabulary was different than the type of computational vocabulary common for that domain. For instance, in the case of Kepler environment, Participant P8 (beginner) had trouble including code blocks. Further more, in the case of SimMan3G simulator, when Participant P5 (beginner) was forced to write events while thinking in terms of dataflow, computational model mismatch was sighted as an important concern.

Here are some statements collected during the interviews to demonstrate what problems end-users faced when they has a mismatch in computation model:

- "Without a worksheet it would be very difficult to fill in the values in the frames. We need to write down all our thoughts and all information organized..." [Participant P5, SimMan3G commenting on difficulty to directly compose frames]
- "Well, it's relatively easy if I have to just combine simple operations. But if I add a differential equation and Kepler thinks about integration of things so I have to rewrite differential equations as integrates, changing code and that would be difficult..." [Participant P8, Kepler commenting on difficulty arising from adding mathematical expressions and code]

## 5 Conclusions

End-User Programming is an activity that has been attributed to allowing end-users — people who are not professional software developers — to program computers. An important class of end-user programming is writing compositions using various domain-specific composition environments such as workflow tools, widget compositions and simulation software. We argue in this paper that while many of these environments may have different computation styles, and a diverse set of application domains, they often have a common set of problems. By getting a better understanding of quality problems for end-users, platforms developers can build better composition environments.

In this paper we describe our qualitative study that throws a light on how end-users use their composition environments, what kind of quality concerns end-user have, and how they can be provided better infrastructures. Furthermore, often the same composition environment could be used for disparate audience with a varying level of skills. A better understanding of the quality requirements could help in better targeting of composition environments.

We presented the findings of our qualitative study in the previous section. Besides the general findings that we discussed in previous section, here are some recommendations for composition environment developers to improve the quality of composition environments.

1. To be effective, composition environments must support all these phases of composition: (i) search and exploration (ii) reuse (iii) construction (iv) analysis (v) execution, and (vi) debugging.
2. Self reuse is a more preferred form of reuse for end-users. However, unless the platforms developers provide curated repositories and specialized compositions for scenarios, the likelihood of external reuse is typically low.

3. Beginners still need tutorials and samples (learning phase). Repositories of compositions are a good mechanism to shorten the learning curve.
4. There is no need to dumb down the vocabulary for end-users. End-users are not overly bothered by complex vocabulary as long as environments provide mechanisms to interact and learn the vocabulary.
5. There is a need for more analytic support across all composition environments. Naive users often require automated analyses to know "what is going on?" with their external reuse scenarios, while Experts need analyses to know "how to get it right?" to modify compositions and adapt them to a different setting in an internal reuse scenario.
6. While construction and execution may seem distinct activities, often execution phase is interleaved with the construction phase. To build high-quality composition environments, platform developers need to support iterative execution that is widely used both as a learning and debugging mechanism.
7. As much as it is possible, compositions should match the computation styles of the domain. A mismatch makes composition process hard and adds an additional burden on end-users to write error-free compositions.

**Acknowledgments.** This work is supported in part by the National Security Agency. The views and conclusions contained herein are those of the authors and should not be interpreted as representing the official policies, either expressed or implied, of the National Security Agency or the U.S. government.

# References

1. Deelman, E., Singh, G., Mei-Hui, S., Blythe, J., Gil, Y., Kesselman, C., Mehta, G., Vahi, K., Berriman, G.B., Good, J., Laity, A.C., Jacob, J.C., Katz, D.S.: Pegasus: a framework for mapping complex scientific workflows onto distributed systems. Sci. Program. **13**(3), 219–237 (2005)
2. Dwivedi, V., Velasco-Elizondo, P., Maria Fernandes, J., Garlan, D., Schmerl, B.: An architectural approach to end user orchestrations. In: Crnkovic, I., Gruhn, V., Book, M. (eds.) ECSA 2011. LNCS, vol. 6903, pp. 370–378. Springer, Heidelberg (2011). doi:10.1007/978-3-642-23798-0_39
3. Edwards, R., Holland, J.: What is Qualitative Interviewing? The 'What is?'. Research Methods Series. Bloomsbury Academic (2013)
4. Garijo, D., Corcho, Ó., Gil, Y., Braskie, M.N., Hibar, D.P., Hua, X., Jahanshad, N., Thompson, P.M., Toga, A.W.: Workflow reuse in practice: a study of neuroimaging pipeline users. In: 10th IEEE International Conference on e-Science, eScience 2014, Sao Paulo, Brazil, 20–24 October 2014, pp. 239–246 (2014)
5. Garlan, D., Dwivedi, V., Ruchkin, I., Schmerl, B.R.: Foundations and tools for end-user architecting. In: Large-Scale Complex IT Systems. Development, Operation and Management - 17th Monterey Workshop, UK, pp. 157–182 (2012)
6. Goodell, H.: End-user computing. In: CHI 1997 Extended Abstracts on Human Factors in Computing Systems: Looking to the Future, CHI EA 1997, NY, USA, p. 132 (1997)
7. Ko, A.J., Abraham, R., Beckwith, L., Blackwell, A.F., Burnett, M.M., Erwig, M., Scaffidi, C., Lawrance, J., Lieberman, H., Myers, B.A., Rosson, M.B., Rothermel, G., Shaw, M., Wiedenbeck, S.: The state of the art in end-user software engineering. ACM Comput. Surv. **43**(3), 21 (2011)

8. Lee, C., Nordstedt, D., Helal, S.: Enabling smart spaces with osgi. IEEE Pervasive Comput. **2**, 89–94 (2003)
9. Letondal, C.: Participatory programming: Developing programmable bioinformatics tools for end-users. End-User Development, pp. 207–242 (2005)
10. McConahy, A.L., Herbsleb, J.D.: Platform design strategies: contrasting case studies of two audio production systems. In: FutureCSD Workshop at CSCW (2011)
11. Miles, M.B., Huberman, A.M., Saldaña, J.: Qualitative Data Analysis. SAGE Publications, Thousand Oaks (2013)
12. Moore, D.M., Crowe, P., Cloutier, R.: Driving major change: The balance between methods and people. Software Technology Support Center Hill AFB UT (2011)
13. Nardi, B.A.: A Small Matter of Programming: Perspectives on End User Computing. MIT Press, Cambridge (1993)
14. Saldana, J.: The Coding Manual for Qualitative Researchers. SAGE Publications, Thousand Oaks (2015)
15. Schmerl, B.R., Garlan, D., Dwivedi, V., Bigrigg, M.W., Carley, K.M.: SORASCS: a case study in SOA-based platform design for socio-cultural analysis. In: International Conference of Software Engineering (ICSE), pp. 643–652 (2011)
16. Segal, J.: Some problems of professional end user developers. In: VL/HCC, pp. 111–118 (2007)
17. Villa, F., Athanasiadis, I.N., Rizzoli, A.E.: Modelling with knowledge: a review of emerging semantic approaches to environmental modelling. Environ. Model Softw. **24**(5), 577–587 (2009)

# Semi-automatic Extraction
# of Cross-Table Data from a Set of Spreadsheets

Alaaeddin Swidan[(⊠)] and Felienne Hermans

Delft University of Technology, Delft, Netherlands
{Alaaeddin.Swidan,F.F.J.Hermans}@tudelft.nl

**Abstract.** Spreadsheets are widely used in companies. End-users often value the high degree of flexibility and freedom spreadsheets provide. However, these features lead to the development of a variety of data forms inside spreadsheets. A *cross-table* is one of these forms of data. A cross-table is defined as a rectangular form of data, which expresses the relations between a set of objects and a set of attributes. Cross-tables are common in spreadsheets: our exploratory analysis found that more than 3.42% of spreadsheets in an industrial open dataset include at least one cross-table. However, current software tools provide no support to analyze data in cross-tables. To address this, we presents a semi-automatic approach to extract cross-table data from a set of spreadsheets, and transform them to a relational table form. We evaluate our approach in a case study, on a set of 333 spreadsheets with 2,801 worksheets. The results show that the approach is successful in extracting over 92% of the data inside the targeted cross-tables. Further, we interview two users of the spreadsheets working in the company; they confirmed the approach is beneficial and provides correct results.

## 1    Introduction

Spreadsheets are used extensively across various domains of expertise, to perform a wide range of tasks [1–4]. In particular, spreadsheets are often used for data analysis and management [5]. In addition to the powerful set of functionalities, the end-users appreciate the flexibility and freedom provided by spreadsheets [6]. This leads, however, to a variety of forms in which data is represented inside a worksheet. One of the special forms of data found in spreadsheets is the *cross-table*. A cross-table in general aims to represent a relation $I$. It consists of $G$ rows and $M$ columns, and can be defined as:

> *A rectangular table with one row for each object and one column for each attribute, having a cross in the intersection of row g with column m iff $(g,m) \in I$. [7]*

Cross-tables, an example of which is shown in Fig. 1, are common in spreadsheets. To explore this, we manually investigated more than 1,500 spreadsheets from the industrial dataset Enron [8]. Our investigation revealed that 552 spreadsheets, or 3.42% of the dataset, include at least one cross-table (Sect. 3). As an

© Springer International Publishing AG 2017
S. Barbosa et al. (Eds.): IS-EUD 2017, LNCS 10303, pp. 84–99, 2017.
DOI: 10.1007/978-3-319-58735-6_6

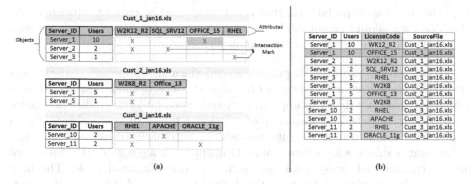

**Fig. 1.** An example showing related data presented in three separate spreadsheets using cross-tables in (a). (b) shows the equivalent data migrated into one relational table.

example of a cross-table in a context, consider Fig. 1a. The example is based on our case study at Solvinity[1], which provides virtual environments and IT services. In the example, the finance department uses spreadsheets to record the data related to third-party licenses sold as part of each virtual environment, in a cross-table. In one scenario, an internal auditor, let us call him Bas, aims to answer management questions such as: do actual billed licenses conform to the specification of the providing third-party? do the actual-billing data on licenses conform to the actual software license-configuration (eg. number of users) on the servers? To answer these, and similar related questions, data analysis on the related cross-tables, which are included in separate files should be carried out.

As a human, Bas can easily read a cross-table. For example, in Fig. 1a, he can read that for *"Cust_1_jan16.xls"*, *"Licence: OFFICE_15"* is related to *"Server_ID:Server_1, Users:10"*. Bas does this *mapping* through a sequence of mental operations, which include linking and relating the two-separate data sets: the objects and the attributes. In addition, Bas incorporates his domain knowledge to recognize that the attribute *"OFFICE_15"* is a data value of type *"License"*.

In reality, Bas is *transforming* each X-marked relation in the cross-table, into one *"record"* in the relational table in Fig. 1b. Therefore, if the data was originally formed in a relational table form, the user would be spared from performing the conversion steps, and focuses on the analysis part of the task. In addition, data in a relational table allows the user to leverage a wide-set of analysis tools and visualizations, including Excel itself. These tools are designed to work best with strictly-formed relational tables. In our case, the user can perform the transformation from a cross-table to a relational-table form manually. However, as the number of cross-tables increases, the task becomes time-consuming, tedious and unrealistic. The previous scenario describes a twofold problem for the end-users:

---

[1] https://www.solvinity.com/.

(a) The data has a special form that is not supported by current software tools.
(b) The data should be consolidated from multiple spreadsheets into one relational table, to be used in other analysis software.

To address this problem, we propose a semi-automatic approach that extracts cross-table data from a set of spreadsheets, and converts them into one (denormalized) relational table. Our approach expands upon previous studies that managed to extract data and hierarchy of relational tables in spreadsheets [9]. In addition to the user input, we incorporate an automatic transformation algorithm that is suitable for a cross-table. Our approach aggregates the data from all the transformed cross-tables, and generates one relational table. The final output is the structure and data of the desired table, encoded in an SQL script.

We perform a mixed method evaluation of our approach, on a set of 333 spreadsheet with 2,801 worksheets found in the company dataset. First, we quantitatively analyze the approach performance in extracting cross-table data. Subsequently, we interview two frequent users of the spreadsheets, to manually validate the approach generated data on a subset of 30 spreadsheets.

The contributions of the paper are:

1. An exploratory study on the incidence of cross-table in spreadsheets. For this, we manually examined a subset of more than 1,500 Enron spreadsheets.
2. A semi-automatic approach that identifies, transforms cross-table data from multiple spreadsheets, aggregating them into one relational table.
3. An industrial evaluation through a case study.

## 2   Background

Before describing the extraction approach, we provide a brief overview of the preliminaries this paper builds upon.

### 2.1   Cross-Tables

There are two types of cross-table: single-valued and many-valued [7]. A single-valued cross-table, shown in Fig. 1a, follows the general definition, where a binary relation $I$ between a row-based object $g$, and a column-based attribute $m$ is marked using the *intersection cell*. A many-valued cross-table, shown in Fig. 2, adds a fourth dimension to the definition, which is the set of data values $W_m$ that are associated with each attribute $m$.

Cross-tables are sometimes called *"matrices"* [10,11]. We find that *"cross-table"* is the frequently used term [7,12,13], so we use it throughout this paper. A cross-table, as a word, suggests the usage of a *"cross"*, or the *"X"* character in *the intersection cell* which indicates the relationship between an object and its attributes. In practice, however, users are not restricted to use the cross, and they can use other marks in the intersection cell, which can be a specific character, a digit or a shape such as a circle or a triangle.

*Price.* An additional value
associated with each attribute

| Licenses and Subscriptions | | W2K8_R2 | Price | OFFICE_15 | Price |
|---|---|---|---|---|---|
| Server_ID | Users | | | | |
| Server_1 | 5 | X | 100 | X | 300 |
| Server_5 | 1 | X | 50 | | |
| Total | | | 150 | | 300 |

**Fig. 2.** An example of a many-valued cross-table. The column *Price* represents an additional data value associated with each attribute in the adjacent column.

In spreadsheets, cross-tables may be developed for various tasks. For a simple example, a spreadsheet with a cross-table can be used by employees (objects) to reserver meeting rooms (attributes). A more complex example is used in *"software requirement traceability"* [14], where the user follows up the progress of customer requirements (objects) against system components under development (attributes). In Sect. 3, we quantify the popularity of using cross-tables in spreadsheets in a business context.

### 2.2    Extraction and Transformation of Spreadsheet Data

In this subsection, we present an overview of previous research work, and software products which targeted the extraction of data from spreadsheets for various goals. One example from previous research is the GyroSAT algorithm, which was developed by Hermans *et al.* [9] to help end-users comprehend the structure of spreadsheets. For that purpose, the GyroSAT visualized the hierarchy and relations between blocks of cells, and worksheets, in a spreadsheet. Another research work is UCheck [15], which extracts header and unit information from all cells, as a means to detecting potential errors in spreadsheets. In software, database and data analysis systems, such as Microsoft SQL Server, consider spreadsheets as a data source, and the user is allowed to import data from a spreadsheet. The aforementioned tools and software products, however, work best with relational tables in spreadsheets. For cross-table data, the user should transform the data inside the spreadsheet into a relational table before being able to use these software tools.

Despite being designed to work on relational tables, some components from previous research can be re-used to extract other forms of data, specifically the cross-table. In our case, our approach expands upon the GyroSAT algorithm, which we choose because: First, the GyroSAT is able to identify a rectangle of adjacent cells, which is called a data block. A cross-table, in essence, is a rectangular area of cells, which makes the identification of a data block is the logical first step in extracting data from a cross-table. Second, a recent study benchmarked the GyroSAT and UCheck performances against the selection made by human users of spreadsheets [16]. The study reveals that GyroSAT has better performance in identifying cell types, which is a prerequisite for the data block identification. Following is the description of the two components that are implemented in GyroSAT, and are used in our approach.

- **Cell Classification:** The GyroSAT approach has four classifications of a cell depending on its content and relations. A *"formula"* type is given to a cell which contains a formula inside. The cells which are referred by the formulas are considered *"data"*. If the cell has an empty content, it is given the *"empty"* type, otherwise the cell is given the *"label"* type. Label cells contain data that are not part of any calculation, thus it is supposed they label other data.
- **Data Blocks:** Using the cell classification, and through a cell-to-cell search algorithm, the approach identifies a rectangular area which includes physically-adjacent cells. The data block, as shown in Fig. 3 is not expanded when each of the current four corners is surrounded by empty cells, from the outside of the block, in the diagonal, vertical and horizontal directions. In Fig. 3 for example, the corner cell A7 is not expanded since the outside neighbor cells A8 and B8 are both empty.

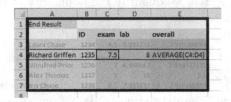

**Fig. 3.** A data block including the cells A1:E7 [6]

## 2.3 Motivation

As the spreadsheet usage grows in organizations, the data in spreadsheets becomes more important for decision making processes [4]. When valuable data are stored in spreadsheets, users such as executives, managers or auditors, become more interested in acquiring knowledge out of the spreadsheets. Many software tools might aid these users in understanding their business, and taking actions accordingly. For instance, Business Intelligence (BI) tools, such as Tableau[2], provide reports and visuals. Traditional database systems provide the ability to perform user-specified queries. In addition, data integration tools, such as Microsoft SSIS[3], allow to compare and aggregate data from different sources.

Despite considering spreadsheets as a potential data source, these software tools require the data inside these spreadsheets to be in a strict relational table form [5]. If this is the case, the user can directly leverage the powerful analysis features provided by these tools. However, when the data is in other forms, such as a cross-table, the users are expected to transform the data beforehand. The transformation can be done manually, though it is tedious and time-consuming especially when the data involved is large in scale. In fact, when working on

---

[2] https://www.tableau.com/.

[3] https://msdn.microsoft.com/en-us/library/ms141026.aspx.

spreadsheet data, a recent survey reveals that users prefer less manual processing and more automatic solutions [4].

In this paper we aim at providing an approach that extracts and transforms data formed in cross-tables, from multiple spreadsheets, into one integrated relational table, with minimum user efforts. The output of our approach, encoded in standard SQL, can be used to further analyze the data by many analysis tools, not limited to the ones described earlier.

## 3    An Exploratory Analysis of Cross-Tables in Industry

Before we address the extraction of cross-table data, it is important to realize how much widespread cross-tables are in spreadsheets. To achieve this, we analyze the Enron spreadsheet dataset in search for the usage of cross-tables. The Enron dataset [8] provides researchers with the opportunity to study a large number of spreadsheets, compared to other known corpora, which were developed and used in an industrial context.

**Setup:** We follow a two-step approach to identify a cross-table in Enron spreadsheets. **First**, we automatically identify all of the spreadsheets which include at least one value of a particular intersection cell. Subsequently, the resulted subset includes the spreadsheet candidates which may have one form of a cross-table inside. To filter out the actual cross-tables from other structures of data, our **second step** consists of manually analyzing the resulted subset of spreadsheets. These two steps are based on self-defined criteria which we detail next.

**Criteria:** For the first step, criteria include the values of intersection cells that the automatic search will use. We recall from Sect. 2.1 that an intersection cell may include many possible values such as a single character, a digit or a shape. Since our analysis is exploratory, and is carried out without previous domain knowledge of the content of Enron spreadsheets, we decide to limit the values we search for to two values:

*X:* Mostly used by users in cross-tables.
*Y:* An abbreviation of Yes, indicating a positive selection of an attribute.

For the second step, the manual verification of the existence of a cross-table, our criteria follow the general definition of a cross-table, examples shown in Fig. 1a. For this, an actual cross-table is identified if it has the following three criteria: (1) The *"objects"* and *"attributes"* are visually recognizable as two separate sets of data. (2) There are one or more intersection cells found in the area between objects and attributes. (3) The value of the intersection cell is used as an indicator to a relation, not as a data value by itself.

**Results:** The summary of our analysis is presented in Table 1. Initially, Enron dataset consists of 16,160 spreadsheets. The first step of the analysis generated a subset of 1,524 spreadsheets. After the manual verification in the second step, we established that 552 spreadsheets in the subset contain at least one form of a

**Table 1.** Results of the analysis performed on the Enron dataset (16,161 spreadsheets), to identify cross-tables structures in the spreadsheets.

| Interaction mark (Case Insensitive) | Spreadsheets with a *"candidate"* cross-table | Spreadsheets with a *"verified"* cross-table |
| --- | --- | --- |
| X | 1,177 | 542 |
| Y | 347 | 10 |
| Total | 1,524 | 552 |

|   | A | B | C | D | E | F | G | H | I | J | K | L | M | N | O |
| --- | --- | --- | --- | --- | --- | --- | --- | --- | --- | --- | --- | --- | --- | --- | --- |
| 1 | | *COUNTERPARTY* | | *BOOK PURPOSE* | | | | | | | | *TAGG* | | | |
| 2 | | | | *Type Of Transactions* | | | | | | | | *Book Mapping* | | | |
| 3 | *CP ID* | *Short Name* | *Long Name* | *Internal* | *External* | *Both* | *Code* | *Region* | *P* | *B* | *Idx* | *GD* | *PHY* | *Y* | *Commodity/UOM/Curr* |
| 4 | *166805* | *FB-Financial1* | *FB-Financial1* | | | *X* | *MF* | *Financial1* | *X* | *X* | *X* | *X* | | *X* | *NG/MMBUT/USD* |
| 5 | *166807* | *FB-Financial2* | *FB-Financial2* | | | *X* | *MF* | *Financial2* | *X* | *X* | *X* | *X* | | *X* | *NG/MMBUT/USD* |
| 6 | *166813* | *FB-Financial3* | *FB-Financial3* | | | *X* | *MF* | *Financial3* | *X* | *X* | *X* | *X* | | *X* | *NG/MMBUT/USD* |
| 7 | *166815* | *FB-Financial4* | *FB-Financial4* | | | *X* | *MF* | *Financial4* | *X* | *X* | *X* | *X* | | *X* | *NG/MMBUT/USD* |
| 8 | *166818* | *FB-Financial5* | *FB-Financial5* | | | *X* | *MF* | *Financial5* | *X* | *X* | *X* | *X* | | *X* | *NG/MMBUT/USD* |
| 9 | *166823* | *FB-Executive* | *FB-Executive* | | | *X* | *MF* | *Financial* | *X* | *X* | *X* | *X* | | *X* | *NG/MMBUT/USD* |
| 10 | *166828* | *FB-Crude* | *FB-Crude* | | | *X* | *MF* | *FinancialC* | *X* | | | | | | *WTI/BBL/USD* |
| 11 | *166831* | *FB-Unleaded* | *FB-Unleaded* | | | *X* | *MF* | *FinancialU* | *X* | | | | | | *HU/BBL/USD* |
| 12 | *166833* | *FB-Heating Oil* | *FB-Heating Oil* | | | *X* | *MF* | *FinancialH* | *X* | | | | | | *HO/BBL/USD* |

**Fig. 4.** A complex cross-table found in Enron dataset: objects are in two columns, attributes are in multiple (hierarchical) rows.

cross-table. In other words, at least 3.42% of spreadsheets in the Enron dataset include one cross-table form. Figure 4 shows one of the cross-tables found in the Enron dataset.

In addition to identifying cross-tables, the analysis shows that particular cross-tables are context-related and found in a subset of spreadsheet files. For example, cross-tables similar to the one shown in Fig. 4 are developed and used frequently in more than 100 spreadsheets in Enron dataset. The content of the cross-table in this example suggests that it was part of a business process of risk book requests. It mentions an information system called *"ERMS"*, standing for Enron Risk Management Services. However, identifying the exact business context remains difficult without the user domain knowledge.

## 4    Approach

Our approach aims to extract cross-tables data from a set of related spreadsheets. The approach follows four steps to achieve its aim, as summarized in Fig. 5.

- Step 1 - Identify the dimensions of a *"potential"* cross-table: For a given worksheet, the approach uses an algorithm based on the GyroSAT, in addition to keywords and configuration parameters specified by the end-user, to decide three attributes of a cross-table rectangle: the minimum row and column, the maximum row and column, and the header row number.
- Step 2 - Transform the cross-table into key-value data tuples: For each detected cross-table, the approach perform transformations on the cross-table to construct the related key-value tuples.

- Step 3 - Decide the common keys from the transformed cross-tables: Our approach considers all the cross-tables identified and transformed from multiple spreadsheet files, and subsequently decides the common keys in the data tuples. These keys will be the column names in the target relational table.
- Step 4 - Generate the output file: The output file, encoded as an SQL script, contains the statements to create the structure, and fill the data of the target relational table.

Prior to the application of the approach, the user should provide the following parameters and textual keywords:

(a) Keywords which can be found in the upper and lower left corners of the cross-table. For example, in Fig. 2, the user may supply {upper: *"licenses"*, upper: *"subscription"*, lower: *"total"*}.
(b) Intersection mark: the value used to indicate an intersection between a cross-table object and its attributes. In Fig. 2, this value is *"X"*.
(c) Number of empty columns to skip: a parameter used in the identification of the cross-table dimensions.
(d) Has adjacent data: A boolean value indicating whether an attribute has related data in the adjacent column to its right. In fact, this value indicates whether the cross-table is of type single-valued or many-valued. Following, we describe in details the algorithm and components of the four steps.

**Step 1 - Identify the dimensions and header row of a *"potential"* cross-table:**

**(a) Dimensions:** The user-specified keywords aid our approach to define the top left corner (minimum row, minimum column) and the bottom left corner (maximum row, minimum column) of a cross-table. To identify the maximum column of the cross-table, our approach performs a ***data-block-based*** search, taking advantage of the data block definition in GyroSAT [17]. First, an initial *"maximum column"* value is retrieved from the first identified data block. Thereafter, the maximum column value is recursively updated whenever a new data block is found under the condition that the data block position is within the values of the three known dimensions (minimum row and column, and maximum row). Once no more data blocks are found, we force an extension of the rectangular area to find adjacent data blocks to the right. The extension allows to skip a number of columns, identified by the end-user. Thereafter, the search locates data blocks starting in the extended area. This is performed because cross-tables may contain empty columns, and an empty column forces the GyroSAT to stop expanding a data block horizontally. We apply the extension action, until no further data blocks are found even with the forced extension.

**(b) Header row:** The header row contains two types of data:

- Label values, which categorize and describe the data cells underneath.
- Data values, when the cells below the header are the intersection cells.

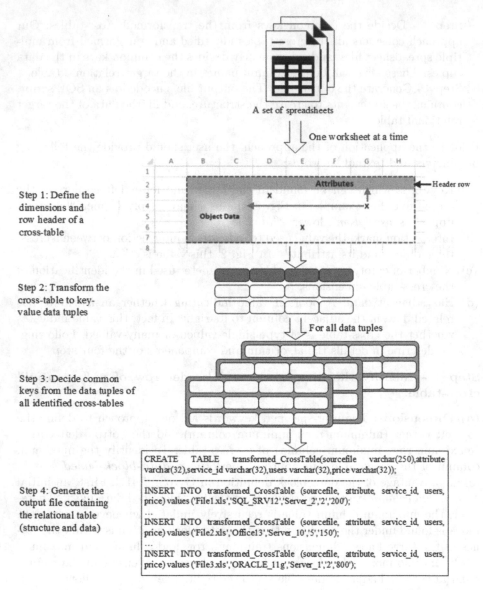

**Fig. 5.** Approach summary showing the steps to extract and transform cross-table data from multiple spreadsheets to one relational table encoded in SQL.

Using the cell classification concept of the GyroSAT, the header row is found as *the row with the largest number of cells of type label, within the dimensions already found.* The search is performed from top to bottom.

The output of this step is the dimensions and header row of a cross-table. When the cross-table cannot be identified; the keywords are not matched or the intersection value is not found, then the approach moves to another worksheet.

**Step 2 - Transform a cross-table:** After identifying the targeted cross-table, data transformations are performed on the cells which lie within the cross-table's dimensions. The transformation starts by identifying the intersection marks, *"X"* in our case. For each intersection mark, the transformation builds a key-value data tuple. Specific transformation actions are followed to generate a data tuple. Following is the description of these actions depending on the type of cell found in the intersection row.

- Intersection: For the intersection cell itself, the data is found in the header. The key which describes this data value is implicit. As a resolution, we introduce the word *"Attribute"* as the key for the intersection cell data. The key-value pair

  | *"Attribute", ValueIn(Intersection column, Header row)* |

  For Fig. 2, the top-left intersection mark has the key-value pair = ( *"Attribute", "W2K8_R2"*).
- Adjacent data: When the cross-table is a many-valued cross-table, a data cell is always adjacent to the right of an intersection cell. In Fig. 2, the cells in the *"Price"* column are always adjacent to the right of the intersection cells. The user defines the boolean parameter *"HasAdjacentData"* to tell the approach whether or not it should consider these data cells in the transformation. In our example, the parameter is set to True and thus we build the key-value pair for the *adjacent data cell* as:

  | *ValueIn(Adjacent column, Header row), ValueIn(Adjacent column, Intersection row)* |

  For Fig. 2, the adjacent cell has the key-value pair = ( *"Price", "100"*).
- Related (object) data: According to the cross-table definition, an intersection mark relates objects data with their attributes. The object data cells are found to the left of an intersection mark; non-empty and does not fall in the ignored type of cells. The key-value pair for a *related object cell* is:

  | *{ ValueIn(Object column, Header row), ValueIn(Object column, Intersection row)}* |

  For Fig. 2, the object cell describing the *"Server ID"* has the key-value pair = ( *"Server_ID", "Server_1"*).
- Ignored: Our approach ignores two types of cells. First, we ignore other intersection cells within the same row, since they will have their own key-value tuple. Secondly, we ignore cells adjacent to other intersection cells, since one adjacent cell is linked to each intersection cell.

**Step 3 - Decide common keys from the transformed cross-tables:** The keys used in the cross-table data tuples are going to be the column names of the target relational table. To decide these keys, from all the transformed cross-tables, we perform two actions. First, we identify the unique keys per cross-table's data tuples. Second, we measure the coverage for each unique key over the whole set of identified cross-tables. The coverage of a key is the division of the count of its unique occurences over the total count of the identified cross-tables. Keys that have a coverage above 80% are included as columns in the target relational table. The integration method we follow may be considered simple, for this we provide further discussion in Sect. 7.

**Step 4 - Generate the output file:** In this step, the approach generates the target relational table, which is encoded in a standard SQL script. The SQL script includes a *"create"* statement representing the structure, and *"insert"* statements representing the data. The columns of the relational table are the common keys decided from the previous step, in addition to the mandatory columns: *"attribute"* and *"sourcefile"*. All columns are assigned a text data type, which is chosen to eliminate additional complexities of type detection and conversion. The generation of the SQL output file starts by making the create statement of the target table. Thereafter, the approach processes the collection of key-value data tuples for each cross-table. For each data tuple an insert statement is generated. Again, the insert statement includes the pairs whose keys are chosen in advance. When a data tuple does not include a pair for one of the chosen keys, we assign to its key the default value *"empty_by_approach"*.

## 5    Evaluation: Case Study

We evaluate our approach presented in the previous sections, through a case study. In this section, we assess the performance of our approach first quantitatively by answering the following:

**RQ1:** How many cross-tables and intersection marks were extracted by the approach?

**RQ2:** Did the approach fail to detect a targeted cross-table completely? If yes, how many?

**RQ3:** Did the approach fail to extract particular intersection marks from the successfully detected cross-tables? If yes, how many?

Following the quantitative analysis, we perform a qualitative assessment through an interview with two frequent spreadsheet users in the company.

### 5.1    Context and Dataset

Solvinity[4] is an IT solution provider. Their finance department uses spreadsheets for calculating the monthly bills for each customer. Within a billing spreadsheet a cross-table, similar to the one in Fig. 2, is used to record the sold third-party licenses. An internal audit required the verification of licenses from all available sources, including the spreadsheets. Collecting the required cross-table data was challenging to users, especially with all the manual work needed. Thus, our approach was applied to extract license data in cross-tables, into one relational table. The output was subsequently used by the auditing team for further analysis. The spreadsheet dataset on which the approach operated includes 333 spreadsheets with 2,801 worksheets.

---

[4] https://www.solvinity.com/.

## 5.2  Results

In a mixed method evaluation, we performed both quantitative and qualitative methods to analyze the results of our approach. Quantitative analysis assesses the performance of the extraction and transformation approach by answering the questions (RQ1, RQ2 and RQ3) presented earlier. In addition, we interview two frequent spreadsheet users, to asses the approach qualititively. Before the interviews, these users were asked to manually validate a selected subset of spreadsheets against their extracted data.

**Table 2.** Summary of the case study results, after applying our approach to extract and transform cross-table data. Further details in Sect. 5.2.

| Result class | Cross-table class | Cross-table count | Cross marks count | Performance (Identify Cross-table) | Performance (Transform Cross Mark) |
|---|---|---|---|---|---|
| Succeeds | Complete cross-tables | 1, 442 | 14, 099 | 99.17% | 92.83% |
|  | Partial cross-tables | 6 | 1, 182 | 0.41% |  |
| Misses | Complete cross-tables | 6 | 1, 139 | 0.41 | 7.17% |
|  | Partial cross-tables | 6 | 41 | 0.41% |  |
| Total |  | 1, 454 | 16, 461 | 100% | 100% |

**Quantitative Evaluation:** Among the 333 spreadsheets, the spreadsheet parser failed to read the contents of two spreadsheets. However, we checked these two files manually, and no cross-tables were detected. This leaves 331 spreadsheet files for the approach to analyze, with a total of 2,801 worksheets. Table 2 represents the summary of the approach performance in extracting and transforming cross-tables, and cross-table marks. To understand the statistics better, we answer the first question:

**RQ1: How many cross-tables and intersection marks were extracted and transformed by the approach?**
The approach detected 1,448 cross-tables. Within these cross-tables, 15,281 intersection marks were extracted and transformed into one relational database table. SQL statements in the output file were syntactically correct. Out of the 2,801 worksheets, we found that no cross-table data were extracted from 1,353 worksheets (48.3%). The reasons for not extracting a cross-table may be that the worksheet did not include a cross-table in the first place, or that the approach detection failed due to wrong keywords for example. To understand the actual reason, we further analyze this result in RQ2 and RQ3.

### RQ2: Did the approach fail to detect a targeted cross-table completely? If yes, how many?

Among the 1,353 worksheets from which no cross-tables were extracted, 1,347 worksheets did not include any cross-table inside. The remaining 6 worksheets included 6 cross-tables, one per worksheet. The approach failed to detect these six cross-tables, because it failed to handle the extra number of empty columns in these cross-tables. The six *"missing"* cross-tables includes 1,139 marks, which as a result, were not transformed to the target relational table. Nevertheless, in another run of the approach, we increased the parameter *"Empty Columns to Skip"* to 2, and these cross-tables were successfully extracted. We refrain from setting the *"Empty Columns to Skip"* parameter to a large value, since this will increase the risk of extracting other irrelevant data lying next to the cross-table form in the worksheet.

### RQ3: Did the approach fail to extract particular intersection marks from successfully detected cross-tables? If yes, how many?

In total 1,448 cross-tables were detected by the approach, one cross-table per worksheet. To verify that all the marks in these cross-table were transformed, we performed a separate analysis. We calculated the counts of all cells with the mark value X, per worksheet. Subsequently, we validated these counts against the number of marks extracted by our approach for each cross-table. What we found is that 1,442 cross-tables were completely migrated into the relational table, while 6 cross-tables were partially transformed. The missing cross-table marks in this case are 41. The root cause for missing these cross-table marks is the same that caused the approach to miss the complete cross-tables: the large number of empty columns within the cross-tables structure.

**Qualitative Evaluation:** In addition to the quantitative evaluation, we interviewed two spreadsheet users. The users worked at the finance department, and their daily job is directly related to the spreadsheets under analysis. One user has been developing and maintaining these spreadsheets for six years within the accounting team. The other user has experience in accounting as a business controller, and he joined the team recently. Prior to the interviews, the end-users were provided with a subset of 30 spreadsheets, selected from both successful and failed cases of the approach. We additionally provided the relational table corresponding to the cross-table data from these 30 files. With these data, the end-users were asked to validate the completeness and contextual correctness of the extracted data by our approach.

**Users perspective:** When asked about the correctness of the information retrieved, according to the context, both users found them, completely correct. One user highlights that *"no factual errors"* were identified in the generated relational table. On the completeness of the retrieved data, one user only was able to detect the missing cross-table marks from the target relational table. The users, after completing their verification, gave a high rating for the approach's extraction capabilities, and regarded it as *"the only gathered data for the sold licenses"*. In addition, the approach was described as *"useful"*, especially for *"these kinds of auditing projects"*, and saving a lot of manual work. However, one user in particular highlighted that *"there will always be a risk"* of extracting *"wrong data"*. He reasoned that the spreadsheets are *"manually designed"* and do not follow a strict template. He concluded that adopting *"more standardized"* designs in the spreadsheets will minimize this risk in the future.

# 6   Related Work

Cunha *et al.* [18] and Hermans *et al.* [17] targeted the transformation of data inside a spreadsheet into a class diagram, for the sake of improving spreadsheet comprehension through visualization. Both works focused on tabular data inside spreadsheets, and were effective in the detection and transformation to class diagrams, one spreadsheet at a time. However, the prototypes were evaluated on a small number of spreadsheets, and no aggregation approach was considered. Cunha *et al.* [19] implemented an approach that maps spreadsheet data into a relational database, with the aim of normalizing data in a spreadsheet. The work, however, was evaluated on simple spreadsheets without addressing any semi-structured data forms. All mentioned work aimed at keeping the end-user working within the spreadsheets, but with an improved environment and understanding. Among the work that aimed at migrating from spreadsheets is Senbazuru [20,21]. They targeted the extraction of hierarchical data from spreadsheets into a relational database. Their approach, however, is more domain specific, and does not consider aggregating similar data in multiple spreadsheets.

# 7   Discussion

In prior sections, we described an approach that extracts data from cross-tables in spreadsheets. In this section, we highlight some issues related to our approach.

**Using the Spreadsheet Formulas:** Formulas are an essential part of spreadsheet development. One cell of data may be the output of a series of formulas which use multiple data cells and ranges. Our current approach considers data in cross-tables, for a more complete migration, the formulas should be considered. Considering formulas' parameters and calculations as part of the data migration may help in building a better relational structure of the extracted data. However, the automatic parsing and translation of formulas to another language is a complex process, therefore it can be an area to explore in future work.

**More Complex Cross-Tables:** Cross-tables may vary in design to some extent because of the flexibility provided to the end-user, and the nature of the cross-table itself. In our approach, we considered cross-tables with simple attributes, with one row of data. However, users may build more complex, and hierarchical headers. Since previous research extracted hierarchical data structures from spreadsheets [20,22], it is a viable option in future to incorporate hierarchical data detection to widen the application of our approach.

**Data Integration:** The process of data integration includes the activities performed, and the approaches followed to combine heterogeneous data from multiple sources [23]. Our approach followed a two-step method: first is to decide the common columns from multiple files, and second is to do an exact match of key names. Even though the method is considered simple, it showed near perfect results in the study evaluation, due to a high level of consistency in the naming of columns. However, variation in the naming may occur in another setup. One way to improve is to consider a general schema resource in order to compare and integrate column headers, or a to build a schema dictionary from within the spreadsheet dataset, prior to the extraction [22].

## 8   Conclusions and Future Work

In this paper we provided the design and implementation of an approach aimed to extract and transform data in cross-tables from multiple spreadsheet files, into one relational table. Our approach was successfully evaluated in an industrial case study, where the resulted table was used in further analysis. The approach succeeded in minimizing the human efforts in the extraction, compared to a manual process. Results show that the approach was able to transform 92.83% of the data in the targeted cross-tables, based on the intersection mark detection. In future work, we aim at eliminating the user role in the extraction, through adopting a machine learning algorithm.

## References

1. Clarke, S., Tobias, A.: Corporate modelling in the UK: a survey. OR Insight **8**(3), 15–20 (1995)
2. Chan, Y.E., Storey, V.C.: The use of spreadsheets in organizations: determinants and consequences. Inf. Manage. **31**(3), 119–134 (1996)
3. Croll, G.J.: The importance and criticality of spreadsheets in the city of London. In: Proceedings of European Spreadsheet Risks Interest Group (EuSpRIG), pp. 82–92 (2005). ISBN: 1-902724-16-X
4. ClusterSeven: ClusterSeven Annual State of the Spreadsheet 2016: The Spreadsheet is Here to Stay (2016)
5. Chen, Z.: Information extraction on para-relational data. Ph.D. thesis, The University of Michigan (2016)
6. Hermans, F.: Analyzing and visualizing spreadsheets. Ph.D. thesis, Technische Universiteit Delft (2012)
7. Bernhard Ganter, G.S.: Formal concept analysis: methods and applications in computer science (2003). http://www.math.tu-dresden.de/~ganter/cl03/stumme/chapter1_2.pdf
8. Hermans, F., Murphy-Hill, E.: Enron's spreadsheets and related emails: a dataset and analysis. In: 2015 IEEE/ACM 37th IEEE International Conference on Software Engineering (2015)
9. Hermans, F., Pinzger, M., van Deursen, A.: Supporting professional spreadsheet users by generating leveled dataflow diagrams. In: Proceeding of the 33rd International Conference on Software Engineering - ICSE 2011 (2011)

10. Ben Nasr, S., Bécan, G., Acher, M., Ferreira Filho, J.B., Baudry, B., Sannier, N., Davril, J.M.: Matrixminer: a red pill to architect informal product descriptions in the matrix. In: Proceedings of the 2015 10th Joint Meeting on Foundations of Software Engineering - ESEC/FSE 2015 (2015)
11. Sannier, N., Acher, M., Baudry, B.: From comparison matrix to variability model: the wikipedia case study. In: 2013 28th IEEE/ACM International Conference on Automated Software Engineering (ASE) (2013)
12. Belohlavek, R.: Introduction to formal concept analysis. Palacky University, Department of Computer Science, Olomouc (2008)
13. Tilley, T.: Formal concept analysis applications to requirements engineering and design. Ph.D. thesis, The University of Queensland (2003)
14. Vitek, D.: Requirements traceability matrix template. http://www2a.cdc.gov/cdcup/library/templates/CDC_UP_Requirements_Traceability_Matrix_Template.xls
15. Abraham, R., Erwig, M.: Ucheck: a spreadsheet type checker for end users. J. Vis. Lang. Comput. 18(1), 71–95 (2007)
16. Roy, S., Hermans, F., Aivaloglou, E., Winter, J., van Deursen, A.: Evaluating automatic spreadsheet metadata extraction on a large set of responses from MOOC participants. In: 2016 IEEE 23rd International Conference on Software Analysis, Evolution, and Reengineering (SANER) (2016)
17. Hermans, F., Pinzger, M., van Deursen, A.: Automatically Extracting Class Diagrams from Spreadsheets. Springer, Heidelberg (2010)
18. Cunha, J., Erwig, M., Saraiva, J.: Automatically inferring classsheet models from spreadsheets. In: 2010 IEEE Symposium on Visual Languages and Human-Centric Computing (2010)
19. Cunha, J., Saraiva, J., Visser, J.: From spreadsheets to relational databases and back. In: Proceedings of the 2009 ACM SIGPLAN Workshop on Partial Evaluation and Program Manipulation - PEPM 2009 (2008)
20. Chen, Z., Cafarella, M., Chen, J., Prevo, D., Zhuang, J.: Senbazuru: a prototype spreadsheet database management system. Proc. VLDB Endow. 6(12), 1202–1205 (2013)
21. Chen, Z., Cafarella, M.: Automatic web spreadsheet data extraction. In: Proceedings of the 3rd International Workshop on Semantic Search Over the Web - SS@2013 (2013)
22. Chen, Z., Cafarella, M.: A semiautomatic approach for accurate and low-effort spreadsheet data extraction. Technical report, University of Michigan (2014)
23. Magnani, M., Rizopoulos, N., Mc.Brien, P., Montesi, D.: Schema integration based on uncertain semantic mappings. In: Delcambre, L., Kop, C., Mayr, H.C., Mylopoulos, J., Pastor, O. (eds.) ER 2005. LNCS, vol. 3716, pp. 31–46. Springer, Heidelberg (2005). doi:10.1007/11568322_3

# Quando: Enabling Museum and Art Gallery Practitioners to Develop Interactive Digital Exhibits

Andrew Stratton[✉], Chris Bates, and Andy Dearden

Cultural Communication and Computing Research Institute,
Sheffield Hallam University, Sheffield, UK
{A.Stratton,C.D.Bates,A.M.Dearden}@shu.ac.uk

**Abstract.** Museums and Art Galleries are challenged to inspire, engage and involve visitors by presenting their collections within physical exhibitions. Curators and exhibition professionals are increasingly telling stories using digital interactivity. This work introduces Quando, a visual programming based toolset that domain experts can use to create interactive exhibits. A small case study demonstrates the language in use at during an archaeological excavation.

**Keywords:** Visual programming · Museums · Programming environments · End-user programming

## 1 Introduction

The nature of museums and galleries is changing as Cultural Heritage Professionals (CHPs), including curators, attempt to bring the past to life by extending visitor exhibits with digital interactivity, including multimedia and new technologies such as augmented reality. CHPs may need, or wish, to create these extensions themselves but, typically, they lack skills and experience in the creation of hardware and software.

This paper discusses the design of the Quando toolset, which includes an event based visual programming language designed for the creation of Visitor Interactive Digital Exhibits (VIDEs). Quando supports Museum and Art Gallery Practitioners in authoring interactive behaviour through rules attached to exhibits. Quando uses connections between blocks to simplify the authoring of interactive multimedia elements whilst eliding notions of programming. The visual editor presents a Domain Specific Language (DSL) using terms that are familiar to CHPs and the editor encourages drag-and-drop creation and configuration.

Section 2 is concerned with background concepts and literature. In Sect. 3 the Quando language and editor are introduced. Section 4 focuses on a preliminary case study involving a local museum, including why we use a visual programming approach and how Quando builds on Google Blockly to support the delivery of complex interactive behaviours in a simple form accessible to non-programmers. Benefits and limitations of the approach are discussed and future directions identified.

© Springer International Publishing AG 2017
S. Barbosa et al. (Eds.): IS-EUD 2017, LNCS 10303, pp. 100–107, 2017.
DOI: 10.1007/978-3-319-58735-6_7

## 2  Background

The nature of museums and galleries is changing as Cultural Heritage Professionals (CHPs), attempt to bring the past to life by extending visitor exhibits with digital interactivity, including multimedia and new technologies such as augmented reality.

CHPs have a deep knowledge of their collections and the ability to present those collections in ways that tell their story and that allow visitors to understand, analyse and reflect. However, they may lack knowledge of, or experience or interest in, the tools and techniques that are used to build immersive multimedia exhibitions.

There are many different approaches being used to augment, supplement or replace displays of objects [4, 5, 12]. A common theme is for designers. developers and CHPs to collaborate through the use of approaches including co-design [1, 7] and the use of supportive frameworks designed to explicitly support the domain of Cultural Heritage [3].

In this work we adopt an approach that seeks to empower CHPs using a visual DSL and block-based editor, with rapid prototyping of executable visitor interactive exhibits, through the co-design of the visual Blocks used to describe behaviour rather than co-design of the behaviour itself. The Quando blocks are similar to the trigger, action approach described in [10], but are also intended to offer a closer match to the domain of Cultural Heritage. The goal of this work is similar to the end goal of EUD (End User Development) stated in [6], i.e. that of *'empowering'* CHPs *'to develop'* digital interactivity for visitors *'themselves'*.

## 3  Quando

Quando is both a DSL and a prototype toolset, including an editor, oriented around a set of visual block tools, building on the Google Blockly visual programming tools [2], that CHPs can use to create VIDEs incorporating interactive media. The augmentations that CHPs may wish to apply to exhibits cover a massive range from playing video or audio on-demand; through physical object and touchless interactions; to location and context-aware tracking of visitors. The range of possible augmentations is large and their style, language and use vary between different contexts making implementation a non-trivial undertaking.

Quando articulates the work of producing interactive exhibits by allowing a programmer to create a library of augmented behavioural components (blocks). Using a visual editor CHPs combine and configure these blocks to define more complex behaviours that enhance visitors' experiences. These behaviours can be revisited by CHPs and updated without resorting to the use of skilled developers.

Quando builds on block-based languages such as Scratch [8]. However, the Quando language is not an imperative language but uses an event-based approach with visual rules and matching action blocks that act as callbacks. This event based approach is not directly visible to, or specified by, CHPs, but the effects of using this approach are evident in the generated artifact interaction. The underlying Quando architecture separates the editor from client run time, so generated behaviour can be executed independently of changes to the blocks used for describing behaviour.

An Agile methodology was adopted to allow the extension and customisation of Quando based on co-design like feedback from CHPs, including modification of terminology, block design and the client side api/library.

## 4   Creswell Crags Case Study

Creswell Crags is an area of limestone cliffs and caves in the English Midlands that were inhabited by nomadic groups during the period 55,000 to 10,000 years ago, including the last ice-age when these were some of humanity's most northerly habitations [11]. Together the limestone gorge, caves and findings tell a story about our ancestors lives during the Palaeolithic. Numerous artefacts left by Palaeolithic people have been found in the caves and are deposited in museums across the UK for study and display. The caves contain both fragile early artworks and areas that have yet to be excavated, currently closed to the public. Such preservation measures alongside the dispersal of findings mean that CHPs have to find new, engaging and informative ways to tell their stories in the Visitor Centre.

The Visitor Centre has an exhibition with physical displays, containing local finds, as well as a variety of multimedia including video loops, interactive touch-screens and projected displays that are suitable for visits by schools and other organized groups. The multimedia content was created for the exhibition by external designers and cannot be edited by the museum's staff. The Exhibition and Event organiser was keen for the exhibition to be both updated and updateable.

The work presented here includes the display of media alongside museum display cases where the media are controlled by visitors using gestures that are sensed with a touchless Leap Motion Controller. The Leap Motion is a small, cheap sensor that detects the motions of hands and fingers in three dimensions as they move in front of it. Early adopters and researchers have typically used the Leap in virtual and augmented reality applications. In this work it is used to control media content, replacing more traditional mouse-driven or newer touch-driven interfaces. Significant complexity and some serious software engineering lie behind the use of these apparently simple controllers.

The remit from Creswell Crags was to display excavation media as the excavation is being performed; the system had to:

- Hold lists of multimedia artefacts (content) and museum displays
- Associate artefacts with displays
- Detect hand movements made by visitors
- Make choices about what media to display and how to display it based on hand movements

The implementation model for Quando is that software developers create visual blocks that implement primitive actions, encapsulate data or wrap coherent blocks of complex functionality. This allows CHPs to create interactive displays containing complex behaviour using visual blocks that express the behaviour in CHP terms and with appropriate complexity.

The case study followed a qualitative evaluation of an initial prototype of Quando [9], which included staff from the museum. Having seen the prototype, the part-time Exhibitions and Event Organiser was keen to use Quando, *'[it] would be brilliant for us to have this...to be able to photograph the excavation whilst it's happening and then upload it with an explanation of what they found and what it means for the site'*.

The full-time Director at Creswell Crags invited the researcher to provide tools to allow staff to create a VIDE for an Archaeological Excavation by Durham University. Discussions with four CHPs identified the need for a *'more interactive'* exhibit than those already at Creswell, where a large screen projection related to climate was described as *'just a (video) loop'*. Staff also identified a desire for audio *'ice age sounds'* to be incorporated. Staff were very keen to use the touchless Leap Motion controller, partly due to the expected increased durability of a non-physically handled interface, and also due to perceived hygiene concerns of visitors.

Multimedia Blocks such as those shown in Fig. 1, which had been used in the previous investigation [9], were included within a starting 'library' for the CHPs:

**Fig. 1.** Initial multi media quando blocks

Further discussions with CHPs led to new blocks being created for representing virtual Vitrines/Display Cases, with navigation between Display Cases being represented through visible 'Labels'. This model is conceptually similar to web page based hyperlinks offering hypertext navigation, but the Creswell staff preferred this terminology.

These concepts were implemented as Blocks and evaluated by Creswell staff, who preferred the term 'Display Cases' over 'Vitrines', so the blocks were redesigned as shown in Fig. 2:

**Fig. 2.** First pass case study blocks

These Blocks were extended to generate browser compliant JavaScript with associated extensions to the Quando runtime library; allowing a Leap Motion controller to be used to select labels to navigate between Display Cases.

The Quando Toolset was deployed to a PC and physically installed within the museum in the paid for exhibition space, including a Leap Motion device. The Leap Motion interaction is handled by the Quando runtime library used from a kiosk web browser and allows user hand movement to move a visible cursor (a filled, partly transparent, circle) in place of a mouse cursor. Hovering over a label then triggers a transparency change with a mouse click being triggered if the hover stays over the same label.

A key requirement for the museum include a robust, kiosk based, presentation that could be powered on and off at the mains and required no interaction to start up. The wireless network availability proved to be too restrictive and staff did not have access to override the security restrictions. The wired network was also limited to registered network cards and could not be changed. To solve this issue, two 'power line' (Ethernet over power) network connections were installed, one in the Exhibition, and the other in a 'back office' accessed through a staff PC. This allowed the staff to develop the interaction remotely through the browser based editor, saving (deploying) any behaviour to the exhibit PC. Content deployment was by physical USB transfer to the exhibit PC.

Four CHPs were involved in the two week authoring of the interaction, with the editor being mainly used by one member of staff, after a short, one hour, training session. Staff requested further extensions to Quando to allow simple changing of Font characteristics, e.g. colours and size. Blocks were quickly implemented to allow these changes to the Labels, Text and Title within different Display Case Blocks. Figure 3 illustrates these blocks.

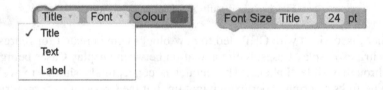

**Fig. 3.** Second pass case study blocks

These blocks were created quickly, generating inefficient code and, as discovered by the staff, including a generated behaviour bug. Since the bug could be avoided by copying the style blocks to each Display Case, it was decided to avoid, rather than fix the bug, to avoid the possibility of introducing new bugs. This bug has since been fixed and the blocks have been incorporated into the Quando library. The staff created a moderately complex behaviour, including the acquisition and editing of the desired content. The quickly implemented font style blocks were found to have two usability issues. A simple workaround was proposed to avoid introducing new issues into the exhibit creation.

The final interaction used images and text contained in a set of six 'Display Cases' with the structure shown in Fig. 4:

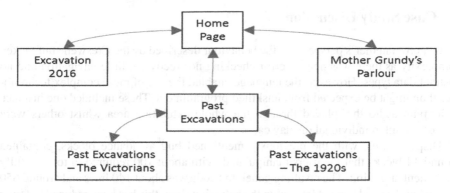

**Fig. 4.** Navigation structure of display case blocks

Each of the Display Case Blocks contained the labels, image, text and configuration for style as set by Creswell staff. Figure 5 shows the finished exhibition specification:

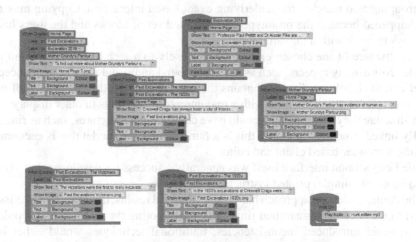

**Fig. 5.** Client behaviour

As also shown in Fig. 5, a new 'Forever' Block was developed at the request of the CHPs to play a continuous audio loop throughout the exhibition space. The Forever block generated code runs asynchronously with the event handling for visitor navigation. The Display block generated code is automatically bound to associated toolset event handling. In this example, only one Display Block will be visible at a time.

Conditional execution is also handled by the When blocks. There was no requirement for explicit iteration from this Case Study, so no iteration blocks were created; iterations are executed within the Client run time library, but the end users did not need domain access to iteration blocks.

# 5    Case Study Discussion

From a programmer's perspective, the behaviour described by the Creswell staff lacked complexity as there was neither error checking nor recovery, little navigation and no abstract data types. However, the language enabled the use of more complex technologies than might be expected from unskilled programmers. These included one instance of looping audio that played through the whole exhibition area whilst others were contained within individual display cases.

Display cases, with the previously mentioned bug avoidance blocks, contained around 14 blocks that the users manipulated, with about 100 required in total to fully implement an exhibit. The resulting generated code was about 140 lines and around 650 'words' of data and code. After fixing the behaviour bug, this has been reduced to fewer than 40 blocks, under 120 lines of generated code and around 550 'words'.

After being shown how to create a simple interaction, users added complexity mainly by copying existing behaviours and modifying them. There appears to be a desire to organise behaviours into groups of blocks that can be associated with a single display; this grouping also matches the underlying event based interaction. Copying may also have happened because the prototype had a limited set of blocks and the users had to find ways to work within this limitation.

The structure of the chosen exhibit maps closely to a web like interface, but also include cross display aspects, such as the background audio and also the staff accepted model that the label to a display contains the same text as the display title. Staff were not limited to a two tier structure with a maximum of three links to other displays; this was a structure they created - they could have chosen other structures, such as ring like or fully linked structures; possibly this is a familiar browser model that is encouraged by using a browser based client and editor.

The Leap Motion interface itself was generally a success for developers but visitors had to be given (simple) printed instructions on its use.

The Agile, co design, approach has produced useful results, though with some issues related to the very fast turnaround time. It is worth noting that workarounds could be used to avoid introduced inconsistencies; traditional techniques would either have stalled with no useful toolset and the CHP requested improvements would likely have been delayed for a subsequent investigation.

Future case studies are planned that will extend the range of activities covered by the blocks to include personalisation of interactions, manipulation of two and three dimensional objects, discovering the temporal models that are used by CHPs and simplifying asynchronous aspects of multimedia. There is also the potential to support more immersive interactions through complex navigation built using the Leap Motion and 3D visualisations.

# 6    Conclusions

In this paper we have shown that using a simple visual language, non-programmers can design, implement and configure moderately complex interactive multimedia experiences.

These experiences can be deployed into settings within museums in which they both disrupt and enhance traditional approaches to displaying and explaining exhibits. The simplicity of the Quando language is not an impediment to its use. CHPs were seen to be capable of modifying and configuring blocks in the editor so that those blocks performed the tasks that they required even when those behaviours were not necessarily built into them by the software developer.

The integration of the visual DSL and editor articulates readily with the ways that professionals working in cultural heritage talk about and understand the idea of an exhibition. Through the DSL they are able to both design and create augmentations for their exhibits and use these to demonstrate areas for future work to software developers.

# References

1. Díaz, P., Aedo, I., Bellucci, A.: Integrating user stories to inspire the co-design of digital futures for cultural heritage. In: Proceedings of the XVII International Conference on Human Computer Interaction, p. 31. ACM (2016)
2. Fraser, N.: Google blockly - a visual programming editor (2016). https://developers.google.com/blockly/. Accessed January 2017
3. Garzotto, F., Megale, L.: CHEF: a user centered perspective for cultural heritage enterprise frameworks. In: Proceedings of the Working Conference on Advanced Visual Interfaces, pp. 293–301. ACM (2006)
4. Grinter, R.E., et al.: Revisiting the visit: understanding how technology can shape the museum visit. In: Proceedings of the 2002 ACM Conference on Computer Supported Cooperative Work, pp. 146–155. ACM (2002)
5. Kocsis, A., Barnes, C.: Making exhibitions, brokering meaning: designing new connections across communities of practice. In: Design Research Society Biennial Conference, p. 13 (2008)
6. Lieberman, H., Paternò, F., Klann, M., Wulf, V.: End-user development: an emerging paradigm. In: Lieberman, H., Paternò, F., Wulf, V. (eds.) End User Development. Human-Computer Interaction Series, vol. 9, pp. 1–8. Springer, Dordrecht (2006)
7. McDermott, F., Maye, L., Avram, G.: Co-designing a collaborative platform with cultural heritage professionals. In: Irish HCI conference, pp. 18–24 (2014)
8. Resnick, M., et al.: Scratch: programming for all. Commun. ACM 52, 60–67 (2009)
9. Stratton, A., et al.: Investigating domain specific visual languages for interactive exhibitions. In: 27th Annual Workshop on Psychology of Programming 2016, pp. 188–191 (2016)
10. Ur, B., McManus, E., Pak Yong Ho, M., Littman, M.L.: Practical trigger-action programming in the smart home. In: Proceedings of the SIGCHI Conference on Human Factors in Computing Systems, pp. 803–812. ACM (2014)
11. Wall, I., et al.: Creswell crags (2009). http://www.creswell-crags.org.uk/. Accessed January 2017
12. Ynnerman, A., et al.: Interactive visualization of 3d scanned mummies at public venues. Commun. ACM 59(12), 72–81 (2016)

# Specification of Complex Logical Expressions for Task Automation: An EUD Approach

Giuseppe Desolda[1(✉)], Carmelo Ardito[1], and Maristella Matera[2]

[1] Dipartimento di Informatica, Università degli Studi di Bari Aldo Moro,
Via Orabona, 70125 Bari, Italy
{giuseppe.desolda,carmelo.ardito}@uniba.it
[2] Dipartimento di Elettronica, Informazione e Bioingegneria, Politecnico di Milano,
Piazza Leonardo da Vinci 32, 20134 Milan, Italy
maristella.matera@polimi.it

**Abstract.** The growing availability of smart objects is stimulating researchers in investigating the IoT phenomenon from different perspectives. In the HCI area, and in particular from the EUD perspective, one prominent goal is to enable non-technical users to be directly involved in configuring smart object behaviour. With this respect, this paper discusses three visual composition techniques to specify logical expressions in Event-Condition-Action rules used for synchronizing the behavior of smart objects.

**Keywords:** End User Development · Internet of Things · Visual languages · Logical expressions

## 1 Introduction and Motivation

In the last years, the computer science landscape has been shifting from the use of personal computer and mobile devices to the adoption in several contexts of integrated, powerful, pervasive devices that offer features like connectivity, sensors, actuators and embedded software, the so-called "smart objects" [5]. The possibility to create easily low-cost smart objects has resulted in the phenomenon known as Internet of Things (IoT), a term indicating a computing platform where the physical world is connected to the Internet via ubiquitous smart objects.

So far, research on IoT has primarily focused on the technological aspects characterizing smart objects; instead, few works have concentrated on how to amplify the social and practical benefits for the end users. We believe that the potential of IoT can be increased if even users with no expertise in computer programming are enabled to manage interoperable smart objects to respond to their situational needs [6].

Smart objects are typically provided with software services (e.g., mobile apps) to interact with them. Unfortunately, it is not possible to go beyond predefined behaviors. For example, a smart bracelet has sensors that can track sleep cycles, heart rate and steps. The measured values are accessible by users through a specific mobile app. However, no communication is allowed between the bracelet and other smart objects. This communication would instead enable the definition of composite behaviors, such as

© Springer International Publishing AG 2017
S. Barbosa et al. (Eds.): IS-EUD 2017, LNCS 10303, pp. 108–116, 2017.
DOI: 10.1007/978-3-319-58735-6_8

controlling the opening of a smart roll-up shutter when the smart bracelet detects that the user is awake. New solutions are needed to allow non-technical users to orchestrate ecologies of smart objects to satisfy the "long tail" of specific – and sometimes unexpected – needs [9, 14]. In other words, adequate End-User Development (EUD) paradigms are needed. Indeed, as largely recognized in the literature [3, 8, 15, 22], EUD methodologies fit very well the requirement of letting users customize their systems to support personal, situational needs.

Several Web tools already address the problem of Task Automation (TA) by supporting the creation of Event-Condition-Action (ECA) rules to synchronize the behavior of smart objects [7, 16]. However, their composition paradigms for rule creation are still far from offering evident benefits for the end users [6]. There are tools [17–19, 23] that claim to address the skills of non-technical users, but they only assist the creation of "basic" rules, for example synchronizing one single event with one single action. Some other tools (e.g., Node-RED [21]) allow one to create more expressive rules, but they also require programming skills.

In this paper we present three novel visual composition techniques for the definition of logical expressions during the creation of Task-Automation rules. The first technique proposes abstraction mechanisms to combine rule events by means of AND/OR logical operators, as well as to group set of conjunctive/disjunctive events, also recursively. The second technique constraints the creation of logic expressions taking into account a principle of the mental model theory [20] saying that people find easier the conceptualization of logical statements as a disjunction of conjunctions (Disjunctive Normal Form - DNF). The third technique is the opposite of DNF, since it allows the combination of rule events as a *conjunction of disjunction* (Conjunctive Normal Form - CNF). Even if the mental model theory prefers the DNF, we believe that CNF can also be a valid support to specify ECA rules.

The paper is organized as follows. Section 2 describes EFESTO-5 W, a Web platform implementing a composition paradigm for defining easily Task-Automation rules. Section 3 then describes the new extensions introduced in EFESTO-5 W to increase the expressive power of logical formulas; it also discusses some works that guided the definition of the new composition mechanisms. Finally, Sect. 4 concludes the paper and outlines our future work.

## 2    EFESTO-5W: A Platform to Create Task-Automation Rules

The research we have conducted in the last years has primarily focused on the definition of composition paradigms assisting non-technical end users in the composition of Web services [2, 4, 10, 11]. Given the diffusion of smart objects that typically expose their sensors and actuators as Web services, we recently started investigating how end users can be enabled to synchronize interoperable smart objects and Web services, to respond to their situational needs [13]. As result, we designed and developed EFESTO-5W, a Task-Automation tool for non-technical users. Its initial design was driven by the 5W model, typically adopted in journalism to analyze the complete story about a fact by answering to the 5 questions: (1) *Who* did it? (2) *What* happened? (3) *When* did it take place? (4) *Where* did it take place? (5) *Why* did it happen?

These five questions were used during an elicitation study to guide participants in proposing user interfaces and interaction techniques for the creation of ECA rules. The design phase resulted in three different user interfaces and interaction paradigms that we then compared during a rigorous study to identify the best one [12].

In order to describe the EFESTO-5W composition paradigm, we illustrate a usage scenario. A user, Jaime, wants to create the following rule: the garage door automatically opens and the smart boiler turns on when his car is close to home and when he taps his smart watch. To start creating this rule, in the visual interface illustrated in Fig. 1 (initially not showing any event and action) Jaime clicks the "New Rule" button (Fig. 1, circle 1) and the "Creating Rule" window is opened. This is the main composition area in which a rule is going to be defined. The left side is for specifying the triggering events, and the right side is to define the actions to be activated.

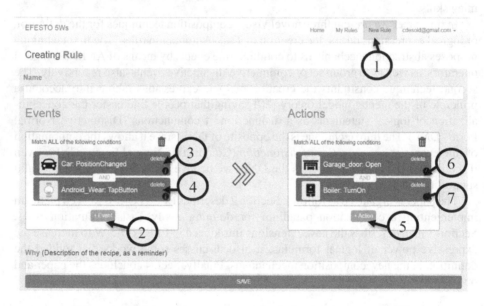

**Fig. 1.** EFESTO-5 W interface for rule creation. (Color figure online)

A wizard procedure, activated by the green "+Event" button (Fig. 1, circle 2), guides Jaime in defining the rule events. The wizard sequentially shows some pop-up windows to select and configure the different elements composing a rule. Jaime first defines the events in a WYSIWYG manner, in terms of *Which* is the service to be monitored for detecting the triggering events, *What* service events have to be monitored, *When* and *Where* the events have to occur. The specification of *When* and *Where* conditions is optional. Thus, following the wizard procedure, Jaime initially selects the *Car* object (Which) and the *Position changed* event (What). He also constraints the event occurrence in the time interval 7.00 p.m.–10.00 p.m. (When) and in proximity of his home address (Where). At the end of the wizard procedure, the summary of the defined event appears in the "Events" area (Fig. 1, circle 3). In a similar way, Jaime adds another event that, in order to activate the rule actions, has to occur together with the first one. He thus selects the *smartwatch* (Which) and its *Tap* event (What) (Fig. 1, circle 4).

The two defined events will trigger the rule as soon as both of them occur. This is expressed by the sentence "Match ALL of the following conditions", on top of the Events blocks, that indicates that all the specified events will be combined by the AND logical operator. The user can click on the "ALL" word (in blue) to switch to the modality "Match AT LEAST ONE of the following conditions", which means that the occurrence of just one event is needed in order to activate the rule; in this case, indeed, the events are combined by the OR logical operator.

After defining the events, Jaime starts adding the actions to be executed in response to the specified events. He clicks on the "+Action" button (Fig. 1, circle 5); a wizard procedure starts, which is similar to the one used for the events. Jaime chooses the *Garage Door* (Which) and its *Open* action (What) (Fig. 1, circle 3). Afterwards, he repeats the same procedure by selecting the *Boiler* (Which) and its *Turn on* action (What) (Fig. 1, circle 4). At the end, he saves the rule; the rule is now active.

# 3   Complex Logical Expressions for Task-Automation Rules

As illustrated in the previous Section, in the first version of EFESTO-5 W users could specify multiple events and actions, but they were allowed to use only one single logical operator to combine rule events: *AND*, if they wanted to activate the rule actions once *all the events* occurred; *OR*, if they wanted to activate the rule actions when *at least one event* occurred. We constrained the rule definition mechanisms in such a way because in the conducted user studies we wanted to focus on the specification of temporal and spatial constraints [12, 13]. Therefore, we purposely did not introduce further elements that could generate side effects deviating from the factors that we wanted to investigate. In the following, we illustrate the extensions of the visual composition paradigm recently introduced to support the combination of multiple events by means of arbitrarily expressive logical expressions.

## 3.1   Logical Expressions in Task-Automation Rules

It is widely recognized that Boolean algebra is a formalism for describing logical relations in the same way as ordinary algebra describes numeric relations. In particular, variables can be combined by using *conjunction, disjunction* and *negation* operators; the values of the variables are the truth values *true* and *false*. Such formalism fits the mental model of computer scientists and engineers, while non-technical users might not be able to use them properly. Often non-technical users tend to interpret "or" as an exclusive OR. Sometimes they have problems managing nested parentheses [20]. In the following we describe some extensions of the EFESTO-5W composition paradigm that aim to alleviate such problems.

As starting point of our design, we surveyed the literature and identified systems that support the definition of logical expressions by using visual techniques. One traditional approach is to represent logic operators graphically with a plumbing or electrical meta-phor [24, 26]. However, in the context of visual composition of Web services, these interaction metaphors did not succeed because they recall concepts that are closer to the background of ICT experts and electronic engineers than to the end users' mental model [25, 27]. Alternative composition paradigms are offered by some commercial and open source systems. For example, Apple *iTunes 9* supports the creation of smart playlists with nested conditionals[1], in order to play songs that match settings within user-defined rules. Apple has also implemented a mechanism inside *Mail*, for creating rules that for example automatize the management of incoming messages, as well as the replying to or the forwarding of messages[2]. A recent open-source project, *QueryBuilder* [1], also provides a Web-based user interface to visually create queries and filters.

Inspired by these approaches, our team of three HCI experts carried out a user-centered design, involving four non-technical end users, to identify alternative visual composition techniques for combining smart-object events by means of logical expres-sions. As a first result, we identified a technique to combine the rule events with the AND/OR logical operators, as well as to group set of conjunctive/disjunctive events, also recursively. With respect to the EFESTO-5W interface shown in Fig. 1, in the Events area we introduced a root-block with the label "Match AT LEAST ONE of the following conditions" (the white block in Fig. 2). This label was conceived to express in natural language the semantics of the OR operator. Inside the white block there are two buttons, i.e., "+Event" and "+Block of Events Conjunction" (see Fig. 2). The first one allows the user to define events as in the previous scenario. The second one permits the creation of sub-blocks grouping set of conjunctive events and is titled "Match ALL of the following conditions" (this label expresses in natural language the semantics of the AND operator). The rule actions are activated when at least one of the events or one of the sub-blocks inside the root are evaluated as true[3].

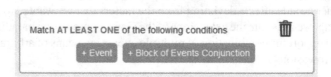

**Fig. 2.** Starting block to define events as logical expressions. (Color figure online)

Inside each sub-block the users can recursively define events or block of events. The logical connectors of the root block and of all the sub-blocks can be switched between OR/AND by clicking on the related label ("Match AT LEAST ONE of the following conditions" and "Match AT LEAST ONE of the following conditions").

The users can exploit this technique to compose different events. For example, the rule depicted in Fig. 3 refers to a scenario where a user, Giuseppe, wants to optimize the home energy consumption by automatically turning on the house heater at 25 °C and

---

[1]  http://www.macworld.com/article/1142846/nested_playlists.html.

[2]  http://www.macworld.com/article/1159394/business/mailrules.html.

[3]  EFESTO-5 W checks events every N minutes, being N a parameter that can be set by the user.

turning on the boiler when one of the following conditions are true: (1) his car (*Giuseppe_Car*) is close to home and he taps his *smartwatch*; (2) his wife car (*Lucy_Car*) is close to home and his wife taps her *smartwatch*; (3) his smart bracelet detects that he is just awake.

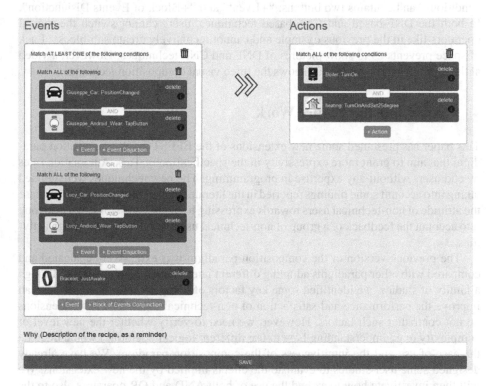

**Fig. 3.**  Example of rule with multiple events.

## 3.2  Simplifying the Creation of Logical Expressions

Even if the visual technique described above introduces abstraction mechanisms that facilitate the creation of logical expression, we designed two further solutions based on the disjunctive normal form (DNF) and the conjunctive normal form (CNF). A DNF is a normalization of a logical formula that is a disjunction of clauses that themselves can be simple terms or a conjunction of terms (terms are smart object events in our case). Contrarily, a CNF is a normalization of a logical formula that is a conjunction of clauses that themselves can be a term or a disjunction of terms. Every propositional formula can be converted into an equivalent DNF and CNF formula. This transformation is based on logical equivalences, such as the double negative law, De Morgan's laws, and the distributive law.

According to the mental model theory [20], people find easier the conceptualization of logical statements as a disjunction of conjunctions. Thus, we designed a DNF-based technique. With respect to Fig. 3, the root-block is titled "Match AT LEAST ONE of the following conditions" and contains two buttons: "+Event" and "+Block of Events Conjunction". Contrarily to what the mental model theory predicts, we believe that also a CNF-based technique can simplify the creation of logical expressions when composing smart objects. With respect to Fig. 3, the root-block is titled "Match ALL of the following conditions" and contains two buttons: "+Event" and "+Block of Events Disjunction". In both the DNF-based and CNF-based techniques, users cannot switch the logical operators like in the previous example and cannot recursively create sub-blocks. Lack of space prevents us to show pictures of DNF and CNF techniques. However, a video at the link https://goo.gl/dn1bde shows the three visual composition techniques.

## 4  Conclusion and Future Work

This paper has presented some new extensions of the EFESTO-5W composition paradigm that aim to grant more expressivity in the specification of Task-Automation rules by end users without any expertise in programming. The new techniques were defined taking into account some findings reported in the literature about factors that can increase the attitude of non-technical users towards expressing logical expressions. We also took into account the feedback of a group of non-technical users involved in the design activities.

The previous version of the composition paradigm was extensively evaluated and compared with other paradigms adopting different interaction metaphors [12]. Through a family of studies, we identified some key factors of composition paradigms that can improve the performance and satisfaction of non-technical users. The new extensions do not contradict such factors. However, we need to verify whether the new level of complexity (e.g., understanding how to use different logical operators) would degrade the ease-of-use and the intuitiveness of the composition paradigm. We have already designed some user studies to evaluate the effects implied by the new extensions. We will then investigate how to extend the use of both AND and OR operators also to the specification of combination of actions.

The overall goal of the research will be to devise an EUD environment where ecosystems of smart objects can be represented through adequate metaphors and easily manipulated and controlled by end users. We are already designing such environment for the definition of smart spaces in museums. From the experience in this specific domain we will also try to derive more general hints for the design of EUD environments for the Internet of Things.

## References

1. StrangePlanet. QueryBuilder (2017). http://querybuilder.js.org/
2. Ardito, C., Bottoni, P., Costabile, M.F., Desolda, G., Matera, M., Picozzi, M.: Creation and use of service-based distributed interactive workspaces. J. Vis. Lang. Comput. **25**(6), 717–726 (2014)
3. Ardito, C., Buono, P., Costabile, M.F., Lanzilotti, R., Piccinno, A.: End users as co-designers of their own tools and products. J. Vis. Lang. Comput. **23**(2), 78–90 (2012)

4. Ardito, C., Costabile, M.F., Desolda, G., Lanzilotti, R., Matera, M., Picozzi, M.: Visual composition of data sources by end-users. In: Proceedings of the International Conference on Advanced Visual Interfaces (AVI 2014), Como (Italy), 28-30 May, pp. 257–260. ACM, New York (2014)

5. Atzori, L., Iera, A., Morabito, G.: The internet of things: a survey. Int. J. Comput. Comput. Netw. **54**(15), 2787–2805 (2010)

6. Barricelli, B.R., Valtolina, S.: Designing for end-user development in the internet of things. In: Díaz, P., Pipek, V., Ardito, C., Jensen, C., Aedo, I., Boden, A. (eds.) IS-EUD 2015. LNCS, vol. 9083, pp. 9–24. Springer, Cham (2015). doi:10.1007/978-3-319-18425-8_2

7. Coronado, M., Iglesias, C.A.: Task automation services: automation for the masses. IEEE Internet Comput. **20**(1), 52–58 (2016)

8. Costabile, M.F., Fogli, D., Mussio, P., Piccinno, A.: Visual interactive systems for end-user development: a model-based design methodology. IEEE Trans. Syst. Man Cybern. Part A Syst. Hum. **37**(6), 1029–1046 (2007)

9. Daniel, F., Matera, M., Weiss, M.: Next in mashup development: user-created apps on the web. IT Prof. Magaz. **13**(5), 22 (2011)

10. Desolda, G.: Enhancing workspace composition by exploiting linked open data as a polymorphic data source. In: Damiani, E., Howlett, Robert J., Jain, L.C., Gallo, L., De Pietro, G. (eds.) Intelligent Interactive Multimedia Systems and Services. SIST, vol. 40, pp. 97–108. Springer, Cham (2015). doi:10.1007/978-3-319-19830-9_9

11. Desolda, G., Ardito, C., Matera, M.: EFESTO: a platform for the end-user development of interactive workspaces for data exploration. In: Daniel, F., Pautasso, C. (eds.) RMC 2015. CCIS, vol. 591, pp. 63–81. Springer, Cham (2016). doi:10.1007/978-3-319-28727-0_5

12. Desolda, G., Ardito, C., Matera, M.: Empowering end users to customize their smart environments: model, composition paradigms and domain-specific tools. ACM Trans. Comput. Hum. Interact. (TOCHI) **24**(2), 53 (2017). Article 12

13. Desolda, G., Ardito, C., Matera, M.: End-user development for the internet of things: EFESTO and the 5W composition paradigm. In: Daniel, F., Gaedke, M. (eds.) RMC 2016. CCIS, vol. 696, pp. 74–93. Springer, Cham (2017). doi:10.1007/978-3-319-53174-8_5

14. Fischer, G.: End-user development and meta-design: foundations for cultures of participation. In: Pipek, V., Rosson, M.B., Ruyter, B., Wulf, V. (eds.) IS-EUD 2009. LNCS, vol. 5435, pp. 3–14. Springer, Heidelberg (2009). doi:10.1007/978-3-642-00427-8_1

15. Fischer, G., Giaccardi, E., Ye, Y., Sutcliffe, A., Mehandjiev, N.: Meta-design: a manifesto for end-user development. Commun. ACM **47**(9), 33–37 (2004)

16. Fogli, D., Lanzilotti, R., Piccinno, A.: End-user development tools for the smart home: a systematic literature review. In: Streitz, N., Markopoulos, P. (eds.) Distributed, Ambient and Pervasive Interactions, in DAPI 2016. LNCS, vol. 9749, pp. 69–79. Springer, Cham (2016)

17. elastic.io GMBH (2016). http://www.elastic.io/

18. IFTTT (2016). https://ifttt.com/

19. Zapier Inc. Zapier (2016). https://zapier.com/

20. Johnson-Laird, P.N.: Mental Models: Towards a Cognitive Science of Language, Inference, and Consciousness. Harvard University Press, Cambridge (1983)

21. JS_Foundation. Node-RED (2016). http://nodered.org/

22. Lieberman, H., Paternò, F., Wulf, V. (eds.) End User Development. Human–Computer Interaction Series, vol. 9. Springer, Dordrecht (2006)

23. Itrios LLC. itDuzzit (2016). http://cloud.itduzzit.com/

24. Murray, N.S., Paton, N.W., Goble, C.A., Bryce, J.: Kaleidoquery—a flow-based visual language and its evaluation. J. Vis. Lang. Comput. **11**(2), 151–189 (2000)

25. Namoun, A., Nestler, T., Angeli, A.: Conceptual and usability issues in the composable web of software services. In: Daniel, F., Facca, F.M. (eds.) ICWE 2010. LNCS, vol. 6385, pp. 396–407. Springer, Heidelberg (2010). doi:10.1007/978-3-642-16985-4_35
26. Shneiderman, B.: Visual user interfaces for information exploration. In: Proceedings of the 54th Annual Meeting of the American Society for Information Sciences (ASIS 1991), pp. 379–384 (1991)
27. Wajid, U., Namoun, A., Mehandjiev, N.: Alternative representations for end user composition of service-based systems. In: Costabile, M.F., Dittrich, Y., Fischer, G., Piccinno, A. (eds.) IS-EUD 2011. LNCS, vol. 6654, pp. 53–66. Springer, Heidelberg (2011). doi: 10.1007/978-3-642-21530-8_6

# The User in EUD

# Public Staff Empowerment in e-Government: A Human Work Interaction Design Approach

Stefano Valtolina[1(✉)], Barbara Rita Barricelli[1], Daniela Fogli[2], Sergio Colosio[3], and Chiara Testa[3]

[1] Dip. di Informatica, Università degli Studi di Milano, Milan, Italy
{valtolin,barricelli}@di.unimi.it
[2] Dip. di Ingegneria dell'Informazione, Università degli Studi di Brescia, Brescia, Italy
daniela.fogli@unibs.it
[3] Settore Informatica e Smart City, Comune di Brescia, Brescia, Italy
{SColosio,CTesta}@comune.brescia.it

**Abstract.** Human Work Interaction Design (HWID) studies the integration of work analysis and interaction design methods to foster new strategies aimed at designing systems that may effectively and efficiently change the way people work. Pervasive technologies and smart places deeply influence traditional physical boundaries and operational modes, leading to important changes in work practice. The goal of this paper is to provide the basis for an improved co-operation and mutual inspiration among public employees by using End-User Development (EUD). EUD in the e-Government context provides non-professional software developers with methods, techniques, and tools for configuring services that citizens can use to interact with public offices. The paper describes how, by using EUD-enabled tools, the work practice of the public staff changes, and how this transformation allows public employees with limited technical background to create services according to their expertise and expectations, and to share them.

**Keywords:** e-Government · End-User Development · Human work interaction design · End-user empowerment

## 1 Introduction

E-government is aimed at supporting administrative processes and improving the quality of services offered by public administration. In particular, digital public services are being studied and developed in order to make the interaction with citizens and businesses faster, more efficient, more transparent, and less expensive [9].

With e-government services, a number of bureaucratic issues can be accomplished without requiring citizens and organization representatives to visit public offices. Enrolling children in school, obtaining a building permit or paying local taxes can be performed through a personal computer or a mobile device, from home or work.

This paper is the result of a long-term collaboration among academic research scholars and some members of a public administration entity, namely the Municipality of Brescia, an Italian town with a population of 200,000 inhabitants. The problem has

© Springer International Publishing AG 2017
S. Barbosa et al. (Eds.): IS-EUD 2017, LNCS 10303, pp. 119–134, 2017.
DOI: 10.1007/978-3-319-58735-6_9

been firstly addressed by proposing a meta-design approach to the development of e-government services, based on meta-modeling techniques [14]. Meta-design has been regarded as a multidisciplinary activity aimed at creating the socio-technical conditions for empowering civil servants to become co-designers of e-government services, according to Fischer and Giaccardi's definition of meta-design [10, 11]. In particular, meta-modeling has been considered as a fundamental activity at the basis of meta-design, aimed at defining a meta-model (namely, from a technical perspective, an XML schema) specifying the characteristics of a class of e-government services, for subsequent instantiation during service creation. In this way, previous work has introduced End-User Development (EUD) [16] in the e-government domain, by providing civil servants with a tailored environment supporting the definition of e-government services. As a result, a set of proof-of-concept tools have been presented in [12, 14] that demonstrated the validity of the idea of transforming domain experts (civil servants) from passive consumers of technology into active contributors, as first-person developers of e-government services according to a cultures of participation philosophy [5].

In this paper, we would like to make a step further in this direction by extending the analysis of the work practice currently adopted at the Municipality of Brescia to develop e-government services, and by providing a deeper understanding on how to improve and transform it through a fully integrated system. We would like to overcome the limitations of the previous proposal, which encompassed a set of separated tools, each one developed with different open source technologies, by proposing a system that takes into careful consideration the stakeholders' know-how and technology currently in use, with the purpose of developing a full-fledged platform, ready for re-use in other public administration contexts.

To this end, the paper describes a Human Work Interaction Design (HWID) approach [1, 7, 8, 15] applied to the e-government domain, with the aim of improving the current work practice of the public administration with the help of EUD methods and techniques. HWID focuses on studying how end users, as workers in specific domains, work both individually and collaboratively for reaching a common objective. The social and organizational dimension that characterizes this approach calls in action concepts like usability and user experience, leading to the definition of Human Work Interaction Design. HWID usually involves a multi-disciplinary approach, which is fundamental to address the complexity of many work practices.

In the frame of the latest Action Plan for e-government [9], the European Commission (EU) advocates the adoption of innovative approaches to design and deliver better public services, in order to satisfy the different needs and demands of citizens and businesses. Fast and high-quality services must be ensured by modern and efficient public administrations, which need to transform their back offices, and to rethink and redesign existing procedures and services [9]. EUD strategies, developed according to a HWID approach, are here proposed as an effective way to accomplish the principles promoted by the EU Action Plan.

The paper is structured as follows: Sect. 2 introduces HWID and discusses its application to the e-government domain; Sect. 3 presents the new system for the development of e-government services based on EUD strategies; Sect. 4 describes the use of the system in an illustrative example; Sect. 5 discusses the main advantages of the system presented in the paper in comparison with literature proposals and commercial solutions, as well as its limitations; Sect. 6 summarizes the main contribution of the paper and presents hints for future work.

## 2   Human Work Interaction Design in the e-Government Domain

Work domains are traditionally studied focusing on the tasks that are usually performed in them, their users' objectives and requirements, the work environments characteristics, and all cognitive and physical factors that may affect the work activities. This human work analysis modus operandi is typically based on Hierarchical Task Analysis [4] and Work Domain Analysis [20, 23] methods. Specifically, the application of ethnographic methods [6] with a sociotechnical perspective [2] is a well-established approach in Human-Computer Interaction (HCI).

HWID, on the other hand, studies the integration of work analysis and interaction design methods for its application to pervasive and smart workplaces. Since 2005 HWID scientific community has studied how technology is changing human life and work practice in numerous, multi-faceted ways.

The outcomes of the research in this field are collected in four books that discuss HWID under four distinct perspectives: (i) the application of work analysis and sketching in the design of human-work interaction [8]; (ii) the concept of usability of human-work practices in different social, cultural, and organizational contexts [15]; (iii) the design of applications for complex and emergent organizational and work contexts (e.g. medical user interfaces, elderly care facilities, green-house climate control, navigating through large oil industry engineering models, crisis management) [7]; and (iv) the integration of work analysis and interaction design methods for pervasive and smart workplaces [1].

Looking at each discipline's workflow is a daunting task, especially in e-government, where workflows may depend on the types of services to provide to citizens and on legal restrictions in data access. Moreover, public authorities are forced to offer their services in a more efficient, more transparent, and more cost effective way. In order to achieve this goal, software developers must learn what citizens will do with an application and how citizens will use information provided by the application; in other words, developers must understand citizens' mental model when the online e-government service is used. Under this perspective, civil servants are the key persons responsible for determining how information across an e-government application has to be displayed and accessed, because they are in the possession of the whole knowledge learned in years of practice in working with citizens. Therefore, they are usually involved in the development of online services, as experts of the application domain.

Particularly, in this paper we present an HWID approach for empowering workers of the e-government domain in improving their work procedures. The following two subsections describe respectively the current work practice adopted for developing e-government applications at the Municipality of Brescia and as it would become by introducing EUD techniques.

## 2.1 Current Approach to the Development of e-Government Applications

In the current work practice, the stakeholders involved in the creation of e-government services devoted to the citizens of Brescia are the domain experts (typically head offices that possess the know-how about government services), the software analysts, the software developers, and the end users (namely, civil servants who will directly manage citizens' requests).

These stakeholders collaborate in the following macro-stages of online service development: Requirements analysis, Development, Testing, Revision, and Deployment.

To describe these stages, in the following we refer to the creation of an online service for children registration to nursery school.

### 2.1.1 Requirements Analysis

At the requirements analysis stage, a set of meetings among domain experts and analysts are carried out. The functionalities that need to be implemented are discussed and defined. The results of the meetings are then organized in a report, also including some mockups, which are transmitted to the software developers who will implement the application.

### 2.1.2 Development

Software developers create a new project in Microsoft.NET, which starts by importing some libraries of the .NET framework and others belonging to an internal framework that enables the basic functionalities of the online services. Stylesheets, scripts, master pages, and images already available in the internal framework are imported as well. The development proceeds with the creation of the steps composing the service, which leads to the development of the objects making up each step. Two types of steps may be included in online services:

- *Predefined* steps: they are related to legal requirements (e.g., privacy policies) or common functionalities to be made available to the citizen (e.g., review of all inserted data before completing an online procedure);
- *Personalized* steps: they are specific to the case at hand.

Specifically, for the online service devoted to nursery school registration, eleven steps must be created, including two predefined steps. Personalized steps gather data about the citizen's requirements and data about the service request. The former data will concern: (i) child's personal and residence details; (ii) data related to parents' work and family status; (iii) child's additional needs (for example, diet, psychological support, etc.). The data about the service request concern: (i) name of the nursery school; (ii) type of attendance (part-time or full-time); (iii) request for an extended period.

As mentioned above, each step is created through the development of a set of software objects, also called *controls* in .NET. Each control is composed by an HTML part for the presentation logic and a C# part for the application logic. Particularly, the HTML part collects all data inserted by the citizen, whilst the application logic implements all functions necessary for the validation of data and their correct storage.

### 2.1.3 Testing
The testing stage is devoted to check if the functionalities and the data collection process work correctly and according to what described in the requirements analysis report. Therefore, once the application is completed, it is published on a dedicated internal Web server, in order to allow domain experts and end users to test it. The publication on the server requires that the developers perform some specific operations: program compilation; copy of files from the development environment to the testing one; creation of a database; and configuration of the Web server to render the application.

This stage is usually critic for the development plan, because domain experts and end users are usually busy with other daily duties, and their unavailability for testing the application as soon as it is completed leads to delays in the process and in the final deployment of the application.

### 2.1.4 Revision
Several changes or integration requests usually arrive during the testing stage, mainly due to misunderstandings at the requirements analysis stage. This stage, however, presents two critical aspects:

- it is almost impossible to plan the duration of the activity because this is highly dependent on the outcomes of the previous testing stage;
- testing is not repeatable on the same application version and, at the end of the revision stage, the new version of the application has to be published again on the server and a new testing has to be organized.

### 2.1.5 Deployment
At the Deployment stage, developers must compile the software application, copy some files from the development environment to the production one, create a database, configure the Web server, and ask system administrators to set up the new domain and the DNS.

## 2.2 Empowering Public Staff with EUD Techniques

With the introduction of a EUD environment for e-government service creation, the domain experts directly define and generate the web pages for the citizens. As a consequence, the community of stakeholders changes significantly: analysts and developers are not needed anymore, so only domain experts, end users and platform administrators are put in charge. In addition, the stages described in the previous section change, and are reduced to Requirements Analysis, Application Creation, and Deployment.

## 2.2.1   Requirements Analysis

Requirements Analysis is now performed entirely by the domain experts in the workplace, without the need of involving developers or analysts. If a domain expert is not yet authorized to access the EUD environment (i.e. a restricted area where s/he is able to create e-government services through the use of EUD tools), platform administrators are required to create a new user profile and to instruct the domain expert on the features of the EUD environment.

## 2.2.2   Application Creation

In this stage, a domain expert uses the EUD environment (like the one presented in Sect. 4) to achieve the following goals:

- set up a new online service by defining its name;
- select service type (only "reservation" or "registration" at the moment) to allow the EUD environment to automatically generate the predefined steps;
- create the personalized steps on the basis of the outcomes of the requirements analysis stage;
- create new user profiles for the other users, eventually assigning them different roles.

As to the last point, the system can indeed be used in different ways by the civil servants, according to their responsibilities and competencies. Therefore, different roles can be associated to each end user depending on the services s/he can create, modify or access. Specifically, in the organizational structure of the Municipality of Brescia four user roles became known, including that one played by the members of the IT sector (*SystemAdministrator*), who can create new users, new service types, and who can access the configurations and data of the stored services.

In particular, the domain expert will play the role of *SystemManager*, which allows her/him to create a new service and specify which civil servants are responsible for accessing this service. Then, for each service there will be civil servants with the role of *ApplicationManager* that allows the management of the service configuration, and other civil servants with the role of *ApplicationViewer* that provides the possibility to display data entered by the citizens.

## 2.2.3   Deployment

The Deployment of the application is carried out in a very simple way: the *ApplicationManager* may change the configuration of the service by selecting a checkbox that declares the service as "published". When this change is saved, a specific database is automatically generated. Since the service is already online as part of the platform itself, it is not needed to proceed with domain and DNS set up anymore.

Section 3 illustrates in more detail how the second stage would be carried out using the new EUD environment proposed in this paper.

# 3  An Integrated System for e-Government

According to the HWID strategy explained in the previous section, the idea is to endow civil servants with a EUD-based visual design environment as a way to represent the connections between different workflow steps and identify how the application will work from a practical perspective. Human information interaction (HII) [3] is an emerging area of research that studies how users interact with information. The proliferation of information-based tasks and activities has led to increased interest in investigating the organization, use, design, communication, flow, and sociotechnical aspects of information. These researches have highlighted how the information architecture of an interactive system can benefit from visual design strategies that can appear to be the best approach for domain experts for setting up and arranging hierarchy and flow of information [21, 27]. Being able to model data, they can define structured content types and data flows that well represent user's needs, business logic and requirements, and internal working practices. Moreover, the visual representation of information flow is also a valuable tool to be used for sharing with colleagues.

Today, Web forms are still the predominant style of interaction for users on the Web for accessing a variety of services. In fact, Web forms are often considered the last and most important stage of the journey to the completion of goals in e-government websites [18, 28].

What civil servants need is a form generator able to support them in the creation of the navigation strategies and information architecture of an online e-government service for citizens. In particular, in this paper only reservation and registration services will be considered, since they cover the majority of online services made currently available to citizens in the municipality web site.

## 3.1  The Form Generator

By using a form generator, civil servants are able to determine how information on the municipal Web site must be displayed and accessed. In order to create the services for requiring reservations or registrations, the civil servants need to consider what the citizen expects to see, as well as what data the public agency wants to collect.

Ultimately, these sorts of decisions create the structure for the online service. The deliverable is thus a wizard that drives the civil servant in the creation of a form structure from the choice of the type of service (reservation or registration) up to the steps that the citizen has to follow for requesting the service.

Once the civil servant makes the decision of where information lives, s/he also needs to decide how the labels might be called, managed, and checked. Labeling ensures that the navigation and hierarchy is appropriately tagged, which plays an important role in whether users will be able to find that information.

For this reason, the civil servant has to choose the most appropriate taxonomies for a Web service based on the mental model of the target audience. For example, in the case of the nursery school service, the labels might cover the personal details and specific requirements concerning the service. For each field of the form, the civil servant has to indicate if it is mandatory or if it is subject to limitations about the value that the citizen has to insert.

## 3.2   The Overall Architecture

The architecture at the basis of the form generator includes two components that aim at generating the JSON document describing the service created by the civil servant and at rendering the final Web application for citizens (see Fig. 1).

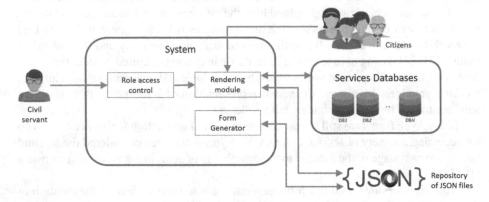

**Fig. 1.** Architecture of the system

JSON is a lightweight data interchange format that uses human-readable text to transfer data objects that are made up of simple attribute-value pairs. The JSON document is used for describing the type of the service to generate (e.g. a registration or a reservation), the steps that make it up, and the visual objects within each step. For each object its name is indicated, as well as the type of data, if it is mandatory or not, and possible constraints. By parsing the JSON document created by the form generator, the second component of the architecture aims at transforming the service description in a responsive website able to satisfy the needs of the users and the devices they are using. Responsive Web allows adjusting a website content into the best layout for the device displaying it. The possibility to separate content and presentation and its applicability to a final desktop or mobile website is what makes transformations so powerful and useful to a broad citizenship.

From the technical point of view, we adopted the React Framework[1] for building user interfaces. This allowed us to implement a component-based approach to EUD [19, 24, 25]. Indeed, React focuses on the View part of the MVC (Model-View-Controller) pattern and revolves around the concept of "components", which are snippets of HTML with functionality attached to them. First of all, for reading a JSON document and transforming it in HTML, any additional libraries in React are needed. HTML templates are a fundamental part of React, especially if the component is

---

[1]  React: a JavaScript Library for building user interfaces: https://facebook.github.io/react/.

written in JSX (an XML-like syntax extension to ECMAScript that is used for producing React "elements"). For producing a responsive Web site, React also uses a concept called the Virtual DOM that selectively renders sub-trees of nodes based upon state changes. It does the least amount of DOM manipulation possible in order to keep the components up to date. React allows creating responsive components, namely components that can respond to screen size changes, adjusting their contents into the optimal layout for the given parameters. React Responsive is a library that provides a wrapper component with a familiar interface to media queries.

The main advantage of this library is that existing components will not need to be modified in any way, and their state and properties will remain the same.

## 4   An Illustrative Example

The form generator that have been developed to support civil servants of the Municipality of Brescia in generating reservation and registration services for citizens is structured as a wizard that presents a sequence of pages containing requests of specific data for the service to compose.

Once a civil servant has been authenticated with the *ApplicationManager* role, s/he can operate for generating a new service or modifying an existing one. Figure 2 illustrates

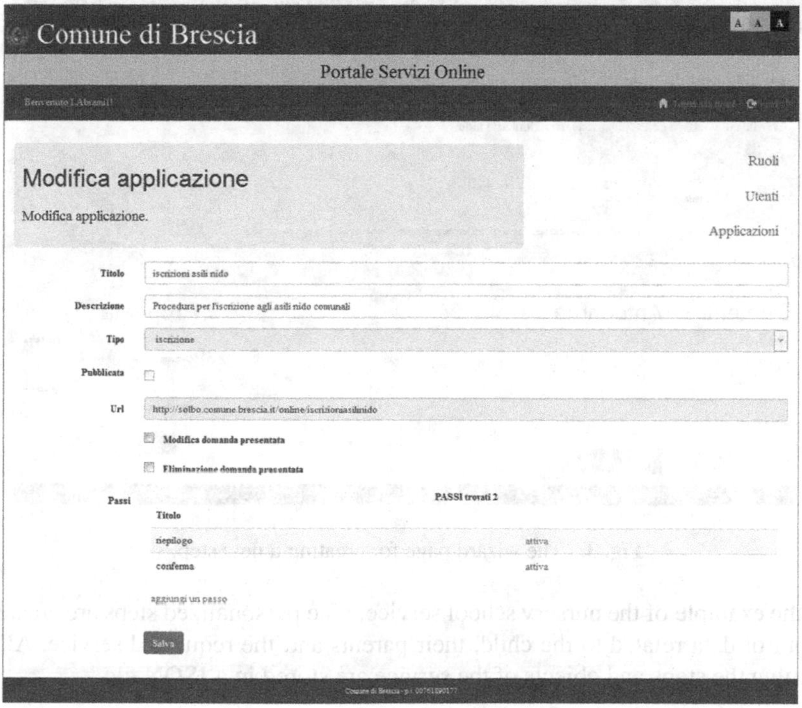

**Fig. 2.**   The wizard page for service modification with predefined steps already available.

the first page of the wizard, where the civil servant has just defined the name of the service and has selected its type ("iscrizione", that means registration in English).

Depending on the type of the selected service, some steps are mandatory and are generated automatically by the platform. For example, since in this case the civil servant wants to create a "registration" service, predefined steps are (see Fig. 2): (i) the summary of inserted data (called "riepilogo" in Italian), and (ii) the confirmation that the instance has been sent to the proper department (called "conferma" in Italian).

Once the type of service to generate has been selected, it is possible to create the logic flow of the service (e.g., its steps) and the objects that compose each step (e.g., fields, labels, controls) by means of a graphic layout and drag-and-drop features that do not require technical competences by the civil servants.

In particular, a preview area ("Anteprima") is shown to the civil servant to see how the fields of the form will appear to the citizens (see Fig. 3). Here, the civil servant can define the data to be required, by adding related objects into the area. S/he can finally define the properties of each object and the validation criteria that the citizen will have to comply. For instance, in Fig. 3, the civil servant has just dragged and dropped a text field for requiring the citizen's surname, whose validation criterion has been set as mandatory.

**Fig. 3.** The wizard page for creating a new step.

In the example of the nursery school service, nine personalized steps are created for the input of data related to the child, their parents and the requested service. All data concerning the steps and objects of the service are stored in a JSON file.

Finally, the civil servant may decide to publish the service so it can be made available to the citizen. When a service is published, a dedicated database is generated for storing the data that citizens will generate by using the service.

### 4.1 Service Rendering for the Citizen

The service-rendering module of the platform can be accessed by the citizens through the municipality Web portal devoted to the online services. Here, a list of available services is displayed. A citizen can filter the list by service name, description, or type, thus obtaining a selection of services that could satisfy her/his current needs. Figure 4 shows the list of available services filtered by name "infanzia" (childhood), including a service for children registration at nursery school and a service for reserving an appointment to the municipality counter providing information about nursery schools.

**Fig. 4.** Online services available on the municipality Web portal.

The citizen who wants to access a specific service may click the corresponding link and a rendering operation is activated for displaying the forms composing the service on her/his device in a proper way. The graphical rendering is performed by reading the JSON file that describes the components of the service and displaying the objects of the Web form according to the registered sequence of steps and the device used by the citizen. By using the React Responsive library, the rendering module allows to tailor presentations to a specific range of output devices without changing the content itself. More precisely, using the special Media Queries directives and inline styles CSS, the module can adapt the styles that fit the content best for a given device. So, when the state of the rendered service changes, it will be updated by re-invoking the rendering method. This behavior allows easily switching from the desktop layout to the mobile one. Figure 5 shows a mobile visualization of the page of an e-government service used to modify the citizen's personal data.

**Fig. 5.** Mobile visualization

Moreover, the final rendering can be provided in two different modalities: (i) standard and (ii) at high contrast. By using two different style sheets, it is possible to display the Web form in order to comply with accessibility requirements of citizens. For example, the "at high contrast" view generates a form with greater character font dimensions, and a high contrast between characters in foreground and background. Figure 6 shows a screenshot of the service used to modify the citizen's personal data rendered by using the "high contrast" view.

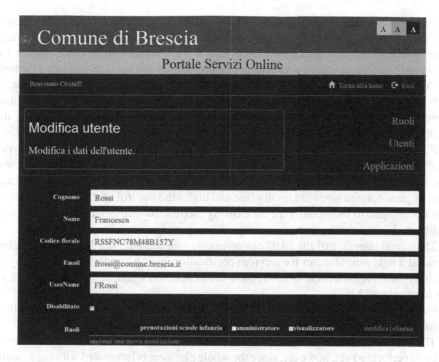

**Fig. 6.** "High contrast" visualization.

## 5 Discussion

A recent market analysis carried out by the IT Sector of the Municipality of Brescia has highlighted that some commercial products for creating interacting forms in an easy and intuitive way are currently being proposed. They can be regarded as EUD-enabling tools that support end users in creating personalized forms. In particular, these tools usually generate PDF forms that could be downloaded by citizens, filled in in an electronic way and then returned to the public administration, e.g. through uploading in the Web site. However, citizens' data collected through these forms cannot be stored in a structured manner in the system database. In this way, civil servants cannot directly process these data through the online application, for example by accessing it with a "viewer" role; the intervention of software developers is necessary to transfer data acquired through the interactive forms into the database of the system used to process them.

The idea of providing civil servants with a unique and integrated system represents an evolution also with respect to the previous proposal of a EUD environment for the e-government domain [12–14]. In that case, a set of different tools with different inter-action styles and different technologies had to be used in a specific operation chain that went from using the EUD environment for creating an XML specification of the service, to running two different parsers taking the XML file as input to generate a Web application devoted to citizens and a Web application devoted to clerks respectively, until publishing the Web applications on the municipality Web site.

Furthermore, the previous version of the EUD environment provided an interaction style completely based on fill-in-forms; the new version, instead, allows civil servants more flexibility through a drag-and-drop interaction and an edit-in-place feature for setting user interface control properties. The preview of the service, provided through a WYSIWYG interface, allows civil servants to directly visualize the outcome of her/his activity, and possibly change it immediately if needed; whilst, in the previous version, the XML generated file had to be processed by the parser before giving the possibility of validating the created service.

Finally, the current system is more general in that it allows creating different types of services that need to gather information from citizens, whilst the previous one was specifically designed for appointment reservation services. Therefore, the number and types of personalized steps are totally free and under the control of the civil servants; s/he is not obliged to only configure the existing predefined steps, but s/he can also add, modify or delete existing steps.

The visual interface of the EUD environment, coupled with the JSON solution, has provided a lightweight mean for service specification, going beyond the complexity of ontology-based approaches, which require either specific training or the support of an ontology expert [22].

Furthermore, different kinds of service rendering have been implemented to allow the use in mobility and to cope with accessibility problems affecting the citizens.

The main limitation of the present work is that usability tests with civil servants have not been performed yet; however, since the whole platform is integrated with the systems and technologies already in use in the workplace, we are confident that civil servants may find the interaction with the platform consistent with the other systems they are using. Similarly, experiments with citizens must be carried out to evaluate the graphics and behavior of the service-rendering module.

## 6   Conclusion

The e-government survey carried out by the United Nations in 2012 would like to promote the development of "citizen-centric services" [26], that is, services customized to citizens' needs and preferences. Public administration workers are the only ones that possess the knowledge about such needs and preferences, since they usually have a direct and continuous contact with citizens. Therefore, empowering them (as domain experts) to directly create online e-government services goes in the direction of closing the gap between software developers and end users.

This paper has presented a possible solution to this problem by proposing a unique and integrated platform for creating, managing and rendering e-government services on the Web portal of any public agency. The solution derives from a long-term collaboration with a town municipality and a novel analysis of the problem performed by following a Human Work Interaction Design approach.

The flexibility and malleability of the proposed platform allows its extension to other kinds of online services that require collecting data from citizens. Moreover, platform fruition could also be realized through a cloud-computing infrastructure, thus saving costs for development and maintenance. In particular, public administrations of small cities and rural areas, which are often excluded from such technological innovation and whose communities thus risk a form of "digital divide" [17], could heavily benefit from this kind of approach. Therefore, in the future, we would like to investigate the possibility of a widespread adoption of the platform, especially in public agencies with limited resources for software development and shortage of technical staff. Another future activity aims at studying design strategies for supporting domain experts in their working activities by means of a Web form generator in other application contexts. In many cases, a design strategy based on visual composition of the information flow can allow domain experts to manage the working processes from their respective domain. This approach can be used in each business process in which we need a visual composition language for defining the information architecture and for controlling flow of information, and the process verification mechanisms that bring to the development of Web forms.

# References

1. Abdelnour Nocera, J., Barricelli, B.R., Lopes, A., Campos, P., Clemmensen, T. (eds.): HWID 2015. IAICT, vol. 468. Springer, Cham (2015). doi:10.1007/978-3-319-27048-7
2. Abdelnour-Nocera, J.A., Dunckley, L., Sharp, H.: An approach to the evaluation of usefulness as a social construct using technological frames. Int. J. Hum. Comput. Interact. **22**(1–2), 153–172 (2007)
3. Agosto, D.E.: Human Information Interaction: An Ecological Approach to Information Behavior by Raya Fidel. MIT Press, Cambridge (2012)
4. Annett, J., Duncan, K.D.: Task analysis and training design. J. Occup. Psychol. **41**, 211–221 (1967)
5. Barricelli, B.R., Fischer, G., Fogli, D., Mørch, A., Piccinno, A., Valtolina, S.: Cultures of participation in the digital age: from "have to" to "want to" participate. In: Proceedings of the 9th Nordic Conference on Human-Computer Interaction (NordiCHI 2016), art. no. 128. ACM, New York (2016). doi:10.1145/2971485.2987668
6. Button, G., Sharrock, W.: Studies of work and the workplace in HCI: concepts and techniques. Synth. Lect. Hum. Centered Inform. **2**(1), 1–96 (2009)
7. Campos, P., Clemmensen, T., Abdelnour Nocera, J., Katre, D., Lopes, A., Ørngreen, R. (eds.): Human Work Interaction Design. Work Analysis and HCI: Third IFIP 13.6 Working Conference, HWID 2012, Copenhagen, Denmark, December 5-6, 2012, Revised Selected Papers. IFIP Advances in Information and Communication Technology, vol. 407. Springer, Heidelberg (2013)
8. Clemmensen, T., Campos, P., Ørngreen, R., Pejtersen, A.M., Wong, W. (eds.): Human Work Interaction Design: Designing for Human Work. Springer, Heidelberg (2006)
9. European Commission. The European eGovernment Action Plan 2016–2020 – Accelerating the digital transformation of government, COM, vol. 179 (2016). http://ec.europa.eu/newsroom/dae/document.cfm?doc_id=15268
10. Fischer, G., Giaccardi, E.: Meta-design: a framework for the future of end user development. In: Lieberman, H., Paternò, F., Wulf, V. (eds.) End-User Development, pp. 427–457. Kluwer Academic Publisher, Dordrecht (2006)
11. Fischer, G., Giaccardi, E., Ye, Y., Sutcliffe, A., Mehandjiev, N.: Meta-design: a manifesto for end-user development. Commun. ACM **47**(9), 33–37 (2004)

12. Fogli, D.: Towards a new work practice in the development of e-government applications. Electron. Gov. Int. J. **10**(3–4), 238–258 (2013)

13. Fogli, D., Parasiliti Provenza, L.: End-user development of e-government services through meta-modeling. In: Costabile, M.F., Dittrich, Y., Fischer, G., Piccinno, A. (eds.) IS-EUD 2011. LNCS, vol. 6654, pp. 107–122. Springer, Heidelberg (2011). doi: 10.1007/978-3-642-21530-8_10

14. Fogli, D., Parasiliti Provenza, L.: A meta-design approach to the development of e-government services. J. Vis. Lang. Comput. **23**(2), 47–62 (2012)

15. Katre, D., Ørngreen, R., Yammiyavar, P., Clemmensen, T. (Eds.): Human Work Interaction Design: Usability in Social, Cultural and Organizational Contexts: Second IFIP WG 13.6 Conference, HWID 2009, Pune, India, October 7-8, 2009, Revised Selected Papers. IFIP Advances in Information and Communication Technology, vol. 316. Springer, Heidelberg (2010)

16. Lieberman, H., Paternò, F., Wulf, V. (eds.): End User Development. Springer, Dordrecht (2006)

17. Manoharan, A., Carrizales, T.J.: Technological equity: an international perspective of e-government and societal divides. Electron. Gov. Int. J. **8**(1), 73–84 (2011)

18. Money, A., Lines, L., Fernando, S., Elliman, A.: E-government online forms: design guidelines for older adults in Europe. Univ. Access Inf. Soc. **10**(1), 1–16 (2011)

19. Mørch, A.I., Zhu, L.: Component-based design and software readymades. In: Dittrich, Y., et al. (eds.) End-User Development: 4th International Symposium, IS-EUD 2013, Copenhagen, Denmark, June 10–13, 2013, pp. 278–283. Springer, Heidelberg (2013)

20. Rasmussen, J., Pejtersen, A., Goodstein, L.P.: Cognitive Systems Engineering. Wiley, New York (1994)

21. Resmini, A., Rosati, L.: Pervasive Information Architecture: Designing Cross-Channel User Experiences, 1st edn. Morgan Kaufmann Publishers Inc., San Francisco (2011)

22. Salhofer, P., Stadhofer, B.: Semantic MDA for e-government service development. In: Proceedings of the 45th Hawaii International Conference on System Sciences (HICSS 2012), pp. 2189–2198. IEEE Computer Society (2012)

23. Stanton, N.A., Salmon, P.M., Jenkins, D.P., Walker, G.H.: Human Factors in the Design and Evaluation of Control Room Operations. Taylor & Francis, Boca Raton (2010)

24. Stevens, G., Pipek, V., Wulf, V.: Appropriation infrastructure: mediating appropriation and production work. J. Organ. End User Comput. (JOEUC) **22**(2), 58–81 (2010)

25. Stevens, G., Quaisser, G., Klann, M.: Breaking it up: an industrial case study of component-based tailorable software design. In: Lieberman, H., et al. (eds.) End User Development, pp. 269–294. Springer, Netherlands, Dordrecht (2006)

26. United Nations: E-Government Survey 2012 – E-Government for the People. United Nations, New York (2012). http://unpan1.un.org/intradoc/groups/public/documents/un/unpan048065.pdf

27. Valtolina, S., Barricelli, B.R., Ariano, F., Padula, M., Scala, P.L.: Knowledge management for designing business workflows through semantic compositions of web services. Int. J. Knowl. Learn. **8**(1–2), 62–85 (2012)

28. Winckler, M., Bernhaupt, R., Pontico, F.: Challenges for the development of user interface pattern languages: a case study on the e-government domain. Int. J. WWW/ Internet **8**(2), 59–84 (2010)

# End User Comprehension
# of Privacy Policy Representations

Sophia Kununka[1(✉)], Nikolay Mehandjiev[1], Pedro Sampaio[1],
and Konstantina Vassilopoulou[2]

[1] Alliance Manchester Business School,
The University of Manchester, Manchester, UK
sophia.Kununka@postgrad.mbs.ac.uk,
{n.mehandjiev,p.sampaio}@manchester.ac.uk
[2] Department of Informatics and Telematics,
Harokopio University, Athens, Greece
kv@hua.gr

**Abstract.** Providers of mobile applications (apps) offer free apps and services but monetise user information and attention, whilst app users have limited control and inadequate understanding over the manner in which apps use their personal data. This study is a first step to taking a user centred approach in the design of app privacy policies to ensure they are easy to understand by non-technical users. To this end we capture the views of 41 users on four different privacy policy representations and analyse them to extract user priorities and needs. We have found that one of the alternative policy representations is liked best by users, and that users focused on data collection and use, neglecting other privacy aspects such as data monetisation and legal issues. As a result of our analysis, we propose a novel interactive representation to enhance the informativeness of privacy policies, especially with respect to data monetisation, whilst facilitating greater user control over personal data privacy. We evaluate our proposal using the cognitive dimensions framework.

**Keywords:** Mobile applications · Privacy policy · End user development

## 1 Introduction

Mobile apps process plentiful personal data that users tend to believe will only be used for a limited set of purposes related to the functionality offered by the app. However, privacy policies tend to state much wider purposes such as marketing, exposure and renting of customer information, and users have been observed to consent to these purposes, which are obfuscated within long and difficult to understand and policies.

Customers are known to favour privacy-friendly providers over privacy-invasive providers, yet the same customers are willing to purchase from privacy-invasive providers if they offer cheaper prices [1, 2]. Achieving an informed user choice thus necessitates that users comprehend the intentions of service providers with respect to personal data, and the value gained by users in exchange for allowing access to their data. This would align user expectations with the extent to which they are willing to

© Springer International Publishing AG 2017
S. Barbosa et al. (Eds.): IS-EUD 2017, LNCS 10303, pp. 135–149, 2017.
DOI: 10.1007/978-3-319-58735-6_10

yield their privacy [3, 4]. Clarity regarding the use of personal data is reinforced by regulatory bodies such as the US Federal Trade Commission and the European Data Protection Act [5], which provide data protection guidance and, increasingly demand that app providers incorporate user privacy requirements into the design of apps. Indeed companies that neglect users' privacy concerns face public anger [3] and the provision of explicit privacy policies is now common, together with the adoption of business models that offer users trade-offs for their information.

Privacy policies are meant to answer user privacy concerns, yet they are often designed from a service provider's perspective, with a focus on validating compliance with regulators and fostering clients' confidence as opposed to facilitating user privacy transparency [6]. While privacy policies have been widely adopted, the traditional full length privacy policies face criticism for their complex content and 'blanket' nature. The 'blanket' nature limits the options available to users to either accepting the entire policy or rejecting it, the latter choice forfeiting the use of the app. App users feel a sense of "hopelessness" when faced with complex policies that offer them limited control over their privacy [7]. Further, users of mobile apps often want access to an app service in the shortest time possible and while users are concerned about their data privacy, they may not be willing to read the lengthy, time consuming and difficult to understand privacy policies. Likewise, mobile phone privacy usability concerns have also been cited [8], a complication that arises from constraints in the display interfaces which limit the amount of privacy information that can be displayed [6]. The necessity for simplification of privacy policies is clear.

We argue that to optimize the way privacy is represented in app policies, we need to find a balance point in the design space where (i) the privacy information representation is simplified, (ii) users are provided with sufficient information about how their data is used and why, (iii) users can consent to specific elements of the policy, and (iv) users understand the trade-off between monetisation interests of providers and privacy protection interests of users. To achieve this, a user centred approach to the design of privacy policies is needed, indeed we are using a user centred design method to incorporate meaningful and relevant user input into system development [9].

In summary, this paper attempts to explore the representation of appropriate interactive mechanisms that allow users to be well informed so they can control their personal privacy. The rest of the paper is organized as follows: the section on related research is followed by a section describing the concept and the method of our study. The paper then presents our results and concludes with discussion.

## 2    Related Research

### 2.1    Privacy Policy Representations

A number of proposals exploring solutions to the complexity of app privacy policies have been put forward with different degrees of success. Efforts in this area have included design of machine readable representations such as a platform for privacy preferences [10] and privacy beacons [11]. User studies comparing privacy policy representations do exist although some have yielded conflicting results. For instance,

[12] reports that users favoured shorter and tabulated privacy policies over the full length policies (see Appendix) while [13] found that the full length policy was perceived as more secure and thorough by participants as compared to other alternatives.

These differences are logical when considering the focus of the two studies, indeed [12] focuses on enjoy ability and ease of finding information in policy, [13] explored comprehension and perceptions on privacy security offered by policies.

However, both studies [12, 13] confirm that full length policies yield the worst accuracy results in terms of users' ability to find and correctly interpret privacy information, as compared to shorter alternative policy representations. This may be a pointer to inadequate user understanding of full length policies. A policy that lacks clarity, readability and is not clearly understood could lead to uninformed user privacy consent increasing opportunities for unanticipated and unwanted uses and disclosures of users' data. The preference of the full length policy in [13] could be attributed to users being hesistant to use policy representations that they are not familiar with and, as such building user trust for alternative policy representations may be attained through repeated use of new alternative policies and user education.

## 2.2 Privacy vs Monetisation Trade-Offs

Related research has studied how users' willingness to disclose their data is influenced by privacy policies [1]; mismatches between users' intention to share information and their actions [14] and trade-offs between privacy and personalization [15].

Achieving a balance in the mobile app ecosystem requires comprehension of the conflict of interests that exist between the service provider and the end user. The service provider is required to find equilibrium between privacy-preservation which greatly limits data monetisation and, privacy-invasiveness that monetises user data in order to ensure business viability [1]. In order to ensure clarity in a policy's privacy preservation or invasiveness, users should be facilitated with means of making and executing specific user choices regarding data monetisation. While privacy policies play a substantial role in expressing these conflicts, [16] stress that there is inadequate research on this subject. The willingness of users to share their data can be enhanced through incentives such as convenience or monetary benefits or discounts [17]. Hence while actual money may not be given to users, trade-offs between sharing their data and use of free apps could be facilitated. The requirement for further research into data handling approaches that optimize monetary and privacy interests such as pricing-by-privacy trade-offs have been recommended [1].

One of the shortcomings of the existing approaches to developing privacy policy representations is that they engage participants at the evaluation stage rather that at the design stage. As such, participants' privacy perceptions are not captured into the design. A lack of user involvement in privacy policy design is an important gap in the development of user centred policies. Secondly, users are limited in understanding how their data is monetized and they cannot control this. This study seeks to address these gaps and uniquely draws on the academic area of end user development, seeking to involve non-technical users in the design of effective privacy representations. The aim is to create a user-centred privacy representation that is simpler, easier to comprehend, facilitates effective user control of their personal data whilst allowing service providers to use business models based on monetizing personal information.

## 3  Conceptual Framework

This study seeks to design a user-friendly privacy policy representation that facilitates user comprehension and control over personal privacy. We follow the user centred design process [9] with its four main stages: determination of user requirements, design, prototyping and assessment. However, the results reported here are from the first iteration through the process, where the focus is on user requirements and preferences, and the other stages are simplified, involving the design and heuristic evaluation of a simple static prototype of the representation. The results will be fed into a second iteration through the process which will focus on producing a high-fidelity interactive prototype and evaluating it through user observation studies.

Our conceptual framework (shown in Fig. 1) incorporates the stages of the user centred design process, focusing on the first iteration through the process.

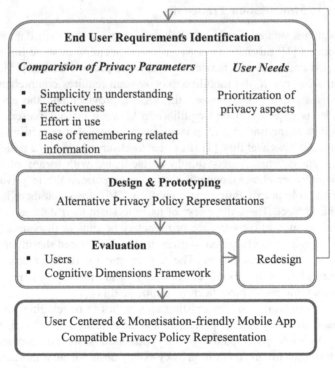

**Fig. 1.** Conceptual framework of study

Our work began by exploring available literature on mobile privacy policies to identify areas of privacy concerns to users which we refer to as privacy parameters. The participants of the study were presented with four alternative privacy policy representations within a questionnaire survey. Three of policy representations were sourced from the literature while the fourth was a design of our own based on qualitative analysis of app privacy policies. Participants were asked to assess the policy representations against the privacy parameters established from the literature. The participants' most liked policy representation from our study was identified. This representation was then used in the design and prototyping stages as a basis to develop the prototype of the final design version presented in this paper which was guided by the participants' opinions regarding the privacy parameters and their representation choices. Evaluation of the prototype design was conducted using the cognitive dimensions framework [18], which is recommended as a suitable means of assessing design artefacts in their initial phases. The feedback received from the evaluation stage is presented here and will be used to guide the next iteration of the prototype design, aiming towards a user centred and monetisation-friendly privacy policy representation for mobile apps.

## 3.1  Privacy Representation Parameters Explored in the Study

Privacy policies have been criticised for their complexity [2], partially arising from the language used to relay information which uses legal terms and structure. This makes policies tuned to demonstrating statutory compliance and hence difficult for non-specialists to understand. As such, we identified *simplicity in understanding* as the first privacy representation parameter to explore in this study.

Further, privacy policies are often deemed ineffective, since they fail to facilitate control by users over information sharing [3]. This view is shared by [19] who assert that an effective privacy policy is one that enhances users' 'perceived control over their information disclosure and the secondary use of personal information'. *Effectiveness* is therefore the second privacy parameter considered in our study.

Likewise, the length of policies is a deterant since reading policies is deemed by users to be a waste of time and burdensome. A study [20] found that a typical user would be required to invest 40 min per day for reading privacy policies. This underpins the necessity of designing policies in a way that reduces the effort to read them required from the users. *Effort in use* is thus the third parameter in our study.

In addition to the amount of user effort required, there is a need to assess how easy it is for users to find specific privacy-related information in a policy. This is to facilitate the granting of informed consent over the user of personal data. However, the current arrangement of privacy information in policies appears not to take this into consideration [21]. *Ease of remembering related information* in the policy is thus the fourth parameter in our study.

The privacy parameters were represented as Likert-scale questions to assess users' privacy perceptions on four alternative policy representations. The privacy policy representations were: the three best representations from the studies by Cranor et al. [12] and Earp et al. [13] plus an initial version of an alternative policy representation that we developed.

The first two representations were based on the Cranor et al. [12] study: the *standardized table policy representation* and the *short text policy representation* (see Appendix). The standardized table shows data collection versus data use and data sharing. It also uses different colours to signify default and non-default data collection and, clearly indicates optional data. The short text policy representation on the other hand is a textual natural language representation of the information presented by the standardized table representation, with related rows combined to ensure conciseness.

Further, we also used the *goals and vulnerabilities policy representation* from Earp et al. [13]. It is based on a traditional full length policy representation in which goals or vulnerability statements relevant to consumer privacy are bolded and highlighted. On "mouse over", these statements present a pop up box with protection goals and vulnerabilities.

The last representation was an initial design of our own, called the *list format policy representation*. It presents key privacy aspects together with a brief description of each aspect. The set of privacy aspects used were established as a result of our qualitative analysis of 100 privacy policies from different business sectors such as: ecommerce, social networking, insurance, traffic and navigation etc.

# 4   Method

## 4.1   Participants and Procedure

Participants were sourced online using an email with a hyperlink to a filtering questionnaire developed in Qualtrics [22]. Participants were offered £15 Amazon vouchers for their participation. A pilot study of 8 participants was conducted and the feedback received used to make improvements on the questionnaire.

A total of 112 responses were received. These were filtered according to availability for scheduled sessions, validity of contact details, gender, age, education and IT proficiency, leaving 41 valid responses with mixed demographics. Gender mix was 63% female and 37% male. Age was under 26 years for 56%, 44% between 26–36 years and 2% above 36 years. In terms of highest level of education attainted, 29% had advanced level, 12% undergraduate, 49% masters, 7% PhD, 2% other. IT proficiency statistics were 22% basic, 44% intermediate, 27% advanced, 7% expert.

Spearman's correlation was used to determine if demographics in terms of age, gender and education impact privacy preferences. Only three statistically significant correlations were observed between gender and privacy preferences: the variant 2 – effectiveness factor ($r_s = .333$, p < .05), the variant 4 – effort factor ($r_s = .400$, p < .05) and, the variant 4 – remember factor ($r_s = .321$, p < .05) where $r_s$ = coefficient. However, they were weak linear relationships and therefore no further tests were conducted on them. As such, the weak relationships observed in the gender factor indicated that the gender imbalance in the sample population of this study has no significant effect on the participants' privacy preferences. Similarly, no significant relationships were observed between the demographic factors of age and education with the participants' preferences. As such further exploration of the preferences across their demographic population was deemed unnecessary.

Each selected participant completed the questionnaire within one of the the six scheduled sessions. Three researchers were present throughout each session to explain any part of the questionnaire that was not clear to participants. Each session began with an identical brief presentation that introduced the purpose of the study, explained basic privacy concepts to participants and answered any questions by participants.

## 4.2    Design of the Questionnaire

We used an example of the privacy policy of a fictitious app we called Jupiter X. The content of privacy information used in the Jupiter X app privacy policy was carefully selected so as to match the real practices of companies. We presented its information as four different types of privacy policy representations. These were: the standardized table (R1), the short text (R2), the goals/vulnerabilities (R3) and, the list format (R4) respectively. Using a mixture of open-ended questions and five point Likert scale questions, the questionnaire captured participants' perceptions on the different policy representations in respect of the four privacy representation parameters: simplicity in understanding, effort required, effectiveness of policy, ease of remembering related information and lastly the participants' overall assessment of the policy representations. The open ended questions invited participants to qualify the responses they provided on the Likert scale questions. This encouraged them to reflect on and consider their answers and also provided the researchers with more insight helpful in the interpretation of participants' responses. The findings contributed to development of improved user centred privacy policies.

In another task, participants were presented with a definition of a privacy policy and a brief description of six key privacy aspects found in privacy policies: data security, user rights, data collection, legal, data use, data exchanges (monetisation). They were then required to rank these privacy aspects according to their importance.

## 4.3    Design and Evaluation of a Prototype Representation

Based on our findings we designed a prototype representation which was based on the most-liked representation and addressed the user needs identified. For example we sought mechanisms of improving the areas of privacy elements in a policy that were least understood and cared for by users. The solution was then evaluated using the cognitive dimensions framework of heuristic evaluation [18].

# 5    Results, Design Effort And Discussion

## 5.1    Variations of Policy Representations

Findings show that the most to the least 'simple to understand' policy representations were: R4, R2, R3 and R1 respectively. In terms of the least to the most required 'effort in use' were: R4, R2, R3 and R1 respectively, an outcome identical to the 'simple to understand' parameter. Results for the most to the least 'effective' policy representation

**Table 1.** User preference of policy representations

|                      | First | Second | Third | Fourth |
|----------------------|-------|--------|-------|--------|
| Simplicity           | R4    | R2     | R3    | R1     |
| Effortlessness       | R4    | R2     | R3    | R1     |
| Effectiveness        | R4    | R2     | R1    | R3     |
| Ease of Identifying  | R4    | R1     | R2    | R3     |
| Overall Results      | R4    | R2     | R3    | R1     |

were: R4, R2, R1 and R3. In light of 'ease of identifying related information', the easiest to the most difficult were: R4, R1, R2 and R3 respectively. The overall assessment of the policy representations by the participants shows that ranking from the most preferred to least preferred representations were: R4, R2, R3 and R1 as shown in Table 1. R4 had the most user preference in terms of simplicity, effort, effectiveness and ease of remembering related information, followed by R2, R3 and R1 the least agreeable representation. A summary is shown in Table 1 with the abbreviations of the policy representations: the standardized table (R1), the short text (R2), the goals & vulnerabilities (R3), the list format (R4).

### 5.2  Ranking of Privacy Elements in Policy

Participants' ranking of the most to the least important privacy aspects in a policy were: data collection, data use, user rights, data security, data exchanges/monetisation and, legal respectively as shown in Fig. 2. The data exchanges/monetisation and the legal were considered the least important. Firstly, a possible explanation for the lowly ranked privacy aspects could be as a result of inadequate user understanding of these privacy aspects whereas participants may have ranked the most important privacy elements (data collection and use) as such because they felt they had a clearer understanding of these aspects. Both Android and iOS operating systems now offer greater permissions granularity during app installation through interfaces that highlight the user data collected together with the corresponding permissions to which users are required to consent for the download to continue. While there are several studies that indicate that there is inadequate user understanding of these permissions [17, 23], permissions requirements give users a clearer idea of the data collected which contributes to user understanding and boosts user confidence. As such, user perceptions about the privacy aspects that were deemed as the least important could be improved by presenting these privacy aspects in more educational and easy to understand ways.

Secondly, the low importance ranking of legal and data exchanges/monetisation could also be an indicator that users feel that these aspects of privacy are out of their control and, thus indicating a need to introduce more user control in these areas. Research indicates that user trust, greater use and willingness to share data have been identified as one of the benefits of facilitating users with more control over their privacy [23].

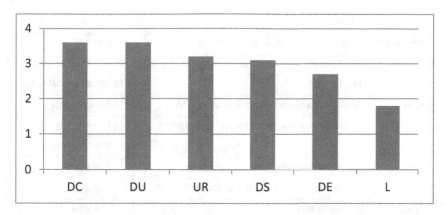

**Fig. 2.** Ranking of the importance of privacy aspects in a policy

## 5.3   Enhancements Contributed to Privacy Policy Representation

To evaluate our proposed artefact, we draw on the cognitive dimensions framework [18] that has been used to evaluate usability [24]. This framework according to [18] should not be confused for rules of design, but should be seen as a means of explaining the artefact-user relationship. The cognitive dimension framework has the following dimensions: Abstraction gradient, diffuseness, closeness of Mapping, visibility and juxaposability, secondary notation and escape from formalism, hidden dependencies, premature commitment, role expressiveness, viscosity, consistency, error-proness, hard mental operations and progressive evaluation. Next, we present a discussion on the evaluation of our design based on these dimensions.

**Abstraction Gradient.** The abstraction dimension of the cognitive dimensions framework addresses the encapsulation or clustering of items into one to achieve simplicity. Depending on users' privacy concerns and it can be subdivided into three degrees of abstraction: abstraction hating, abstraction tolerant and abstraction hungry. "Privacy freaks" [14] are likely to fall under the "abstraction hating" category as they desire may much privacy information as possible, the average user is interested in privacy [6] given empowerment exercise it and is aligned with the "abstraction toler-ant" category and, the "abstraction hungry" category could represent careless users [8], which take no thought of privacy either due to lack of awareness or interest. The relevance of representation is asserted by [3] who state that the transformation of data into information and thus the extent of its usability is greatly impacted by how the data is represented. A major focus in improving app privacy policy representations is content minimization due to the limitations of mobile phone interfaces. While a privacy balance is challenging to achieve we sought to attain a means of catering for the different abstractions that are represented by users.

Our artefact seeks to provide content minimization which is consistent with abstraction-hungry representation. To this end, the artefact presents privacy information in a tabular two column format that presents a particular privacy aspect with its brief description adjust to it. At the same time, our artefact seeks to cater for abstraction-tolerant

| Jupiter X App | | | |
|---|---|---|---|
| Requires access to | Contacts, location, financials, demographics, cookies | | App costs £ 10 |
| Why | Service provision, site maintenance, personalized service, user support | | Allow use of your data with a tick<br>Each tick reduces cost by £ 2 |
| Your rights | Consent to data collection, access & update date, opt-out | ☑ | Service Provision |
| Data security | Data encryption; staff adheres the company's data privacy policy | ☐ | Marketing |
| | | ☐ | Order catalogues |
| | Your responsibility - use strong, careful kept passwords | ☑ | Third parties |
| | Storage of data - Deletes 3 month after you opt-out | ☑ | Data spread |
| To keep app free | Data may be shared | | ▪App now costs £ 6    OK |
| | Data may be sold e.g. marketing          more . . . | | |
| Legal requests | Changes in policy - Email notification 7 days before change | | |

**Fig. 3.** Proposed artefact: new list privacy policy representation

by providing a more link to another interface with a brief description a particular privacy aspect such as the data monetisation. Further, for abstraction-hating, the full privacy policy is provided through an easily accessible link (Fig. 3).

**Diffuseness.** Depending on the objective, representations may be tabular, graphical, textual, visual etc. The number of symbols or space required to convey information differs with different notations. In order to enhance readability the word count of sentences was reduced. The result is a reduction in the amount of information held in memory and as such facilitates faster information processing [8]. This facilitates better view of the policy on the limited mobile phone interfaces. Likewise, in some sections such the 'Why' section, comma separated key words were used to replace whole sentences therefore facilitating simpler relaying of privacy information.

**Closeness of Mapping.** The cognitive dimensions framework dimension of 'closeness of mapping' explores mapping of the problem world and a solution. Our artefact seeks to address the problem of representing privacy information such that it reflects what users deem as most important to their privacy problem. While there is limited research on the order in which privacy information is presented in a policy, [25] argue that the aspects of privacy that users are interested in differ. Based on our findings on their prioritisation of the different aspects of privacy information, our artefact rearranged the order in which privacy information is presented to users to reflect their needs. For instance, to highlight the key aspects of user privacy, the 'your rights' privacy aspect was moved from the bottom to third position in order of appearance. Our motivation here was to support informed consent as much as possible even in instances where users may be in a hurry to download apps. This enables them to quickly and easily access the aspects of privacy that are most important to them even in the event they do not want to explore all the privacy aspects of an app. In addition, the 'your responsibility' section was collapsed under the 'data security' privacy aspect where it rightfully belongs and also as a result makes the policy appearance less cluttered. The importance of this action is underpinned by [3] who state that 'every notation highlights some kinds of information at the expense of obscuring other kinds'.

**Visibility and Juxaposability.** The ability to display relevant information or provision of intuitive access to information or further being able to display related information adjust to each other is underlined in the visibility and juxaposbility dimension of the cognitive dimension framework. This is particularly important due to the insurmountable amount of information presented to users in traditional full length privacy policy representations. Specifically the 'To keep app free' section was developed to be more intuitive by appending a 'more' link at its right hand side (see Fig. 3). A study [26] recommends that simplified representations could have mechanisms through which users can obtain more comprehensive details should they be required. Juxaposability comes into effect by clicking the 'more' link, which provides an interface presenting a summary of several ways in which data may be monetized for instance: service provision, marketing, order catalogues, third parties, data spread etc. In addition, the interface displays the cost of the app which for example is £ 10. Further, it informs uses that they can consent to the different ways shown through which their data may be monetized by checking adjacent checkboxes. Users are also informed that for each type of data monetisation they consent to, the price of the app reduces by a certain amount for instance £2. At the bottom of that interface, the final cost of the app is automatically calculated and displayed based on the number of consent checks a user has provided. An 'ok' option together with an option to exit the interface is provided returning the user to the policy representation. Visibility and juxaposability are particularly important in helping address the challenge of how to improve users' perceptions of privacy aspects such as the data exchanges/monetisation which users ranked lowest in importance. By designing the artefact as described above, the data exchanges/monetisation was developed to be more informative and to facilitate greater user control over user privacy.

**Secondary Notation and Escape from Formalism.** The cognitive dimensions framework dimension of secondary notation and escape from formalism focuses on how information may be relayed in unconventional ways. This could include use of aesthetics to enhance readability. The use of secondary notation has at times been critique as being a platform via which service providers try to influence users' by stressing certain information while ignoring what is 'truely' important to the users. However, our artefact seeks to support users in the in the privacy aspect of data exchanges/monetisation by using colour highlights to emphasis prices and checkboxes to indicate user consent and thus to facilitate user interactiveness and control over their privacy.

**Hidden Dependencies.** The cognitive dimensions framework dimension of 'hidden dependencies' which deals with exposing interdependencies between or within privacy aspects that may not be obvious to the users. Our enhancement of the data exchanges/monetisation privacy aspect is only a first step in dealing with this challenge. This is because while the user knows and thus consent on the ways in which their data may be monetised, they are not aware of how their data will spread out in the data market places especially through third parties associated to the app/s they are using. This is important as sensitive user data exposure without knowledgable consent could have significant consequences for instances health data [21]. This underpins the necessity for more research into how to express hidden dependencies in privacy policy representations.

**Premature Commitment.** There are several instances or factors in privacy policy representation that could result in premature commitment or consent by users. As discussed earlier, hidden dependencies could be a contributing factor, the ordering of privacy information may be another contributor as a user may not be ready to ready the entire policy, or yet still the complexity and ambiguity of privacy as it's represented in the traditional full length policy representation. The enhancements that our artefact proposes curb premature committement to an extent. However, research into user centred design of all the key privacy aspects in a policy is required in order to minimize premature commitment.

**Other Dimensions in the Cognitive Dimensions Framework.** The role expressiveness dimension addresses the ease of identifying the use of each entity within the overall representation. In our artefact, role expressiveness is reflected through it structuring, use of secondary notation and and 'explicit description level' [18].

Viscosity another dimension deals with resistance to local and the amount of changes required to implement changes in a policy representation. Our artefact uses abstraction, a measure cited by [3] as a means of limiting user resistance.

Further, consistency is a dimension that deals with users' ability to infer a part of a representation from another earlier mastered representation part. Our artefact endeavours to maintain consistency by ensuring simplicity and a similar structuring throughout the representation.

Error-proness is a dimension that enables recovery from mistakes. Whereas a user does not have the option of opting out once they agree to the traditional full length policy, our enhanced data exchanges/monetisation facility enables users not only to careless express their choices or also to cancel or change any undesired option.

The hard mental operations dimension addresses the degree of mental processing necessary as opposed to the semantic process. Our artefact seeks to limit the effort of mental processing involved in the use of the representation as this eases understanding. Hence the artefact design involved the simplifion of terminologies that participants had identified as 'jargons'. For example, the statement 'we may monetize your data' was changed to 'we may sell some of your data', 'profiling' changed to 'personalized service' etc. The last dimension, progressive evaluation was conducted by seeking expert feedback during the design process. The artefact went through several processes of refininement enhancing its effectiveness in privacy policy representation.

# 6 Conclusion and Future Work

We use a user-centred approach in designing a privacy policy representation which balances information with ease-of-understanding, and allows communicating important monetisation trade-offs to end users. Drawing on literature, we establish privacy representation parameters that are pertinent for achieving a more usable and thus effective privacy policy design. A study of 41 users assessed four privacy policy representations using the privacy representation parameters. The most preferred privacy policy representation by users was the list policy representation, followed by the short text policy representation, then the goals and vulnerabilities policy representation and last was the standardized table policy representation.

Users' focus was mainly on the data collection and use as opposed to the data monetisation and legal privacy aspects. We propose a solution to enhance the limited understanding of the data monetisation aspect and checked its usability using the cognitive dimensions framework. The end result is a privacy policy representation that empowers user to provide more informed consent about the use of their personal information and facilitates user interaction and control over the data monetisation privacy aspects. In future research we plan to investigate ways of refining and testing the language or terminology used so as to further enhance user understanding.

# Appendix

**R 1:** The standardized table policy                    **R 2:** The short text policy

**R 3**: The goals and vulnerabilities policy          **R 4** : The list format policy

# References

1. Gerlach, J., Widjaja, T., Buxmann, P.: Handle with care: how online social network providers' privacy policies impact users' information sharing behavior. J. Strateg. Inf. Syst. **24**(1), 33–43 (2015). doi:10.1016/j.jsis.2014.09.001
2. Jentzsch, N., Preibusch, S., Harasser, A.: Study on monetising privacy: an economic model for pricing personal information. In: ENISA (2012)
3. Acquisti, A., Taylor, C.R., Wagman, L.: The economics of privacy (2016). doi:10.1257/jel. 54.2.442
4. Taylor, C., Webb, R.: HBR Blog Network (2012). http://blogs.hbr.org/cs/2012/10/a_penny_ for_your_privacy.html
5. Steinke, G.: Data privacy approaches from US and EU perspectives. Telematics Inform. **19** (2), 193–200 (2002)
6. Schaub, F., Balebako, R., Durity, A.L., Cranor, L.F.: A design space for effective privacy notices. In: Eleventh Symposium On Usable Privacy and Security (SOUPS 2015), pp. 1–17 (2015)
7. Patil, S., Schlegel, R., Kapadia, A., Lee, A.J.: Reflection or action? How feedback and control. In: CHI (2014). doi:10.1145/2556288.2557121
8. Wesson, J.L., Akash, S., van Tonder, B.: Can Adaptive Interfaces Improve the Usability of Mobile Applications? Brisbane (2010). doi:10.1007/978-3-642-15231-3_19
9. Sharp, H., Rogers, Y., Preece, J.: Interaction Design: Beyond Human-Computer Interaction, 2nd edn. Wiley, West Sussex (2006)
10. P3P. Platform for privacy preferences (2007). https://www.w3.org/P3P/
11. Langheinrich, M.: Privacy by design — principles of privacy-aware ubiquitous systems. In: Abowd, Gregory D., Brumitt, B., Shafer, S. (eds.) UbiComp 2001. LNCS, vol. 2201, pp. 273–291. Springer, Heidelberg (2001). doi:10.1007/3-540-45427-6_23
12. Cranor, L., Kelley, P.G., Cesca, L., Bresee, J.: Standardizing privacy notices: an online study of the nutrition label approach. In: Human Factors in Computing Systems: Proceedings of the SIGCHI Conference, pp. 1573–1582 (2010). doi:10.1145/1753326.1753561

13. Earp, J.B., Vail, M., Anton, A.I.: Privacy policy representation in web-based healthcare. In: 40th Annual Hawaii International Conference, p. 138 (2007). doi:10.1109/HICSS.2007.445
14. Norberg, P.A., Horne, D.R.: Privacy attitudes and privacy-related behavior. Psychol. Market. **24**(10), 829–847 (2007)
15. Li, T., Unger, T.: Willing to pay for quality personalization? Trade-off between quality and privacy. Eur. J. Inf. Syst. **21**(6), 621–642 (2012). doi:10.1057/ejis.2012.13
16. Bélanger, F., Crossler, R.E.: Privacy in the digital age: a review of information privacy research in information systems. MIS Q. **35**(4), 1017–1042 (2011)
17. Dinev, T.: Why would we care about privacy? EJIS **23**(2), 97–102 (2014). doi:10.1057/ejis. 2014.1
18. Green, G., Petre, M.: Usability analysis of visual programming environments: a 'cognitive dimensions' framework. J. Visual Lang. Comput. **7**(2), 131–174 (1996). doi:10.1006/jvlc. 1996.0009
19. Wu, J.J., Chen, Y.H., Chung, Y.S.: Trust factors influencing virtual community members: a study of transaction communities. J. Bus. Res. **63**(9), 1025–1032 (2010). doi:10.1016/j. jbusres.2009.03.022
20. McDonald, A.M., Cranor, L.F.: The cost of reading privacy policies. J. Law Policy Inf. Soc. (ISJLP) **4**, 543 (2008)
21. Lin, J., et al.: Expectation and purpose: understanding users' mental models of mobile app privacy through crowdsourcing (2012). doi:10.1145/2370216.2370290
22. Qualtrics. Qualtrics.com (2017). https://www.qualtrics.com/
23. Brandimarte, L., Acquisti, A., Loewenstein, G.: Misplaced confidences privacy and the control paradox. Soc. Psychol. Pers. Sci. **4**(3), 340–347 (2013)
24. Clarke, S., Becker, C.: Using the cognitive dimensions framework to evaluate the usability of a class library (2003)
25. Nielsen, J.: (1995). www.nngroup.com, https://www.nngroup.com/articles/ten-usability-heuristics/
26. Mehandjiev, N., Namoune, A., Wajid, U., Macaulay, L., Sutcliffe, A.: End user service composition: perceptions and requirements. In: Eighth IEEE European Conference on Web Services, pp. 139–146 (2010)

# An Integration of Empirical Study Participants into the Mobile Data Analysis Through Information Visualization

Thomas Ludwig[✉], Kevin Schneider, and Volkmar Pipek

Institute for Information Systems, University of Siegen, Siegen, Germany
thomas.ludwig@uni-siegen.de

**Abstract.** Visualizations are mainly used for providing an easy access to complex information and data. Collaborative visualization as the shared use of computer supported, visual representations of data by more than one person aims to joint information processing activities. Within this paper we apply the concept of collaborative information visualization to the field of analysis of mobile device data. By linking the concept of Quantified Self to our approach, we derive an application for integrating end users into the analysis of mobile device data provided by them. Based on its evaluation we were able to make informed statements about the main enablers for data analysis from an end-user's perspective such as the interest in the own behavior, the comparison with other study participants as well as the importance of an appropriate baseline.

**Keywords:** Collaborative information visualization · End-user · Research empirical studies · Mobile devices

## 1 Introduction

In recent years, mobile and wearable technologies have become a ubiquitous constant in people's everyday activities. The arising mobile data of these devices therefore are brought into attention as an interesting source for empirical research aiming to provide additional valuable information about the behavior of the end users' mobile devices and connected habits/practices in various contexts [9, 11]. At that point, the main challenge is not generating the data builts utilization. Modern research approaches make use of concepts such as *Participatory Sensing* to integrate not only data but also the users themselves [22]. Participatory sensing "tasks everyday mobile devices, such as cellular phones, to form interactive, participatory sensor networks that enable public and professional users to gather, analyze and share local knowledge" [2]. In contrast to other methods of enquiry, the participants of such studies want to find out something about themselves or their "community". They are considered as intrinsically motivated "citizen scientists" [17]. Participatory sensing studies are often conducted with the support of professional researchers and traditionally focus on quantitative data.

The inclusion of the end users of smartphones ("the data provider") as external stakeholders in the analysis of data offers a great potential for both, involved researchers

© Springer International Publishing AG 2017
S. Barbosa et al. (Eds.): IS-EUD 2017, LNCS 10303, pp. 150–166, 2017.
DOI: 10.1007/978-3-319-58735-6_11

and participants [22]. On the one hand, researchers benefit from new options to access knowledge about the emergence of data because end users are personally connected to their data in an intimate way in which researchers could never be. In consequence they generate a different knowledge than researchers do. On the other hand, end users gain an insight into the field of data analysis and their data by using technological possibilities of research which are usually inaccessible to them.

However, people who are not familiar with empirical research and its procedures, often lack knowledge about how to analyze data appropriately. In this sense, the visualization of data becomes an indispensable tool for non-experts to tap into this field since the range of information perception is the highest on the visual level [26]. The visualization of information is therefore essential to data analysis in empirical research and simultaneously creates a ground for understanding of how to analyze relevant content for both, researchers and non-experts. Nevertheless, the main research question is how to involve end users of mobile devices on the basis of information visualization in the research process and data analysis.

## 2  Theoretical Background and Related Work

The related work shows possibilities of the inclusion of external stakeholders in empirical research and data analysis through the visualization of information. We base our research on two discourses, one on collaborative information visualization and the other one on the concept of a quantified self.

### 2.1  (Collaborative) Information Visualization

Visualizations are not a modern-day invention. Cartography and astronomy have been using visual representations since 200 B.C. and the 10th-century respectively. Visualizations and graphics are used for a wide range of fields even beyond research contexts: for instance, in journalism, to provide a broad audience with easy access to complex information. Computer science provides various approaches and tools for gathering, processing and analyzing huge amounts of data. Chen et al. [4] describe different processes of how interactive visualizations are created and how they can be supported by existing information. Data visualization is 'the use of computer-supported, interactive, visual representations of data to amplify cognition' [3] and can be subdivided into information visualization and scientific visualization, whereby scientific visualization focuses on physically-based, scientific data and information visualization on abstract, non-physically-based data [3].

Collaborative visualization can be understood as "the shared use of computer supported, (interactive,) visual representations of data by more than one person with the common goal of contribution to joint information processing activities" [18]. The idea of collaborative visualization resulted from the need to overcome the traditional design of single-user visualization systems and to allow the collective exploration and analysis of large data sets through visualization. First approaches of collaborative visualizations were redefined extensions of existing modular systems for collaborative use cases. These were mainly achieved by duplicating views or sharing some selected parts – or a mixture of both approaches [29]. Former research has shown visualizations are significant for collaborative work, e.g. the benefits of using visualizations compared to not using them [1]; or that groups obtain better results with visualization systems in comparison to individuals [23]. Isenberg et al. (2011) differentiate collaborative visualization systems into the two categories of distributed and co-located approaches. In both cases, various approaches exist, such as Hugin [19], Many-Eyes [8, 27], Sense.us [14] and Comment Space [28]. These approaches show tagging and linking, if used, can have a positive impact on the collaborative analysis tasks. During deployments, it was noted that tags and links were not used as often as in laboratory evaluations. Willett et al. (2011) assume motivational factors and emphasize the need for guidance and incentives to facilitate the benefits of the provided mechanisms.

Ludwig et al. (2015) examined how visualization serves as a collaborative aspect in mutual, asynchronous team work. A study on users developed and elaborated implications of design for collaborative systems visualizing information which especially refers to empirical questions of research:

1. An application should support the user to select relevant datasets and to focus on areas of personalized interest within the data.
2. An application should support filtering and aggregating of data. In this case, filtering refers to functionality permitting the exploration of data within the dataset so that unappealing data are removed. By using aggregation, users are enabled to change levels of the dataset's abstraction.
3. An application should enrich data with information from external data sources.
4. An application should offer options to connect visualizations and interim findings.
5. An application should structure the cooperation of participants to empower effective work and collaboration.
6. An application should offer features encouraging users to communicate.
7. An application should reveal relations between special entities (for instance by connecting visualizations with their aim).
8. An application should promote and maintain engagement of external stakeholders encouraging them attending research projects.
9. An application should include external stakeholders in the process of the visualization of information. The research context must not only focus on formally predefined groups but also on the informally.

## 2.2  Quantified Self

Because end users of smartphones (in the process of research) interact with data provided by them, the concept of *Quantified Self* plays a big role. Quantified Self contains a growing community dealing with recording and analyzing user's data so that the user develops an understanding/awareness of personalized behavior [6]. Aiming to achieve significant conclusions, problems are exposed and behavior is changed if necessary [6]. Most end users collect data about their activities (40%), their eating habits (31%), about their weight (29%), sleeping habits (25%) and mood (13%) [6].

The analysis of collected data in the context of Quantified Self is often realized through the visualization of data. The current challenge is not to present data in an appropriate visualization but to gain knowledge about personalized behavior from the visualized data [6]. In this sense, end users visualize data in a personalized context by using quantified self because of a personal incentive (Huang et al., 2015). End users are usually neither professionals, nor experts in mobile data analysis who differ in their personal abilities and their cultural backgrounds. The most common motives to collect data about personal behaviors are (1) improvement of health, (2) improvement of other relevant aspects such as maximization of effectivity, (3) making new experiences [6]. Following Choe et al. (2015) end users thereby intend to:

1. examine data in detail and to place these linking to peaks in the dataset,
2. explain certain points in the visualized dataset by including external data or to reflect personal behavior by the confirmation or rejection of existing knowledge,
3. gain insights through the reveal of trends
4. compare existing dataset with external data considering different criteria
5. reveal correlations and specific interdependence of two variables in the dataset
6. overview the dataset
7. be aware of the distribution of single data points/spots within the dataset
8. identify aberrations because these are of special interest to the user.

The process from gathering data to its analysis in the field of quantified self can be divided in different phases [20]. First, a user prepares to collect and analyze data. During this process, the user's motivation to collect personal data is essential and s/he decides how data is ought to be collected [20].

The second phase aims at collecting and recording data. Problems according to used application can occur – for instance caused through lack of time or absent motivation – or referring to data itself – for instance caused through dependencies of subjective assessment [20]. Another common issue of the second phase is the lack of scientific accuracy while recording data so that misleading conclusions are drawn [6]. Missing scientific accuracy means that a user argues due to deficient accuracy while recording or the ignorance of contextualized data.

During the phase of integration, collected data must be combined and transformed. Most applications only require the user to do this marginally. Problems occur if data is transformed much before the user works with it [20]. The development of appropriate visualization is the most essential approach to gain knowledge from data in this phase [6]. The most commonly used types of visualization are line charts, bar diagrams or scatter grams [5]. To convey knowledge from these types, labels, shapes, trend lines and textual segments are popular [5].

In later phases of reflection, end users confront prepared dataful visualizations, to achieve knowledge. This happens either directly after collecting data ("short-term") or after several days or weeks ("long-term") Statistical methods such as comparison are often used to gain knowledge. Here users compare their personal data with data of others, mostly similar persons from a demographic view [6]. Problems arise due to a lack of time and often difficulties in understanding information [20].

## 2.3   Information Visualization and Quantified Self

To gain knowledge about personal behavior, several tools exist that support users to record and analyze data. The plain noticing of personal information without any help of tools contains errors because people possess a limited ability to memorize [20]. Further, it is not possible to observe some behavior by oneself such as sleeping habits (Li et al., 2010). The reflection of data through user's memory makes it hard to detect patterns and trends, and not anyone has sufficient knowledge and expertise to generate useful findings. Quantified self-tools support users in recording and saving personal data and offer functionality for drawing conclusions in the process of analysis and reflection [20]. By using these tools, it is essential that they empower users to autonomously recognize the relevance of data, to detect coherence, to experiment with data and therefore to promote generating of knowledge [6, 20].

Information visualization often facilitates experimenting with data. Nevertheless, following Pousman et al. (2007), end users are usually no expert but a novice to the field of visualization of information in the context of quantified self. Furthermore, the types of certain data are to be visualized because they are personally relevant to the user and as a result correlating with the knowledge which the user develops from the data [24]. It is therefore important to understand the challenges for novices in the field of visualization of information and in constructing visualized information by themselves. A requirement is visualizing information and offer functionality for filtering.

End users face three challenges [12]: (1) The user needs to select suitable data to answer the generated question of interest, (2) this selected data ought to be transformed into an appropriate visualization, (3) this visualization need to be interpreted usefully to gain knowledge. These three challenges, applying to tools for visualizing information and simultaneously addressing users without experience in the field of research, result in certain demands [12]: (1) Tools ought to provide search engines helping the user to look for data attributes based on key words, (2) suggest suitable visualizations based on provided information, (3) support iterative refinement/elaboration of visualization, (4) cope with an incomplete specification of visualization caused by the user, (5) provide explanations of existing content and as a result, launch a learning effect by the user and (6) involve the user closely in the entire process of visual analysis so that the user firstly establishes visualization and secondly achieves an answer to the question of interest. Heer et al. (2008) define similar demands for these specific applications: Applications ought to provide a user-friendly supply of data, provide an automatic selection of the optimal type of visualization based on useful criteria, offer information in context which explain which data are presented and how these are processed [13].

Huang et al. (2015) describe further special challenges for tools visualizing information in this context: (1) An appropriate application ought to fit into personal environment and routines of the user, (2) support the user in identifying personally relevant data and (3) provide suitable generalized data (a "baseline") so the user can organize personal data. A baseline should be personalized by creating referring to people demographically similar to the respective user because comparisons with similar people help gaining a higher knowledge [10]. Further tools should enable the sharing of data with regard to aspects of privacy and (5) allow making decisions autonomously referring to how personal data is visualized. (6) Such tools should support offering automatic pattern detection and (7) include in the user's daily procedure easily.

## 3   Research Gap and Research Question

Information visualization uses interactive, visual representation of abstract data to facilitate the understanding of data and the gaining of knowledge for end users [3]. Here, users create a suitable presentation of personal data by identifying relevant data and adapting all important information [25]. An appropriate presentation crucially depends on the existing data [26]. Thus, an application for visualizing information should offer different interaction types for users [30]. Collaborative information visualization is the shared usage of computer supported, visual representation of data involving more than one person with the aim of a common contribution to activities processing information [18]. Here from a researchers' perspective it is crucial to involve external stakeholders. In consequence, this higly collaborative context demands applications which provide a "common ground" between all collaborating users [7] and enable reference to single data objects [15]. Further, these applications must structure the cooperation between participants and encourage communication [21, 22]. Applications such as 'PartS' [22], 'ManyEyes' [27], and 'sense.us' [14] already offer some functionality addressing these requirements. Quantified self deals with the gathering and analysis of personal data of a particular user supporting this user to gain insights of individual behaviors [6, 16]. Thereby, not the visualization itself, but the gain of knowledge is the main issue [6]. The entire process should support the recording of data from the analysis of data and allow experimenting with personal data [6, 20, 22].

Currently, approaches already exist which facilitate collaboration to the visualization of information and involve quantified self as vehicle for the visualization of information. Within our paper, we contribute with a view on the involvement of end users in collaborative data analysis of research data, where the users visualize information of own data, which relates to the fields of collaborative information visualization and quantified self. Previous work already provide a tool (name: PartS) for recording and analyzing mobile usage data which serves as a basis for further exploration of the paper's research question [21, 22].

## 4   Concept and Implementation

To explore our research question, we have designed and implemented a web application to involve end users in the process of research through suitable visualization of information and to empower them to analyze mobile data provided by themselves. The client was implemented in AngularJS and the server backend as an instantiation of a BaasBox. The aim is to visualize data suitable for end users and involve them in the collaborative process of research through visualization and process data in a way that other end users could make use of. A specification of our concept is that the data is generated by users themselves because of their participation in respective empirical studies. We assume that end users gain different knowledge from their self-generated data than experts who do not have knowledge about the emergence of these personal data as the user has an additional insight about the own self. Our concept focusses on end users which have no (or hardly any) experience with regard to information visualization tools [16].

## 4.1  Data

Before the implementation we defined some pre-specifications for our data: (1) A data set exactly refers to one research project, (2) participants and users can collect data for different research projects, (3) metadata about the users exist. In the following, the terms "data set" and "data object" are used. A data set is the amount of data provided for one respective research project and a data object is an entity from this data set. Due to the concept's context in empirical research, personal data from users generated by them-selves as participants of a previous study and data generated by all users exist. We differentiate between two data types: (1) The data which the user has personally produced as a participant of an empirical research study and (2) the data which all the others users has produced. A user can use both data types; however, the data are pooled by the community whereby the user cannot access single data objects or dedicate data to a specific user. We decided for such a differentiation because no additional entrance barrier is raised due to the uncontrolled access of data by other users and the complexity of data structure is distinctly reduced through containment of data accessible to the user. A user has the possibility to see a data set (meaning a research project) to which s/he has contributed data previously (Fig. 1).

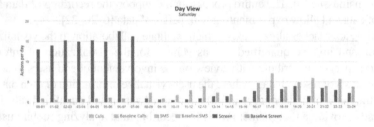

**Fig. 1.**  Available data sets (here: saturday and screen activations)

To generate an appropriate set of data we used PartS (Ludwig et al., 2016). Here we gathered mobile smartphone data within a period from July 1st to September 1st 2016. We gathered the number of screen activations (on/off), the number of received phone calls as well as the number of sent and received SMS. We decided to use these three data types because we assume these data as typical and easy to understand for the end users and most of the users identify with these data. We pick one specific user from the data set ("imaginary user") who has some abnormalities in data compared to the other. The data of this imaginary user serves as the data set for the later evaluation. The imag-inary user of our application sends one SMS a day, receives six phone calls a day and turns on the smartphone screen 71 times a day. The other users sent two SMS a day, receive four phone calls a day and turn on the smartphone screen 58 times a day. The imaginary user of the application has a significant higher use on a weekend and on Saturdays the value of the user's received phone calls is an average of 12, the SMS value

2,75 and the screen value 152,5. The imaginary user uses the smartphone from Monday until Friday similar to the other users of the application. The values increase from 12:00 at night constantly to 12 pm. However, on Saturdays and Sundays the values of the imaginary user increase rapidly instead of decreasing like the values of the others. The data remain on a high level until the morning, then these decrease and start increasing again at 4 pm. The values of the other users start increasing at 8 am (Fig. 2).

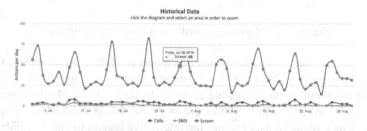

**Fig. 2.** Timeline-based visualization (Color figure online)

## 4.2  Information Visualization

While our concept involves the end user in the data analysis process through the visualization of information, it is firstly necessary that we offer possibilities for information visualization. The user's abstract process of gaining knowledge from data usually starts with raw data being transformed into a chart which is secondly presented through a suitable visualization [3]. To support these steps our applications facilitates an understanding of the data set for a user by providing not only a visualized presentation of data set but also a presentation of data in a chart. The tabular representation should always mark which data objects are used in the currently displayed visualization. Hence, the user is not forced to visualize personal data in detail which is useful especially if the user wants to satisfy a need for information faster in the sense of time saving without using graphic visualization [3].

During visualizing the data, the user has the possibility to decide autonomously which type of visualization fits personally. Thereby, the application suggests suitable types of visualization based on the user's data [24]. The application supports simple types of visualization such as bar diagram, line diagram and scatter gram because these are familiar to potential users [5]. The application should allow the exploration of a data set in a way the user gain knowledge from the visualized data [26]. The end user has the option to use a visualization based on a timeline (that represents the entire period of data gathering) and the summarized amounts of phone calls (blue), SMS (green) as well as screen activations (red) (Fig. 2).The application provides functionality to visualize the data in an aggregated form, whereby the average amounts of weekdays (Fig. 3) or just one specific weekday are presented. Based on the used specification, the data sets of phone calls, SMS as well as screen activations are visualized.

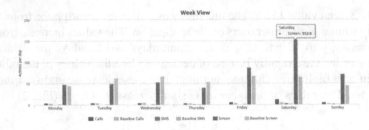

**Fig. 3.** Weekday-based visualization (Color figure online)

Based on literature, visualization should support the following functions for inter-action: (1) An overview about the entire data set, (2) the filtering out of specific data objects, (3) the zooming on interesting spots in the data set and (4) the displaying of details to a selected data object. All of our implemented visualizations are therefore interactive, which means a user can use the interactive legend to show or hide specific data objects. Further by hovering over the graphs, the detailed values of the data objects are accessible (Fig. 3). Further zooming is possible and the timeline adapts to the zoom level. To support the user actively while gaining knowledge, the application offers auto-matic pattern detection in a data set [13, 21, 31]. If a link between two data objects exits, the application highlights them, even if both data objects are not displayed [21, 30, 31]. As the application primarily addresses end users who lack experience with data analysis, we avoided the implementation of complex functions.

### 4.3    Baseline

To support the user's gain of knowledge, the application empowers the user to validate the data about personal behavior in comparison to data of the others. In fact, to gain knowledge from personal data, users compare themselves with others [6, 16]. We there-fore implemented a baseline that is calculated based on the average values of all other users (Fig. 3, red). The user has the option to integrate the baseline in the visualization to existing, personal data. As people reach a higher gain of knowledge if they compare themselves with others who match with them per relevant features [10], the applications empowers the user to individualize the baseline (Fig. 4).

**Fig. 4.** Baseline filter

The user can decide about specific users being included or excluded in the calculation of the baseline. This personal accommodation is based on demographic data such as age, sex, profession, residence etc. The user then can assess personal data in relation to other persons who resemble them in the baseline's observed features. It is, ofcourse, necessary to provide metadata about each user to offer this functionality. Within our example, a user chose male users aged between 30 and 47.

## 4.4  Collaboration

To involve users into the collaborative data analysis, the application offers users the functionality to collaborate with researchers. A common ground serves as a base for a fruitful collaboration [7]. To reach a common ground, all participants must operate with the exact same visualization which creates a base for discussion [27]. A user can therefore produce an extract based on the visualization of a data set and collaborate with the participating researchers through discussion based on this particular extract. We assume the researchers benefit from the user's knowledge about the personal data, and on the other side the user benefit from the researcher's knowledge about analyzing and explaining data phenomena.

To foster collaboration and discussion, a user should clarify to which data object s/he refer [15]. Hence, our application enables functionality for annotations to mark or highlight data objects (Fig. 5). The annotation is realized in the form of free-hand annotations, labels, shapes and trend lines or colored and textual segments because these are most common in personal context [5]. Once an extract of the visualization was saved, a user is not allowed to edit it anymore. However, there is the option to save more than one visualization. Users expect sharing extracts via social media or e-mail o gain a larger attention [16].

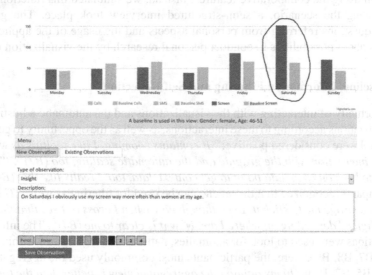

**Fig. 5.** Annotation and discussion screen

The application's functionality for discussion is orientated with regard to the application "ManyEyes" [27]. As already mentioned, the discussion about an extract of a (specific) visualization serves as base for any discussion intending to build a common ground. In each discussion, participants collaborate by exchanging comments and based on the visualization, a new extract can be generated and stored.

## 5   Evaluation

To evaluate our prototype, we conducted an evaluation with a total of 9 users. The participants' age ranges from 20 to 50 and their experiences from being affine to technical contexts (students of information systems) to those who are less IT affine (social worker). We aimed at testing usability and how the application supports the involvement of users into data analysis in empirical research and what challenges as well as obstacles exists. We were primarily concerned with identifying whether and in what ways the application would be used, and what difficulties in use might be encountered. The evaluations took place on the basis of a scenario to simulate a better understanding of the application's goal and to provide a frame for comparing the results. Each evaluation lasted about 60 min per participant during which the participants were asked to think aloud and were audio-recorded. The scenario demands participation in empirical study over a certain period of time in which the users collects data through smartphones. These data and data of other participants are provided simultaneously and the user involves in data analysis in context of this empirical research by use the application. After describing the tasks, the participants were asked to perform these by using our application. During the evaluation the participants were not able to engage with researchers in real-time discussion using the collaborative features. Instead, we simulated this functionality.

Following the scenario, a semi-structured interview took place. The guideline contains questions referring from personal aspects and the usage of the application to questions about possibilities to conduct personal research by the visualization of data.

### 5.1   Baseline, Information Filtering and Self Reflection

The opportunity of interacting with the visualizations and the automatic adjustments of the visualizations according to these interactions, as well as the opportunity to get details on demand were considered positive: *"It contains zooming, I like tooltips as well. [...] I like the interaction with the graphic and the automatic scaling, too (B7)". "That it's possible to klick on each data point to get context data, too. I really like that (B4)".* Not all participants recognized that the legend can be used for filtering as well: *"The legend did not encourage me to klick it. Even though now when I cross it, I see that the graphs are highlighted depending on where I am. Now it is clear to me (B4)".* The information visualizations were used to look for anomalies, patterns and regularities within the data set (B1, B7, B8, B9). Here, the participants most commonly used the aggregated view (B3, B4, B5, B7, B8): *"In my opinion the aggregated view is better than the timeline to make comparisons in any case, because I find everything a bit more divided and split here. I also find the baseline is directly next to it here, is bit better to compare myself to others (B5)".*

Even though there were problems of the term 'baseline' at first, the opportunity of a baseline was used to see the own data in relation to general data in particular. Thereby the majority of participants adjusted the baseline to their own gender and rough own age, to be able to classify the own data better: *"I am interested in comparing myself to other people. Just to get a feel for it (B4)"*. Assessing the own data in relation to an anonymous crowd of other users is considered as sufficient by the participants: *"For me personally it is perfectly fine that it is anonymous. I do not need any information about who it is (B7)"*. Especially it is highlighted positively that the graph adapts to baseline changes immediately: *"Now I narrow it all down a bit more. The graph changes live, that's very interesting of course. (B6)"*. The baseline was not only used to see the user's own data in relation to other data. It was also used for examining general data, without considering the own data. For this purpose, only the desired baseline data was plotted in the visualization: *"Now there are only males left. Cool. So, women look at their screen more often in average. And then it is possible to limit the age. Okay, the younger ones have a higher average of looking at it. [...] The youngest women look the most... use their smartphone the most (B7)"*.

Each of the participants discovered the pattern of particularly high values at weekends in the aggregated week view: *"Well, and then I see that my values at the weekend are far above the average. The calls are far above the average for the whole weekend and during the week it is quite usual (B4)"*. After discovering the special usage behaviour at weekends in the aggregated week view, the participants used the opportunity to zoom into relevant data objects using the day-view. Participants used the day-views of Friday, Saturday and Sunday to identify, when the specifics were caused. They tried to find the specifics' reason and gain knowledge in that way: *"So, from Friday night to Saturday I obviously was out. Or I was awake because I looked at the screen obviously. If I would not have been awake, that would be fatal because then someone else would have done it. Am I always like that? Do I do this on Sunday, too? Indeed. On Monday, too? No. Boah. I look... Friday and Saturday I obviously go for some parties. Or I just used my smartphone intensively for the whole night (B7)"*.

For gaining knowledge the participants tried to associate the observations, they made using the visualizations, with their daily routine (B1, B4, B7). Most commonly participants tried to extrapolate from patterns in the data set to when they sleep or not: *"But spontaneously screen on/off, sure. I can look how long I sleep at night, because I use the phone when I go to bed for example, to read something or get distracted a little and get tired (B4)"*.

The participants made further observations in the data set, which do not relate to daytime. They try to make insights from in the ratio of calls, text messages and screen activations. The participants made these observations in the timeline more frequently than in the aggregated view. One participant tries to extrapolate from the ratio of screen activations and number of text messages and calls to how often the smartphone is used for its usual purpose of communication and how often it is used for other things: *"Something you can see really well here is that the number of screen activations of the smartphone, which in the end is some kind of phone to be used for calls and sending text messages, is much higher than the actual usage of the phone for calls. So out of that I see, that you look at the screen much more often just to see if there is something new (B8)"*. Another participant tried to extrapolate from the ratio of calls and text messages to his own communication behaviour and if a text message flat rate in his smartphone rate makes sense or not (B4). For that purpose, he analyzed how many text messages he wrote within one calendar month. By doing that it becomes apparent, that a sum function about a specific period within the timeline would be very useful: *"I would like to know how many... But now I would have to count how many text messages I wrote last month. But that is nothing at all, anyway. Maybe there are two, four, six, eight, ten, 14, some more. There are not even 20 text messages. I would claim that my flat rate is not worth it (B4)"*. For a better classification and interpretation of the aggregated view's values, the participants would like to know the number of values a single data point is based on (B3, B4, B9): *"Here, it would be interesting to show the period of time that has been considered (B3)"*.

To assess the baseline and its validity, the participants wish additional information about the baseline data (B1, B2, B7). The participants are particularly interested in the number of persons included in the computation of the baseline: *"It would be nice to see the number of persons the baseline is composed of. Are there five people included or five thousand? With a baseline of five, I can't claim: All young women check their phone more frequently. Well, actually one is interested in gaining knowledge [...] and if the baseline is composed of ten people – that's not enough. The expression 'baseline' somehow implies a general validity, which requires the disclosure of the baseline population (B7)"*.

Regarding the baseline, several participants raise the question whether their own data is included in the baseline calculation and therefore biases its value. For that reason, the opportunity to exclude oneself from the baseline is requested: *"Maybe it would be an option to exclude oneself from the baseline. Easily by using a check mark that excludes the data automatically. So I can see what the others are do, myself excluded. [...] If I consider myself as an extreme user, I could use the tick mark to check whether the baseline values are biased by my data or not. That is, of course, just one point to consider if you compare yourself to only ten or twelve other users (B2)"*. Although the filter information was considered as useful, it was noted that the number of filter options is not sufficient: *"I think it is difficult to compare oneself solely by age and gender. That falls to short. [...] A person is characterized by more than age and gender"*. *(B4)* In addition to the existing filter options, the participants want to filter the baseline data by location (B2, B3, B4, B9), and include smartphone users from a certain area exclusively: *"A user could be requested to insert his zip code. So one could see if there are considerable differences in the frequency of using a smartphone between certain areas in Germany for example (B2)"*.

## 5.2   Annotations and Collaboration

Most of the participants use simple annotations, such as circles, arrows, or exclamation marks to highlight specific data points (Fig. 6). In the evaluation, the participants noted that they would like more annotation options, for example text fields (B3, B4, B5, B8), arrows (B4) or bullet points (B7). Not all the participants recognized that their feedback is incorporated in the research process by saving views and feedback. Some of them therefore demanded that the application should clearly state what happens to saved extracts: *"Here it should perhaps be explicated, whether the pictures are for private use only or if they are stored anywhere else (B1)"*. The second purpose of saving extracts – the incorporation into the research process by sharing insights with involved researchers – is viewed as valuable by the participants: *"If it is about sharing information with the researcher, I think saving insights makes sense (B3)"*.

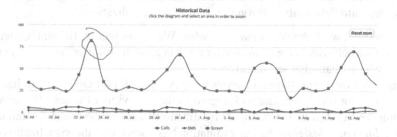

**Fig. 6.** Annotated visualization

To make the incorporation of users into the research process more effective, the participants request more information about the types of insights that are valuable to researchers. With that information, participants can also analyze and interpret their own data more efficiently: *"Regarding the insights, it would be interesting to know: What are insights a researcher would like to know at this point? (B3)"*.

One participant claimed that the opportunity to collaborate with other users is necessary, so that he could share his insights in a forum to profit from other users' experiences and opinions: *"I would like to have the opportunity to share my insights in a forum and attach the statement: I was asleep. Why did my smartphone display light up constantly? Of course, you could also ask other users: I recognized a strange pattern, how do you interpret it? Simply an opportunity to exchange ideas with other users to whom you are already linked to by the baseline (B2)"*.

The use of collaboration functionality between users is considered as especially valuable by the participants if they can collaborate with people they know personally (B5, B6). Thereby, the focus is not on the collaborative data analysis, but on the opportunity to compare oneself with single persons (B1, B5, B6, B8). Regarding this kind of data sharing, some participants consider it as more problematic than sharing data with researchers (B1, B8). To satisfy one's own interest in information, some participants demand the inclusion of individual research questions. They note that the research questions are essential for the involvement of users in the research process: *"It would be great to have leading questions that are in the interest of researchers, in order to deliberate in the same direction. [...] The research interest should be stated somewhere to contribute insights and findings regarding this interest and thereby contribute to research in a better way (B1)"*.

# 6   Conclusion

The aim of this paper was to explore the involvement of end users in the analysis of mobile device data generated by themselves in empirical studies through collaborative information visualization. The unique characteristic of our approach is the involvement of end users in analysis of their own provided data. We therefore conceptualized and implemented an application that offers the comparisons of data sets (and their visualizations) as well as collaborative features such as annotations and discussions. The evaluation revealed potentials as well as obstacles when aiming for the integration of external stakeholders into data analysis through information visualization:

(1) *Interest in own behavior is main enabler:* We argue that participant's interest in their own behavior is the main enabler for data analysis from an end user's perspective within quantified self research.
(2) *Exploring own data through comparison:* Almost all participants were interested in exploring their own data with regard to the behaviors of others. Fostering this comparison helps appropriating a visualization-based analysis tool for end users.
(3) *Baseline gains insights:* As our evaluation has shown that the visualization of the baseline is an appropriate tool for a comparison of the own data with others as it is easy to understand and handle.
(4) *Aggregated view vs. timeline-based view:* Our evaluation revealed that the aggregated view was much more often used than a timeline-based view. It seems the time plays a secondary role when focusing on the comparison with others.
(5) *End user interested in expert knowledge:* As our evaluation has shown, the participants are always interested in how experts make sense from their data and how they analyze and visualize the data. We assume users interested in quantified self are more willing to learn from experts about their own behavior.
(6) *Common ground:* Unsurprisingly, a common ground is needed when aiming at deep discussions between end users and experts. Visualization is able to support the common ground based on quantified self data.
(7) *Sharing data with researchers:* Our evaluation has shown that end users are more willing to share their data with researchers.

Data protection and thoughts about privacy play an important role for almost every participant. Especially if the data is be extended with further data types such as location data. According to the participants' thoughts of data protection it is a fundamental interest of the users to find out, what kind of data about them is being collected within the whole research context (B1, B3). However, going into detail about privacy issues would require an own paper. As a next step we aim to open the research platform PartS [22] to other users to pave the way for mobile data based citizen scientists.

# References

1. Bresciani, S., Eppler, M.J.: The benefits of synchronous collaborative information visualization: evidence from an experimental evaluation. IEEE Trans. Vis. Comput. Graph. **15**(6), 1073–1080 (2009)
2. Burke, J.A., et al.: Participatory sensing. Center for Embedded Networked Sensor System (2006)
3. Card, S.K., et al.: Readings in Information Visualization: Using Vision to Think. Morgan Kaufmann, San Francisco (1999)

4. Chen, M., et al.: Data information, and knowledge in visualization. IEEE Comput. Graph. Appl. **29**(1), 12–19 (2009)
5. Choe, E.K., et al.: Characterizing visualization insights from quantified selfers' personal data presentations. IEEE Comput. Graph. Appl. **35**(4), 28–37 (2015)
6. Choe, E.K., et al.: Understanding quantified-selfers' practices in collecting and exploring personal data. In: Proceedings of CHI, pp. 1143–1152 (2014)
7. Clark, H.H., Brennan, S.E.: Grounding in communication. Perspect. Soc. Shar. Cogn. **13**, 127–149 (1991)
8. Danis, C.M., et al.: Your place or mine? Visualization as a community component. In: Proceedings of CHI, pp. 275–284, NY, USA (2008)
9. Ferreira, D., et al.: Contextual experience sampling of mobile application micro-usage. In: Proceedings of MobileHCI, NY, USA (2014)
10. Festinger, L.: A theory of social comparison processes. Hum. Relations **7**(2), 117–140 (1954)
11. Froehlich, J., et al.: MyExperience: a system for in situ tracing and capturing of user feedback on mobile phones. In: Design, pp. 57–70. ACM (2007)
12. Grammel, L., et al.: How information visualization novices construct visualizations. IEEE Trans. Vis. Comput. Graph. **16**(6), 943–952 (2010)
13. Heer, J., Ham, F., Carpendale, S., Weaver, C., Isenberg, P.: Creation and collaboration: engaging new audiences for information visualization. In: Kerren, A., Stasko, J.T., Fekete, J.-D., North, C. (eds.) Information Visualization. LNCS, vol. 4950, pp. 92–133. Springer, Heidelberg (2008). doi: 10.1007/978-3-540-70956-5_5
14. Heer, J., et al.: Voyagers and voyeurs: supporting asynchronous collaborative visualization. Commun. ACM **52**(1), 87–97 (2009)
15. Heer, J., Agrawala, M.: Design considerations for collaborative visual analytics. In: Information Visualization, pp. 171–178 (2007)
16. Huang, D., et al.: Personal visualization and personal visual analytics. IEEE Trans. Vis. Comput. Graph. **21**(3), 420–433 (2015)
17. Irwin, A.: Citizen Science: A Study of People, Expertise and Sustainable Development (Environment and Society). Routledge, London (1995)
18. Isenberg, P., et al.: Collaborative visualization: definition, challenges, and research agenda. Inf. Vis. **10**(4), 310–326 (2011)
19. Kim, K., et al.: Hugin: a framework for awareness and coordination in mixed-presence collaborative information visualization. In: Proceedings of ITS, pp. 231–240. ACM (2010)
20. Li, I., et al.: A stage-based model of personal informatics systems. In: Proceedings of Conference on Human Factors in Computing Systems, pp. 557–566. ACM, New York (2010)
21. Ludwig, T., Hilbert, T., Pipek, V.: Collaborative visualization for supporting the analysis of mobile device data. In: Boulus-Rødje, N., Ellingsen, G., Bratteteig, T., Aanestad, M., Bjørn, P. (eds.) ECSCW 2015: Proceedings of the 14th European Conference on Computer Supported Cooperative Work, 19-23 September 2015, Oslo, Norway, pp. 305–316. Springer, Cham (2015). doi:10.1007/978-3-319-20499-4_17
22. Ludwig, T., et al.: Work or leisure? Designing a user-centered approach for researching activity "in the wild". Pers. Ubiquit. Comput. **20**(4), 487–515 (2016)
23. Mark, G., et al.: Do four eyes see better than two? Collaborative versus individual discovery in data visualization systems. In: Proceedings on Information Visualization, pp. 249–255 (2002)
24. Pousman, Z., et al.: Casual information visualization: depictions of data in everyday life. IEEE Trans. Vis. Comput. Graph. **13**(6), 1145–1152 (2007)
25. Russell, D.M., et al.: The cost structure of sensemaking. In: Proceedings of CHI, pp. 269–276 (1993)

26. Shneiderman, B.: The eyes have it: a task by data type taxonomy for information visualizations. In: Proceedings of IEEE Symposium on Visual Languages, pp. 336–343 (1996)

27. Viegas, F., et al.: Manyeyes: a site for visualization at internet scale. Trans. Vis. Comput. Graph. **13**(6), 1121–1128 (2007)

28. Willett, W., et al.: CommentSpace: structured support for collaborative visual analysis. In: Proceedings of CHI, pp. 3131–3140, Vancouver, BC, Canada (2011)

29. Wood, J., et al.: Collaborative visualization. In: Proceedings of IEEE Visualization, pp. 253–259 (1997)

30. Yi, J.S., et al.: Toward a deeper understanding of the role of interaction in information visualization. IEEE Trans. Vis. Comput. Graph. **13**(6), 1224–1231 (2007)

31. Yi, J.S., et al.: Understanding and characterizing insights: how do people gain insights using information visualization? In: Proceedings of 2008 Conference on BEyond Time and Errors Novel Evaluation Methods for Information Visualization, vol. 1 (2008)

# The Participatory Design Process of Tangibles for Children's Socio-Emotional Learning

Rosella Gennari[✉], Alessandra Melonio, and Mehdi Rizvi

Faculty of Computer Science, Free University of Bozen-Bolzano,
Piazza Domenicani 3, 39100 Bolzano, Italy
gennari@inf.unibz.it, {alessandra.melonio,srizvi}@unibz.it

**Abstract.** Education researchers voice the need of technology that can aid in the scaffolding of socio-emotional learning of primary-school children. In particular supporting norms for conversing with peers can enhance children's engagement in school activities, which can positively impact on their academic achievements in turn. This paper reports on a participatory design process of tangibles for socio-emotional learning, conducted with different children, education experts and designers over time. It focuses on a specific tangible, TurnTalk, for the scaffolding of turn-sharing in group conversations with 8–13 year old children. The paper discusses how the process was organised so that all participants had a voice in the development of the tangible, bringing in design possibilities, and how these were carried over in the next design solution. The paper focuses on the most recent version of TurnTalk and field study. It concludes by reflecting on the results of the study as well as on the benefits and limitations of the design process.

**Keywords:** Participatory design · Tangible design · Rapid design · Children · Families · Socio-emotional learning

## 1 Introduction

Schools or other learning environments offer plenty of interaction opportunities to children: when children have positive social interactions, they tend to show positive self esteem, emotion management, attitudes towards schools, school performances and quality of life in general, whereas negative social interactions are related to the reverse [1]. Education experts increasingly voice the need of *socio-emotional learning* (SEL) in learning contexts for promoting positive social interactions among children.

This paper focuses on the promotion of SEL in conversations of groups of children, from primary school onwards, e.g., [2]. SEL can then be supported by social interaction norms and roles for group conversations [3], which are common to different SEL methods such as cooperative learning or scripted collaboration [1]. A basic norm, trasversal to different methods, is the *sharing of turns* in conversations: (1) children take turns one at a time, so as not to overlap in conversation;

S. Barbosa et al. (Eds.): IS-EUD 2017, LNCS 10303, pp. 167–182, 2017.
DOI: 10.1007/978-3-319-58735-6_12

(2) turns are balanced among children. Turn-sharing has been assessed as one of the most salient features of conversations to teach primary school children but, being a rather abstract and complex norm, it does not occur automatically and takes educators' scaffolding [4].

Educators themselves need support for teaching this norm and similar others to different children. Interaction design solutions can play a vital role in their scaffolding; more generally, how to design interactive solutions that promote SEL is an emerging area of research in human computer interaction [5].

This paper leverages on the idea that tangibles are natural solutions for supporting social interaction norms for SEL (briefly, *SEL tangibles*), such as turn-sharing. The idea is not completely new: tangibles have been since long considered the most natural way of bringing children together, as they mirror the collaboration that occurs with physical objects and promote multi-sensory experiences, reinforcing learning [6].

The design of such SEL tangibles is anyhow complex as it should consider their usability, experience of children, besides how to support the scaffolding of social interaction norms for SEL. In view of that, it is not surprising that the existing body of work in interaction design for SEL is still in early stages, according to the literature review in [5]. According to Slovak and coauthors, most of the research so far is limited in scope, focusing on specific disadvantaged populations, especially people with autism; this choice crucially leaves out mainstream schools and family environments. Moreover, the majority of the existing work is not conducted in ecological settings, or over a long term.

Participatory design approaches could remedy the situation and help move forward research concerning SEL tangibles: participatory approaches, which recommend the deployment of exploratory tangible solutions in real-world contexts and explore their usage over time, could help design technologies informed by repeated usage practices and gain insights from the end-user's viewpoint [7].

This paper purports such a view on the design of SEL tangibles. It explores related work (Sect. 2) and motivates the importance of participatory design for SEL tangibles in learning contexts with end users, that is children, but also their educators and SEL experts (Subsect. 3.1). The design process crucially proceeds over time, through actions with field studies, and reflections about their results. The paper focuses on the design process of a specific tangible, TurnTalk, for the scaffolding of the norm of sharing turns in conversations (Subsect. 3.2). It shows its evolution and then it concentrates on the latest field study (Sect. 4), its results and reflections stirred by it (Sect. 5).

The conclusions of the paper reflect over the proposed participatory design process, by considering its advantages and limitations (Sect. 6).

## 2    Related Work

In spite of their potentials for educational contexts, so far little research has been devoted to tangibles for supporting SEL in conversations among children. Most work done is primarily focused on adults in work related meetings instead of children in educational contexts. Even so, key ideas behind those solutions can aid in the design of tangibles for children and hence they are overviewed briefly in the following. The literature review shows that end-user development approaches have potentials for the design of SEL tangibles. This sections ends by overviewing relevant end-user development studies or methods for tangibles.

## 2.1   Tangibles for Conversations

**Visual Modality.** Tabletop or screen-based solutions often implement complex visualisations concerning conversation progress for adults so as to influence their behaviours. For instance, *Second Messenger* experimented different visualisations to make adults reflect on participation [8]. Most interestingly for this paper, in [9], authors observe that tabletop collaboration can be enhanced if the tabletop surface is partitioned radially or in angular sections. This is implemented by [10] in the form of a tabletop display with different regions acting as personal, group and storage space. Another realisation of this idea is the *ArgueTable* [11], with an interactive tabletop display for two users with 4 storage spaces, 2 personal spaces and one common group or shared space.

Solutions such as *Collaborative Workspace* or *Reflect* also visualise conversation patterns and act essentially as mirroring devices: they aim to inform users about their conversation and leave it to group members (all adults) to reflect upon the feedback and see if anything needs to be changed in their conversation behaviours [12,13]. Similar design solutions based on times taken in conversations are [14,15]. Few of them implement and experiment complex technology in lab settings for visualising conversation progression, e.g., scene analysis via 4 Kinect cameras [16].

Instead, solutions such as *ACSS* [17] are on purpose designed as low-technology solutions, easy to deploy in real contexts, for enabling rapid design over time, as we do in this paper. By using cheap micro-controllers and LEDs, ACSS implements different types of conversation progression feedback for group meetings, which is then rapidly assessed and re-designed.

**Other Modalities.** Besides the visual modality, different modalities for feedback about conversation progression have also been investigated. *Grouper* is one such solution for coordinating team work [18]. Developed as a proof-of-concept wireless wearable, it is a group coordinator: through sensory cues, it alerts its users to pay attention to the leader or current speaker of the group. The device vibrates to indicate if a person is too far away from other users. *Interactive Benches* [19] also aim at promoting collaboration in conversations: benches communicate with each other and light up to encourage people to sit closer.

**For Learning Contexts.** Not many tabletop or screen-based solutions focus on children and learning contexts. Solutions for younger children usually enable them to exchange and manipulate objects through their surface, without addressing specifically conversation. For example, *Ely the Explorer* [20] is intended for school children for fostering collaboration through the exchange of physical objects. In this solution, each child uses physical objects such as dolls, rotary knobs and RFID cards to interact with the system, which interacts back with the children through animations. The animations are designed in such a manner to encourage discussion.

Technology-enhanced solutions for conversations among university students have been designed and evaluated in field studies [21]: university students used a shared surface or screen which is touch sensitive, while data, such as verbal communication and gestures, is recorded. Students collaborate through the shared work-space, but they are not given any live input or feedback for their collaboration, which is instead given to teachers.

Overall the literature review shows a number of tabletop surfaces for supporting conversations among adults, but it misses assessed design principles and patterns that designers can immediately apply to SEL tangibles for children. End-user development becomes then an ideal approach for finding together with users novel design possibilities for them and their contexts.

## 2.2   End-User Development of Tangibles

Design solutions for social contexts are subject to evolution, and meta-design has been proposed as the ideal design approach for them [22]. Meta-design and other end-user development approaches, such as [23], do not provide fixed solutions but a framework within which end users and designers alike can continuously contribute to the development. An interesting study of meta-design for social products (physical objects interacting with social medias) is reported in [24].

In spite of their potentials, so far meta-design end other end-user development approaches have been scarcely used for tangibles over long periods of time, in a continuous manner, as done for instance in [25, 26]. The former is a participatory design study over time with elderly people. The latter describes the CoDICE software that enables designers to trace the rationale of co-design decisions. The participatory design of this paper shares the same concern of enabling a continuous evolution of SEL tangibles over time.

The participatory approach also shares concerns with the Extreme Co-design approach of [27]. They have the same ambition to enable end-users to co-design tangibles for themselves in their environments. They have also differences.

In Extreme Co-design, prototype tangibles for families have undefined purposes, besides open-ended usages. In the participatory approach of this paper, instead, SEL tangibles are for children and educators, but their SEL purposes (specific social interaction norms for group conversations) are identified with experts of SEL, besides educators.

Moreover, Extreme Co-design promotes *extreme* rapidity, which was feasible in Bellucci and coauthors' work also because only one family was involved and for one month. Instead SEL tangibles or other novel solutions for learning take time to appropriate and different end users to gain insights representative of their normal usage in learning contexts. The features of the participatory approach, embraced in this paper, are described next.

# 3   Participatory Design of SEL Tangibles

A participatory design approach is adopted in this paper for developing SEL tangibles with end users and relevant stakeholders in learning contexts over time [28]. This section explains the reasons why this approach was chosen and how it was implemented in the case of TurnTalk over time.

## 3.1   Key Features and Their Rationale

**How.** The adopted participatory design of SEL tangibles is essentially an action-research process, spiralling through: (1) *planning* of SEL tangibles, (2) *acting in the field* for (3) *reflecting about their end-users' usage*, like in [25]. Tangible solutions for SEL, open-ended for unexpected usage and with few functionalities, are used along the process. Early solutions take the form of *probes* [29]; these should be cheap and easy to abandon solutions, or solutions that can rapidly evolve into interactive prototypes over time, introducing small changes. The rationale for this spiral process is that solutions like SEL tangibles, which are for social processes, can be studied best by introducing small changes into these processes and observing the effects of these changes in it over time [30].

**Who.** The participatory design of SEL tangibles moves through the continuous involvement of designers, SEL experts (e.g., SEL researchers) and especially end users—children and teachers, in our case. Designers are experts of interaction design and usability evaluation for children; they are present across all design stages (planning, action and reflection). The involvement of SEL experts is critical in the planning stage to identify the SEL purposes and benefits for end users; it is critical in the reflection stage to assess them. The involvement of end users is critical across almost all stages for addressing usability and user experience goals as well as disclosing unforeseen design possibilities for tangibles [31].

**Where.** Design of novel tangibles for everyday usages with end users requires designers to embed and assess the design of tangibles in ecological settings [32]. Also in this paper the participatory design of SEL tangibles is carried over with field studies in learning contexts, which enables end users' appropriation and allows designers to gather reliable usability and experience data [33].

The next part details the participatory design process for the TurnTalk SEL tangible, recapped in Fig. 1.

## 3.2   The Design Process of TurnTalk

As the Fig. 1 shows, TurnTalk was initially ideated with SEL experts and teachers for the scaffolding of turn-sharing in group conversations: each member should take a turn, so that taken turns are balanced across group members; there should be no conversation overlaps, that is, members should speak one at a time [4]. TurnTalk was then realised as a cultural probe, which was re-designed first into a technology probe and then into an interactive prototype for children's usage. Each of them is discussed next.

| Solution | Cultural Probe | | | Technology Probe | | | Interactive Prototype | | |
|---|---|---|---|---|---|---|---|---|---|
| Design stage | Planning | Action | Reflection | Planning | Action | Reflection | Planning | Action | Reflection |
| Usage sessions | contextual inquiries | pilot    field | | contextual inquiries | pilot    field | | contextual inquiries | pilot    field | |
| Children | No | Yes | Yes | No | Yes | Yes | No | Yes | Yes |
| Teachers | Yes | Yes | Yes | Yes | Yes | Yes | Yes | No | No |
| SEL experts | Yes | No | Yes | Yes | Yes | Yes | Yes | No | Yes |
| Technology components | | No | | Yes: Arduino; NFC cards | | | Yes: Arduino; LED bars; LED pins; cards | | |
| Play-card | | No | | | Yes | | | Yes | |
| Progression feedback | | No | | | No | | | Yes | |

**Fig. 1.** The participatory design process for TurnTalk, spiralling through planning, actions in the field, reflections.

**Cultural Probe.** Cultural probes are simple artefacts (e.g., post-it notes, diaries) with the social science goal of collecting information about contexts and end-users, and the design goal of inspiring users and designers to think of new design possibilities. The cultural probe incarnation of TurnTalk was a scepter [34], one per group of children, inspired by talking sticks used in cooperative learning classes, e.g., [35]. See the left-most column in Fig. 1.

The scepter was a no-technology solution for making tangible the norm of sharing turns in speaking, and to enable designers to explore how the probe would stir the conversation turns. It was adopted in a repeated-measure field study by 35 children, aged 8–10 year old, in 5 conversation sessions in primary schools, each half an hour long. This action (the field study) stirred reflections. The main *reflections* concerning the probe (briefly, RC) are listed as follows.

According to observations of children's interventions and behaviours, the probe was generally used for sharing conversation turns. Scepters were also used in manners that were indeed unexpected by designers but also dysfunctional with respect to the school activity (RC1).

Most importantly, the scepter was not sufficiently prominent: older children in particular, aged 9 to 10 year old, often forgot about it (RC2). Such observations were backed up by children's preferences, which were collected via a survey; children rarely selected the probe as preferred, and some children expressed the desire to have "something for themselves" to take their turns (RC3).

Finally, the observation of taken-turns in groups (who took a turn and how often) was exceedingly time-consuming for designers or teachers and not sufficiently reliable. Teachers asked whether the computation of turns in a group could be tracked by the probe itself (RC4). Such reflections made designers conceive a different design solution for Turn-Talk, enhanced with technology.

**Technology Probe.** Technology probes evolve from cultural probes: they add the user experience goal of field-testing a design solution, and use technology in order to log relevant data for opening up new design possibilities. The cultural probe of TurnTak became a technology probe. It was realised as a tabletop pentagon-shaped box, endowed with technology. See the central column in Fig. 1.

In view of RC1, it was made of wood so that children could not easily shuffle it around. In view of RC2, it was placed at the centre of the table around which group members gathered. In view of RC3, group members were given cards to play and place in a dedicated area of the box in order to share their turns in conversations, so that only one card per turn could be played. In view of RC4, technology took the form of micro-controllers and sensors for logging taken turns for usage analyses. The probe was used in a repeated-measure field study by 42 children, aged 9–10 year old, in 5 conversation sessions in primary schools, each half an hour long. Children grow and change school, hence new children were involved but they were explained where the probe was coming from. This action (the field study) stirred novel reflections. The main reflections concerning the technology probe (RT) are listed as follows.

The probe was well received and the play-card mechanism was generally understood. Having a single area in the box for group members' cards raised issues: some children placed cards in the box area facing them and not in the dedicated area. Interestingly, a group placed cards one on top of the other to reserve turns, a design possibility that was not implemented in the probe (RT1).

Observations and log analysis concerning the repeated usage of the probe revealed that turn-sharing tended to improve over time; these specific results were published in [36], and hence they are not discussed in this paper.

Observations, log analysis and interviews concerning the repeated usage of the probe also stirred reflections concerning further design possibilities. Teachers were given the log analysis concerning turns taken in conversation sessions, and reflected on the relevance of the information for children. They and designers agreed that the probe could be turned into a tool for supporting groups' self reflections about turn-sharing. Observation results, backed up by log analysis, also purported the need of avoiding that over-participating members treated TurnTalk as means for dominating conversations. Information concerning over-participation was also judged important for children's reflection (RT2).

In light of such reflections, a novel TurnTalk design was planned and advanced in [37]. This was revised in view of expert reviews, a novel literature review, partly reported in Sect. 2, and pilot studies with children as well as adults. The result is explained next.

**Interactive Prototype.** The current TurnTalk is a tabletop pentagon-shaped device, like the technology probe described above. See the right-most column in

Fig. 1. Technology takes again the form of micro-controllers, sensors and actuators, all hidden in the device. It also implements new features: a slightly refined play-card mechanism, designed in light of the RT1 reflection; a completely novel conversation progression feedback, designed in light of RT2. They are explained separately as follows, and illustrated in Fig. 2.

**Fig. 2.** The TurnTalk interactive prototype: play-card mechanism (left); progression feedback concerning turns taken by group members and their balance (right). (Color figure online)

*Play-Card Mechanism for RT1.* Like the technology probe, the current TurnTalk device has a play-card per group member, which identifies him or her. See the left side of Fig. 2. The play-card mechanism is however slightly changed with respect to the technology probe version. The device has a dedicated slot for the card of each group member, indicated with a number. LED pins were introduced to signal the conversation source even more and to enable turn reservations: a LED pin flashes green for signalling who is speaking, and yellow for signalling who has reserved the next turn.

*Progression Feedback for RT2.* A novel progression feedback was introduced in TurnTalk. See the right-side of Fig. 2.

According to the literature [9], a division in sectors of a tabletop surface is beneficial for promoting positive social interactions. Accordingly, the surface of TurnTalk is divided into triangular slices, one per child. The slice of the surface for a child is lighted up with hidden LED bars in a manner proportional to the turns taken by the child, thereby delivering a simple visual progression feedback on turns taken and their balance in the group: a group conversation is balanced if approximately the same number of LED bars lights up for all group members. The right more photo in Fig. 2 shows unbalance.

The progression feedback of the current TurnTalk also tracks over-participation and under-participation data; they are defined as outliers, computed using upper and lower fences with quartiles, respectively. In line with literature review, over-participants tend to moderate their participation in conversation once aware of over-participating; thus if a member has been over-participating then his or her LED-bar slice flashes to signal it. Under-participation is not highlighted as it may even further inhibit under-participants from interacting in conversation, in line with studies with adults, e.g., [8].

The delivery of the progression feedback can be co-adapted according to teachers' and children's needs. For instance, the progression feedback can be given in real-time during a conversation, at specific moments chosen by the teacher, or between conversation sessions.

## 4   The Field Study

A field study was organised for primary and middle school children in a learning context. Groups were composed of children from the same schools. The study used a mixed-method approach so as to gather different data concerning children's usage of the interactive TurnTalk prototype, described in Sect. 3.2. This section elaborates on the research questions of the study and the related data collection instruments. Then it describes the participants and outlines the protocol of the group conversation for children, specifying the role of the designers.

### 4.1   Questions and Data Collection

The field-study questions concerning the interaction of children with TurnTalk were related to its usability, children's experience with it and usage.

*Usability Questions.* Usability questions were mainly related to the design changes of TurnTalk, that is, the novelties in the play-card mechanism and the progression feedback. Questions for designers' attention were as follows: Would children be able to use the play-card mechanism, after an initial training? Would the progression feedback be understandable for children?

*Experience and Usage Questions.* According to [6], children are more likely to value the quality of the experience they have using a technology than adults do. Given that and the fact that the major usability issues were resolved with the TurnTalk technology probe, the field study questions concentrated on children's experience as well as unexpected usages of TurnTalk: Is TurnTalk engaging? Will children use it differently than expected and how?

*Data Collection.* Data were collected through logs and mainly videos. A camera was positioned so as to record all children and the TurnTalk prototype as well. Videos were then analysed and transcribed by two designers, in relation to the usability questions and children's unexpected usages of TurnTalk. The designers worked independently and then compared their transcriptions. Children were also interviewed for gathering their ideas concerning further design possibilities.

Data concerning children's engagement were mainly collected via the Again-and-Again survey [38]. It asks children whether they "would do it again", using a 3-Likert scale with answers: yes, maybe, no. Additionally, parents can act as proxies for their children; parents were also asked about what children reported of their experience with TurnTalk with unstructured interviews.

## 4.2  Participants

The study was conducted with 9 children, 8–13 year old, and 2 designers; one was acting as moderator, for interacting with children, the other as observer, taking notes, and as technical-problem solver. Only one of the children had participated in the evolution of TurnTalk, whereas the others were explained its history, e.g., through photos. Children were organised into 3 groups of 3 members. The first group had 2 females and 1 male, all aged 13 year old; the second group had 2 females, aged 9 year old, and 1 male, aged 7 year old; the third group had 3 males, all aged 9 year old. All children participated on a voluntary basis, and their parents authorised their participation.

## 4.3  Group Conversation Protocol

The group conversation was about a science topic and it was adapted from [39], a protocol for conversations among primary school children, which encourages discussion to reveal differences in opinions. Groups are provided with three cups, one made of thick plastic, one made of thin plastic and one made of glass. They have to discuss about features of the cups and choose the cup for their group party. The conversation is organised as follows.

*Welcome.* Initially, participants are invited to sit. The designer, acting as moderator, introduces the study goal ("you can help us to shape TurnTalk") and the goal of the group conversation. The introduction takes no longer than 5 min.

*Training.* Then the training session starts for training participants to the play-card mechanism of TurnTalk for about 5 min. At the start of the training, the moderator asks children to present themselves using the TurnTalk play-card mechanism. Then the moderator introduces a topic and children carry on the conversation with TurnTalk.

*Conversation Sessions.* The first and second session require conversations with TurnTalk, driven by topics proposed by the moderator. The first conversation session takes c. 15–20 min. The second conversation session takes c. 5–10 min. At the end of both sessions, TurnTalk shows the progression feedback concerning the group conversation (in terms of turns taken and their balance) and the moderator invites children to reflect on it and elaborate their ideas.

## 5  Study Results and Reflections

Results of the study are reported as follows in relation to its guiding questions.

## 5.1   Results for TurnTalk

*Usability of the Play-Card Mechanism.* TurnTalk logs allowed designers to track each child's conversation *turn* taken with his or her TurnTalk card, if superior to 1 s in duration. Specifically, TurnTalk tracked its *start* and its *conclusion*, and also the time duration of a turn, in relation to the card usage. The minimum time duration was calibrated through pilot studies and set to 1 s, in line with [8], because shorter feedback (e.g., "yes" or "no") is not considered a contribution to conversations [40].

Two designers independently analysed all videos and marked: when a child started a turn, and if the child used or not the card; when the child concluded it, and if the child removed or not the card; relevant usability issues. Then the designers compared their transcriptions and resolved differences through discussions of video snippets.

Comparison of turns tracked in videos and turns tracked with TurnTalk was used to identify situations in which children had a conversation turn without using TurnTalk, or TurnTalk did not register it. The latter never happened during the two conversation sessions. Situations when a child forgot to use their cards for their turn occurred during training only; then the moderator reminded the child to do so. Such results seem to purport the usability of the overall play-card mechanism. However designers also tracked that at times children forgot to remove their cards to conclude their turn; when this happened, other group members reminded them to do so. Designers also noted that children forgot to remove their cards when they were busy with another task (e.g., listening to the moderator) and their cards were out of their line of sight.

*Understandability of the Progression Feedback.* The progression feedback was delivered at the end of the conversation sessions only. Its understandability was assessed through video analysis by the two designers. The two designers considered, separately and then together, how children reacted to the moderator's questions concerning the feedback. Children's answers denoted an intuitive understanding of the feedback. For instance, in Group 2, the moderator said: "the green (LED) bars tell how often each of you took a turn with cards; how did the conversation go?". All children answered: "well". When the moderator further probed "why", the youngest child answered: "it's because all bars are switched on and green". As situations with outliers for under or over-participation never occurred, the related design features could not be assessed in the field study.

*Experience and Usages of TurnTalk.* All children answered in the positive ("yes") to the Again-and-Again survey concerning their engagement with TurnTalk (100%). Survey results are backed up and confirmed by feedback from children's parents. All children voluntarily explained their parents what they had done with TurnTalk in details. All younger children (6 out of 9) asked their parents to ask designers whether it was possible to "do it again".

The two designers also analysed videos and tracked children's acts that denoted unexpected usages or emotional reactions to TurnTalk that pointed to new design possibilities. After working separately, they compared their transcriptions. The major results are reported as follows.

The progression feedback for the group conversation was generally perceived with curiosity or enjoyment. For instance, in Group 3, a child continued exploring the tabletop surface moving around it; another one moved it closer to himself for inspecting the feedback concerning the progression in conversation. However, in Group 2, a child was disappointed with the feedback for the progression in conversation, according to which she had taken less turns; her lips curled downwards and she inspected the feedback more closely as expecting something else to happen. The video analysis shows that her interventions were all task related and long, which is not reflected in the feedback, which is only concerned with the number of turns taken.

The designer observing children had noticed it during the study and informed the moderator. Through interviews, the moderator reflected with children on the idea of introducing a progression feedback that considers also turn times.

During the interviews, another child pointed out that he would like to see his number of turns displayed during the entire conversation, so as to better reflect on the number of turns of group members and balance them. The moderator reasoned with the child about the potential distraction effect of such feedback, and the child himself suggested that the feedback should be displayed only when children take new turns, and then it could fade away.

## 5.2    Reflections on TurnTalk

The play-card mechanism was used as intended and raised few usability issues, mainly related to children forgetting to remove cards when out of sight. It is thus speculated that the play-card mechanism should remain a tangible visual signal for turn sharing but it should be somehow improved, embodied and perceived as part of the child's body so as to minimise errors in forgetting to remove cards.

Understandability was also investigated through video analysis of questions-answers concerning the progression feedback for the group conversation. According to the available data, the visual metaphor of the progression feedback seem to be understandable for 8–13 children, e.g., they easily grasped that the progression feedback shows approximately the number of taken turns, and balance means that all children have similar numbers of LED bars on.

Engagement and novel design possibilities were carefully explored. Engagement, investigated through the Again-and-Again survey and parents' feedback, was in general high. Most critical was the emotional reaction of a child who interacted for conversation aims and for longer turns, but the feedback did not render such information and did not "make her justice". On the one hand, the progression feedback of TurnTalk was designed on purpose with SEL experts for the scaffolding of interacting and taking more turns. On the other hand, it can be improved by considering time-related data in conversation turns and displaying it gradually to children, in line with [8,12]. Children's reflection on turn balance could be displayed on request by children, as suggested by a child. Some SEL experts are however contrary to it as it may be a distraction factor.

The novel design features are currently under assessment with a SEL expert for future usages in a school class with 9–10 year old children.

# 6   Conclusions and Reflections for Future Work

This paper posits that interactive tangible objects can aid in the scaffolding of abstract conversation norms for children's SEL. The paper concentrated on a tangible, TurnTalk, for the scaffolding of turn-sharing in conversations in groups with 3–5 children, aged 8–13 year old.

The paper motivated and presented the participatory approach to the design of the SEL tangible. It shows how the participatory design process started with cultural and then technology probes, which led to the recent TurnTalk version: a tangible interactive tabletop solution for the scaffolding of turn-sharing. The participatory design process was carried on with different end-users and other stakeholders over time, in a spiral fashion, through planning, actions in the field and reflections over their results. Actions progressively advanced design features in small chunks, as suggested in [30].

The paper presents the most recent field study in which children used and appropriated TurnTalk. The study allowed designers to collect multiple data concerning the usability of TurnTalk, the user experience and unexpected usages that it promoted, besides information concerning the design process itself. The former data were analysed, and reflected upon in relation to TurnTalk and tangibles for SEL. The paper concludes by reflecting on the design process itself, how it facilitated the design of SEL tangibles and its limitations.

**Advantages.** In line with the advocated participatory process, the designed solutions were always economic and rapid to design. In this manner, they turned out to be easy to abandon in case of failure, and to replicate for school classes.

In each field study, the usability of design solutions was assessed together with children's experience and unexpected usages. The presence of designers, experienced of usability and interaction design for children, facilitated the reflections over solutions, and so did the possibility to log data and videos.

Another essential ingredient of the process was the cross-disciplinary and cross-generational amalgama of participants. SEL experts brought their own experience of SEL. Children brought their own unique perspective into the process and envisioned design possibilites that adults did not (dare) think of.

**Limitations.** Continuing participatory design over time was an essential feature of the work presented in this paper. However, children grow, have a number of school committments and hence the same children could not participate in studies over time. Even though the consistent commitment of the same children over time was not always possible, the participatory design process implemented several strategies for supporting the experience of continuity. For instance, designers explained the evolution of the tangibles, sharing memories (e.g., photos, design parts of older TurnTalk versions) for showing children that other children had contributed to TurnTalk, as done in [25].

Moreover, tangibles for SEL have the ambitious goal of being SEL devices and engaging children into different usages. Merging such requirements into the participatory design process proved challenging at points. For instance, designers tracked different unexpected usages of the technology probe for TurnTalk but they were dysfunctional to SEL scaffolding. This is backed up by similar findings in the participatory design literature of educational games, e.g., [41]. Teaming with end-users and SEL experts were key factors for designing solutions that were engaging for children and yet promoting SEL.

**Acknowledgements.** We thank parents and classes, the SEL and product design experts involved in the study, the Makerspace of UniBZ for their assistance. The work reported in this paper was supported through the GOST grant.

# References

1. Durlak, J.A., Weissberg, R.P., Dymnicki, A.B., Taylor, R.D., Schellinger, K.B.: The impact of enhancing student's social and emotional learning: a meta-analysis of school-based universal interventions. Child Dev. **82**(1), 405–432 (2011)
2. Cefai, C., Ferrario, E., Cavioni, V., Carter, A., Grech, T.: Circle time for social and emotional learning in primary school. Pastoral Care Educ. **32**(2), 116–130 (2014)
3. Forsyth, D.R.: Group Dynamics. Wadsworth Cengage Learning, Belmont (2014)
4. Wiemann, J.M., Knapp, M.L.: Turn-taking in conversations. J. Commun. **25**(2), 75–92 (1975)
5. Slovák, P., Fitzpatrick, G.: Teaching and developing social and emotional skills with technology. ACM Trans. Comput.-Hum. Interact. **22**(4), 19:1–19:34 (2015)
6. Hourcade, J.P.: Child-Computer Interaction (2015)
7. Botero, A., Kommonen, K., Marttila, S.: Design from the everyday: continuously evolving, embedded exploratory prototypes. In: Proceeding of DIS 2010, pp. 282–291. ACM (2011)
8. DiMicco, J.M., Hollenbach, K.J., Pandolfo, A., Bender, W.: The impact of increased awareness while face-to-face. Hum.-Comput. Interact. **22**(1), 47–96 (2007)
9. Scott, S.D.: Territory-based interaction techniques for tabletop collaboration. In: Proceeding of UIST 2003 Conference Companion (2003)
10. Habelski, S.: Realisation of territory-based interaction techniques for supporting tabletop collaboration. Internship Thesis (2004)
11. Streng, S., Stegmann, K., Wagner, C., Böhm, S., Hussmann, H., Fischer, F.: Supporting argumentative knowledge construction in face-to-face settings: from Arguetable to Arguewall. In: Proceeding of the Conference on Computer-Supported Collaborative Learning (2011)
12. Leonardi, C., Pianesi, F., Tomasini, D., Zancanaro, M.: The collaborative workspace: a co-located tabletop device to support meetings. In: Waibel, A., Stiefelhagen, R. (eds.) Computers in the Human Interaction Loop, pp. 187–205. Springer, London (2009)
13. Bachour, K., Kaplan, F., Dillenbourg, P.: An interactive table for supporting participation balance in face-to-face collaborative learning. IEEE Trans. Learn. Technol. **3**(3), 203–213 (2010)

14. Waibel, A., Stiefelhagen, R., Carlson, R., Casas, J., Kleindienst, J., Lamel, L., Lanz, O., Mostefa, D., Omologo, M., Pianesi, F., Polymenakos, L., Potamianos, G., Soldatos, J., Sutschet, G., Terken, J.: Computers in the human interaction loop. In: Nakashima, H., Aghajan, H., Augusto, J.C. (eds.) Handbook of Ambient Intelligence and Smart Environments, pp. 1071–1116. Springer, New York (2010)
15. Terken, J., Sturm, J.: Multimodal support for social dynamics in co-located meetings. Pers. Ubiquit. Comput. **14**(8), 703–714 (2010)
16. Schiavo, G., Cappelletti, A., Mencarini, E., Stock, O., Zancanaro, M.: Overt or subtle? Supporting group conversations with automatically targeted directives. In: Proceeding of the 19th International Conference on Intelligent User Interfaces, IUI 2014, pp. 225–234. ACM, New York (2014)
17. Hirai, Y., Kaneko, K.: Ambient conversation support in small face-to-face group meetings. In: Proceeding of the Sixth International Symposium on Information and Communication Technology, SoICT 2015, pp. 239–246. ACM, New York (2015)
18. Shaw, F.W., Klavins, E.: Grouper: a proof-of-concept wearable wireless group coordinator. In: Proceeding of the 12th ACM International Conference Adjunct Papers on Ubiquitous Computing, pp. 379–380. ACM (2010)
19. Remin, J.S., Ignac, M., Kjaergard, S.: Interactive benches (2016). http://ciid.dk/education/portfolio/py/courses/physical-computing/projects/interactive-benches/
20. Africano, D., Berg, S., Lindbergh, K., Lundholm, P., Nilbrink, F., Persson, A.: Designing tangible interfaces for children's collaboration. In: CHI 2004 Extended Abstracts on Human Factors in Computing Systems, CHI EA 2004, pp. 853–868. ACM, New York (2004)
21. Martinez Maldonado, R., Kay, J., Yacef, K., Schwendimann, B.: An interactive teacher's dashboard for monitoring groups in a multi-tabletop learning environment. In: Cerri, S.A., Clancey, W.J., Papadourakis, G., Panourgia, K. (eds.) ITS 2012. LNCS, vol. 7315, pp. 482–492. Springer, Heidelberg (2012). doi:10.1007/978-3-642-30950-2_62
22. Fischer, G., Herrmann, T.: Meta-design: transforming and enriching the design and use of socio-technical systems. In: Wulf, V., Schmidt, K., Randall, D. (eds.) Designing Socially Embedded Technologies in the Real-World. CSCW, pp. 79–109. Springer, London (2015). doi:10.1007/978-1-4471-6720-4_6
23. Costabile, M.F., Fogli, D., Mussio, P., Piccinno, A.: Visual interactive systems for end-user development: a model-based design methodology. IEEE Trans. Syst. Man Cybern. Part A Syst. Hum. **37**(6), 1029–1046 (2007)
24. Fogli, D., Giaccardi, E., Acerbis, A., Filisetti, F.: Physical prototyping of social products through end-user development. In: Díaz, P., Pipek, V., Ardito, C., Jensen, C., Aedo, I., Boden, A. (eds.) IS-EUD 2015. LNCS, vol. 9083, pp. 217–222. Springer, Cham (2015). doi:10.1007/978-3-319-18425-8_19
25. Joshi, S.G., Bratteteig, T.: Designing for prolonged mastery. On involving old people in participatory design. Scand. J. Inf. Syst. **28**(1), 3–36 (2016)
26. Díaz, P., Aedo, I., Vaart, M.: Engineering the creative co-design of augmented digital experiences with cultural heritage. In: Díaz, P., Pipek, V., Ardito, C., Jensen, C., Aedo, I., Boden, A. (eds.) IS-EUD 2015. LNCS, vol. 9083, pp. 42–57. Springer, Cham (2015). doi:10.1007/978-3-319-18425-8_4
27. Bellucci, A., Jacucci, G., Kotkavuori, V., Serim, B., Ahmed, I., Ylirisku, S.: Extreme co-design: prototyping with and by the user for appropriation of web-connected tags. In: Díaz, P., Pipek, V., Ardito, C., Jensen, C., Aedo, I., Boden, A. (eds.) IS-EUD 2015. LNCS, vol. 9083, pp. 109–124. Springer, Cham (2015). doi:10.1007/978-3-319-18425-8_8

28. Halskov, K., Hansen, N.B.: The diversity of participatory design research practice at PDC 2002–2012. Int. J. Hum. Comput. Stud. **74**, 81–92 (2015)
29. Hutchinson, H., Mackay, W., Westerlund, B., Bederson, B.B., Druin, A., Plaisant, C., Beaudouin-Lafon, M., Conversy, S., Evans, H., Hansen, H., Roussel, N., Eiderbäck, B.: Technology probes: inspiring design for and with families. In: Proc. of the SIGCHI Conference on Human Factors in Computing Systems, CHI 2003, pp. 17–24. ACM, New York (2003)
30. Baskerville, R.L.: Investigating information systems with action research. Commun. AIS **2**(3es), Article No. 4 (1999)
31. Botero, A., Kommonen, K., Marttila, S.: Expanding design space: design-in-use activities and strategies. In: Proceeding of DRS 2010 (2011)
32. Binder, T., De Michelis, G., Ehn, P., Jacucci, G., Linde, P., Wagner, I.: Design Things. MIT Press, Cambridge (2011)
33. Tetteroo, D., Markopoulos, P.: A review of research methods in end user development. In: Díaz, P., Pipek, V., Ardito, C., Jensen, C., Aedo, I., Boden, A. (eds.) IS-EUD 2015. LNCS, vol. 9083, pp. 58–75. Springer, Cham (2015). doi:10.1007/978-3-319-18425-8_5
34. Dodero, G., Gennari, R., Melonio, A., Torello, S.: "There Is No Rose Without A Thorn": an assessment of a game design experience for children. In: Proceeding of 11th Biannual Conference on Italian SIGCHI Chapter, CHItaly 2015. ACM, New York (2015). doi:10.1145/2808435.2808436
35. Ransdell, M.: Using cooperative learning in elementary science classrooms. Prof. Educ. **26**(1), 23–35 (2003)
36. Gennari, R., Melonio, A., Torello, S.: Gamified probes for cooperative learning: a case study. In: Multimedia Tools and Applications (2016)
37. Melonio, A., Rizvi, M.: The design of turntalk for the scaffolding of balanced conversations in groups of children. In: Wu, T.T., Gennari, R., Huang, Y.M., Xie, H., Cao, Y. (eds.) SETE 2016. LNCS, vol. 10108, pp. 278–287. Springer, Cham (2017). doi:10.1007/978-3-319-52836-6_28
38. Read, J.C., MacFarlane, S.: Using the fun toolkit and other survey methods to gather opinions in child computer interaction. In: Proceeding of the 2006 Conference on Interaction Design and Children, IDC 2006, pp. 81–88. ACM, New York (2006)
39. Simon, S., Maloney, J.: Activities for promoting small-group discussion and argumentation. Sch. Sci. Rev. **88**(324), 49–58 (2007)
40. Bales, R.: Interaction Process Analysis: A Method for the Study of Small Groups. Addison-Wesley, Cambridge (1950)
41. Khaled, R., Vasalou, A.: Bridging serious games and participatory design. Int. J. Child-Comp. Interact. **2**(2), 93–100 (2014)

# Potential Financial Payoffs to End-User Developers

Christopher Scaffidi[✉]

Oregon State University, Corvallis, OR, USA
cscaffid@eecs.oregonstate.edu

**Abstract.** What are the benefits of end-user development (EUD) to the average worker? This paper provides one quantitative answer to this question by using historical data to analyze the relationship between worker earnings and two forms of EUD. The analysis indicates that American workers who used both spreadsheets/databases, and who also each did programming, earned on the order of 10% more than peers who did neither of these activities.

**Keywords:** End-user development · Earnings · Workers

## 1 Introduction

End-user development (EUD) takes many forms such as spreadsheet use [4], end-user programming [12], co-design [6], participatory and/or pair programming [5], and tailoring [9]. Yet not all computer users engage in EUD. For example, one study of therapists found they rarely chose to engage in EUD, and that the main incentives that would prompt them to begin doing more EUD were additional *financial compensation, additional free time, and intellectual ownership of the result* [8]. We should therefore not be surprised if workers want *personal benefits* from doing EUD. They may be interested, for example, in whether EUD will advance their earnings, their career, or their job satisfaction.

Driven by these concerns, this paper uses historical worker data from the United States government to statistically analyze the relationship between earnings and two forms of EUD, namely spreadsheet/database use and programming on the job. It goes beyond two prior studies that looked at this same issue by controlling for employment and demographic variables not considered in earlier analyses.

## 2 Related Work

Formal empirical research on the relationship between earnings and programming, or other aspects of software development, is limited. One source of information is the United States Bureau of Labor and Statistics (BLS), which projected that American employment in software publishing would grow at an annualized rate of 3.1% between 2010–2020 to 351,600 [7]. Other sources of information include annual industry surveys of software engineers, which tabulate salary versus programming languages and job

© Springer International Publishing AG 2017
S. Barbosa et al. (Eds.): IS-EUD 2017, LNCS 10303, pp. 183–190, 2017.
DOI: 10.1007/978-3-319-58735-6_13

descriptions. Yet such workfocuses on the experiences of professional software engineers, offering limited insight into the benefits of EUD.

Perhaps the first research to investigate the relationship between earnings and EUD was a study that analyzed job posts across a broad range of occupations [2]. It found that a subset of job posts mentioned, on average, a 13% higher salary to applicants if they could use office productivity software, such as Excel. A limitation of the study was that it conflated use of Excel with use of other office productivity software(Word, Outlook, PowerPoint, SAP, and Oracle) that lack the pedigree of spreadsheets as EUD tools. Moreover, the study only looked at job posts for occupations that offered an average of at least $15 per hour and that usually did not require a bachelor's degree. Thus, though this study was a useful first step, it is difficult to generalize from the results to the full range of jobs that workers occupy.

The only other study to quantitatively examine the relationship between EUD and career impacts was an analysis of how earnings varied as a function of whether workers used spreadsheets or databases and/or whether they did programming at work [11]. This research statistically analyzed survey data collected from workers by the BLS in October 2003. The study revealed that workers who used spreadsheets or databases, and each of whom also did programming, reported 14% higher earnings than workers who reported neither of these behaviors at work. A key limitation of that study was it did not control for worker characteristics other than occupation. For example, it did not control for educational background. It is possible well-educated workers happened to be heavy tool users (due to education) and also well-paid (due to education), so the tool use might not have caused the higher earnings; in this case, the correlation between tool use and earnings could have been spurious. The current study addresses this limitation by repeating the analysis in ways that further test validity.

## 3   Study Design

As in the prior study [11], the current study used data from the BLS Current Population Survey (CPS) [1], which is one of the longest-running, nationally-representative, and widely-cited surveys on the American population. It includes questions concerning demographics, employment and earnings. In addition, at several points up until 2003, this monthly survey incorporated questions concerning whether and how workers used computers on the job. These data make it possible to assess the relationship between earnings and forms of EUD at work, while controlling for employment and demographic characteristics.

### 3.1   Data Acquisition

The study used the CPS datasets from August 2001 and October 2003, which were the last two occasions that the survey included questions regarding computer use at work. Over a dozen variables were extracted and/or constructed for the study. The relevant questions from the August 2001 and October 2003 instances differed only slightly between surveys.

**Table 1.** Variables used; refer to [1] for details on source CPS variables.

| Employment data | |
|---|---|
| Earnings | Per-week earnings (capped at $2884.61 in the CPS dataset) |
| Employment status | Boolean indicating if the worker was employed and at work in the month prior to the study, or if the worker was employed but absent from the job |
| Multiple jobs | Boolean indicating if the subject had >1 job; variables below refer to the "main" job |
| Occupation | A four-digit code based on the worker's job |
| Class of work | 8-category, indicating classifications of employment in government, non-profits, self-run, and for-profit |
| Employer type | 4-category plus "unknown," indicating types of manufacturing, wholesale, retail, other employers |
| **Demographic data** | |
| Age | In years, capped at 90 |
| Education | 5-category code |
| Marital status | 6-category code |
| Metro | Indicating if subject lived in metropolitan or non-metropolitan area |
| Race | For 2001 data, 4-category value; for 2003 data, 21-category value |
| Sex | From the Boolean CPS variable PESEX (within which the US government only offered male/female as options, with no distinction between sex and gender) |
| **Computer-use data** | |
| Used Computer | Boolean indicating if the subject used a computer at work |
| Used Spreadsheets or Databases | Boolean indicating if the subject used a computer at work to create spreadsheets or databases |
| Wrote Programs | Boolean indicating if the subject used a computer at work for programming |
| Number of EUD behaviors (NDEV) | 0 if the subject used neither spreadsheets/databases nor did programming, 2 if the subject did both, and 1 otherwise |

*Filtering data*: Records were filtered to include only those of people who had positive earnings and who used a computer at work, yielding 8345 records for the 2001 dataset and 8468 for the 2003. Examining the Employment Status variable confirmed these filters retained only workers who were employed, although some of them were on vacation or otherwise absent from their jobs in the month covered by the survey.

*Control variables*: Eleven control variables were computed from the data, covering a wide range of employment and demographic characteristics (Table 1). Controlling for these variables in the analyses below made it possible to rule out these variables as the source of any correlation between earnings and EUD.

*Constructing EUD variables*: The prior study using this same 2003 CPS dataset indicated that spreadsheet/database usage and programming were strongly related to one another, rather than independent variables [11]. That study revealed that 34% of workers used neither spreadsheets/databases nor did programming, 51% used spreadsheets/databases but did not program, and 13% did both. In total, this three-level classification accounted for 98% of all workers; in other words, only 2% wrote programs but did not use spreadsheets/databases, and use of a computer by a worker for programming implied (in almost every case) that he or she also used spreadsheets/databases.

Therefore, these variables for use of spreadsheets/databases and use of programming tools were combined for the current study into a single variable indicating the number of EUD behaviors (NDEV), equaling 0, 1, or 2 depending on whether the subject indicated neither, one, or both of these behaviors at work. When NDEV = 1, this almost always meant (96% of the time) that the worker used spreadsheets or databases but did not do programming. (Due to its construction from Booleans, NDEV was treated as a categorical variable in analyses below.)

*Limitations*: The NDEV variable, above, did not capture all possible forms of EUD, nor was the variable constructed with the intent of characterizing all possible forms of EUD. It merely flagged *people who used spreadsheets/databases at work and/or who did programming.* Using spreadsheets/databases at work and/or doing programming represent a limited range of EUD behaviors. Future work can expand beyond this analysis (see Sect. 5).

### 3.2 Analytical Methods

*Analysis 1*: The first analysis estimated how workers' earnings varied depending on NDEV. Using the 2003 dataset, a linear regression was performed of Earnings versus the 11 control variables. This yielded a model for how Earnings varied depending on the workers' employment and demographic variables alone. This model was then used to generate a fitted Earnings estimate, which was subtracted from the actual Earnings, thereby extracting as much variance in Earnings as possible based on the control variables. The remaining residual was regressed against NDEV to determine the difference in Earnings attributable to NDEV after having corrected for the employment and demographic variables.

*Analysis 2*: In recognition of the fact that Earnings were log-normally distributed (rather than normally distributed), which can affect the validity of p values generated by a simple linear regression, a second analysis was performed. This analysis used the 2003 dataset to perform a linear regression of log (Earnings) against all 11 control variables and NDEV, thereby testing the relationship versus NDEV while simultaneously controlling for employment and demographic characteristics.

*Analyses 3 and 4*: To assess an aspect of external validity, namely the extent to which findings above generalized over multiple points in time, Analyses 1 and 2 were repeated using the 2001 dataset. Each analysis was identical to the corresponding analysis with the 2003 data, except for taking into account the minor difference in the Race variable (Table 1).

*Analysis 5*: The final analysis investigated internal validity by focusing on whether occupations with the largest apparent dependence of residual Earnings on NDEVwere, plausibly, ones in which spreadsheet and/or programming activities might be deemed to have substantial value. If, for example, a large positive relationship between residual Earnings and NDEV appeared among garbage collectors but not among accountants, then one might suppose that the findings were due to a systematic error of some sort rather than a true relationship.

To avoid undue influence from small-sample statistics, this final analysis focused on the 2940 workers in occupations for which the 2003 dataset contained at least 100 records. For each occupation, the average residual (from Analysis 1 above) was calculated among workers with NDEV = 2, as well as the average residual among workers with NDEV = 0. The 10 occupations with the most positive difference between these averages were then identified and reviewed to assess whether they each had a plausible relationship between earnings and EUD.

*Limitations*: The analysis did not examine causation, nor was it intended to do so. Moreover, the data are too old to give insight about the current causative impact of EUD. Future work can go beyond the current study (Sect. 5).

# 4 Results

## 4.1 Relationship Between Earnings and EUD

*Analysis 1*: The linear regression of Earnings against the 11 control variables was significant ($F_{(448, 8019)} = 13.8$, N = 8468, $p < 0.0001$). Among these, variables with a highly significant relationship to Earnings ($p < 0.0001$) were those for all levels of education, never-married marital status, sex (male/female), having multiple jobs, metropolitan residence, occupation, and class of work. After subtracting fitted from actual Earnings to control for these 11 variables, the resulting residual appeared normally distributed.

In addition, the linear regression of the residual against NDEV was significant ($F_{(2,8465)} = 20.6$, N = 8468, $p < 0.0001$), as was the coefficient for each level of NDEV (at $p < 0.0001$). Relative to workers with NDEV = 0, those with NDEV = 1 earned $59.32 (± $10.13 standard error) more per week, and those with NDEV = 2 earned a total of $71.72 (± $14.91) more per week.

Thus, after controlling for the 11 employment and demographic variables, workers who used spreadsheets/databases and who did programming at work averaged $3729 more per year than workers who did neither of these while using a computer at work. Because the average annualized earnings among all computer-using workers was $42,812, the marginal difference amounted to 8.7%.

*Analysis 2*: The linear regression of log (Earnings) versus all 11 control variables and NDEV was significant ($F_{(450, 8017)} = 9.7$, N = 8468, $p < 0.0001$). The coefficients for NDEV = 1 and NDEV = 2 were both significant ($t = 6.1$ and $t = 5.6$, respectively, both $p < 0.0001$) and (at 0.05 and 0.06) were comparable in magnitude to 8.7% above.

**Table 2.** The 10 occupations that had the largest gap between residual weekly Earnings among workers at NDEV = 2 and workers at NDEV = 0 (among all occupations with at least 100 workers that reported using a computer at work in the October 2003 CPS).

| Occupation | Gap in residual weekly Earnings |
|---|---|
| Accountants & auditors | $353 |
| Retail sales managers | $316 |
| Retail salespersons | $281 |
| Wholesale salespersons | $281 |
| Financial managers | $234 |
| Postsecondary teachers | $219 |
| Registered nurses | $184 |
| Chief executives | $167 |
| Managers, all other | $55 |
| Administrative assistants | $52 |

### 4.2 Generalizability to Other Data

*Analysis 3*: The replicated analysis with 2001 data yielded similar results. Specifically, the linear regression of Earnings versus control variables was significant ($F(397, 7947) = 13.0$, $N = 8345$, $p < 0.0001$), as was residual Earnings versus NDEV ($F(2,8342) = 37.6$, $N = 8345$, $p < 0.0001$). Workers at NDEV = 1 earned $75.77 more than workers at NDEV = 0, and those at NDEV = 2 earned a total of $99.60 more than those at NDEV = 0. Relative to the overall average of $785 per week, this difference from NDEV = 0 to NDEV = 2 was an increase of 12.7%.

*Analysis 4*: The regression of log (Earnings) against all variables was significant ($F(399, 7945) = 11.7$, $N = 8345$, $p < 0.0001$), as were the individual coefficients of NDEV = 1 and NDEV = 2 ($t = 8.4$ and $t = 6.2$, $p < 0.0001$ in each case) relative to NDEV = 0, and each of these coefficients (0.06 and 0.07, respectively) was close to the corresponding value resulting from Analysis 2.

To summarize, both datasets yielded two findings: workers at NDEV = 2 earned on the order of 10% more than those at NDEV = 0 after correcting for control variables; second, the Earnings gap between NDEV = 0 and NDEV = 1 was clearly larger than that between NDEV = 1 and NDEV = 2.

### 4.3 Occupations with the Largest Differences in Earnings Relative to NDEV

*Analysis 5*: Management and sales jobs predominated among the occupations that had the highest gap in residual Earnings for NDEV = 2 versus NDEV = 0, and for which at least 100 workers indicated using a computer in the 2003 CPS data (Table 2).

For example, accountants and auditors had the highest difference in residual Earnings. Those with NDEV = 2 earned $353 per week more than those with NDEV = 0 (i.e., a gap of over $18,000 per year). Compared to the average Earnings of $911 among all accountants and auditors, this amounted to an increase of 39%.

Most occupations in Table 2 are information-centric and can involve spreadsheets, databases and/or programming. Spreadsheets were, in fact, invented for the purpose of helping managers to more effectively track expenses and make financial forecasts [10]. Studies have also hinted at the growing importance of spreadsheets among salespeople for tracking sales, analyzing costs and making sales forecasts [3]. Other occupations shown in Table 2, such as nursing, also involve use of spreadsheets to the extent that informatics has taken hold of these professions [13]. These results help confirm that the statistical relationship between Earnings and NDEV is not attributable to systematic error.

# 5   Discussion

This study revealed a positive statistical relationship between workers' earnings and two forms of EUD. Using spreadsheets/databases and doing programming correlated with a positive difference in earnings on the order of 10% when averaged across all occupations. The results are consistent with the expectation that employers might place a premium on EUD skills, which could affect hiring. Differences in earnings were much more sensitive to spreadsheet/database use than to programming. This result is consistent with the fact that people frequently create spreadsheets that have no formulas or other sign of programming [4], and with the view that EUD encompasses far more than explicit programming. The 10 occupations with the biggest correlation between earnings and these two forms of EUD were generally information-centric.

The current study has a number of extreme limitations that demand additional research building upon these results.

(1) Spreadsheets and programming were considered as indicators for EUD, and although much EUD takes place in these contexts, no precise data were available for what *specific* activities occurred. Some might therefore question the extent to which using a spreadsheet and doing programming constituted EUD. Satisfying such doubts may call for further, more fine-grained research of specific activities versus earnings.

(2) A more interesting question is how other forms of EUD relate to earnings. These, as mentioned in Sect. 1, include co-design [6], participatory and/or pair programming [5], and tailoring [9]. Further research could investigate the relationships between each of these and earnings as well as other measures of career success.

(3) The data are too old to give sufficient insight about the current economic impact of doing EUD. The spread of social media and mobile devices, as well as other technologies since 2003, might have boosted computer literacy and impacted the economic value of practicing EUD. The only way to address this limitation is to replicate the study again, this time with more contemporary sources of data.

(4) Professional programmers comprise only a tiny fraction of all programmers [12], so their presence in the current data set is unlikely to substantially skew results. In particular, not one of the occupations having a sizable sample and a large earnings gap (Table 2) is associated with professional programmers, so it is safe to conclude that many information-centric occupations do offer an earnings premium for forms of EUD to workers other than professional programmers. Nonetheless if we want

to be maximally precise when focusing solely on EUD, it could be beneficial in future studies to separate out professional programmers.

(5) Finally, correlative analysis, such as in the current study, cannot establish causation. The analysis of historical data could be complemented by a study, perhaps based on a random assignment experiment, aimed at measuring the impact that changing individuals' EUD practices has on earnings or other measures of career success.

In short, this work illustrates a broad new avenue for EUD research aimed at quantifying the many ways in which EUD can benefit workers.

# References

1. Bureau of Labor Statistics. Current Population Survey (CPS) Computer Ownership/Internet Usage Supplement (2003). http://dataferrett.census.gov/
2. Burning Glass Technologies: Crunched by the Numbers: The Digital Skills Gap in the Workforce (2015)
3. Byrne, T., Moon, M., Mentzer, J.: Motivating the industrial sales force in the sales forecasting process. Ind. Mark. Manage. **40**(1), 128–138 (2011)
4. Chambers, C., Scaffidi, C.: Struggling to excel: a field study of challenges faced by spreadsheet users. In: IEEE Symposium on Visual Languages and Human-Centric Computing (VL/HCC), pp. 187–194 (2010)
5. de la Flor, G., Jirotka, M.: Blurring the distinction between software design and work practice. In: International Symposium on End User Development (IS-EUD), pp. 24–31 (2009)
6. Fischer, G., Herrmann, T.: Meta-design: transforming and enriching the design and use of socio-technical systems. In: Designing Socially Embedded Technologies in the Real-World, pp. 79–109 (2015)
7. Henderson, R.: Industry employment and output projections to 2020. Monthly Labor Rev. **135**, 65–83 (2012)
8. Kierkegaard, P., Markopoulos, P.: From top to bottom: end user development, motivation, creativity and organisational support. In: Costabile, M.F., Dittrich, Y., Fischer, G., Piccinno, A. (eds.) IS-EUD 2011. LNCS, vol. 6654, pp. 307–312. Springer, Heidelberg (2011). doi: 10.1007/978-3-642-21530-8_31
9. Mørch, A.: Tailoring tools for system development. J. Organ. End User Comput. (JOEUC) **10**(2), 22–29 (1998)
10. Power, D.: A history of microcomputer spreadsheets. Communications of the Association for Information Systems, vol. 4, Article 9 (2000)
11. Scaffidi, C.: Potential financial motivations for end-user programming. In: IEEE Symposium on Visual Languages and Human-Centric Computing (VL/HCC), pp. 180–184 (2016)
12. Scaffidi, C., Shaw, M., Myers, B.: Estimating the numbers of end users and end user programmers. IEEE Symposium on Visual Languages and Human-Centric Computing (VL/HCC), pp. 207–214 (2005)
13. Staggers, N., Gassert, C., Curran, C.: A delphi study to determine informatics competencies for nurses at four levels of practice. Nurs. Res. **51**(6), 383–390 (2002)

# Author Index

Ardito, Carmelo 108

Barricelli, Barbara Rita 119
Bates, Chris 100

Chen, Fanglin 3
Colosio, Sergio 119
Corcella, Luca 18

Dearden, Andy 100
Desolda, Giuseppe 108
Dwivedi, Vishal 66

Fogli, Daniela 119

Garlan, David 66
Gennari, Rosella 167

Herbsleb, James D. 66
Hermans, Felienne 84
Hutchinson, Kevin 34

Khan, Vassilis-Javed 34
Kununka, Sophia 135

Li, Toby Jia-Jun 3
Li, Yuanchun 3
Ludwig, Thomas 150

Maceli, Monica G. 49
Manca, Marco 18
Markopoulos, Panos 34
Matera, Maristella 108
Mehandjiev, Nikolay 135
Melonio, Alessandra 167
Myers, Brad A. 3

Paternò, Fabio 18
Pipek, Volkmar 150

Rizvi, Mehdi 167

Sampaio, Pedro 135
Santos, Carlos Pereira 34
Scaffidi, Christopher 183
Schneider, Kevin 150
Stratton, Andrew 100
Swidan, Alaaeddin 84

Testa, Chiara 119

Valtolina, Stefano 119
van de Haterd, Jeroen 34
Vassilopoulou, Konstantina 135

Printed in the United States
By Bookmasters

Printed in the United States
By Bookmasters